TEACHING YOURSELF IN LIBRARIES

A GUIDE TO THE HIGH SCHOOL MEDIA CENTER AND OTHER LIBRARIES

LILLIAN L. SHAPIRO SCHOOL LIBRARY CONSULTANT,
FORMERLY SUPERVISOR SENIOR HIGH SCHOOL LIBRARIES,
NEW YORK CITY BOARD OF EDUCATION

1978 THE H. W. WILSON COMPANY NEW YORK

Printed in the United States of America

Library of Congress Cataloging in Publication Data
Shapiro, Lillian L
Teaching yourself in libraries.

Bibliography; p.
Includes index.
SUMMARY: Explains the usage of a variety of library resources including indexes, reference books, and the card catalog and outlines procedures for researching different types of questions.
1. Libraries—Juvenile literature. 2. Instructional materials centers—Juvenile literature. 3. Self-culture—Juvenile literature. [1. Libraries] I. Title.
Z665.5.S52 027.82'23 78-16616
ISBN 0-8242-0628-2

ACKNOWLEDGMENTS

The author wishes to thank the following publishers for permission to reprint copyrighted material: Barron's Educational Series (Woodbury, New York) for *Barron's Handbook of American College Financial Aid* by Nicholas Proia (page 197), copyright 1974. Reprinted by permission of the publisher; Europa Publications Ltd. (18 Bedford Square, London, WCIB 3JN, England) for *The International Who's Who 1977–78* (page 1506). Reprinted by permission of the publisher; Facts on File for page 8 of *Facts on File*. Reprinted by special permission, © 1977 Facts on File, Inc.; Columbia University Press for *Granger's Index to Poetry* (pages xxvii and 1058), 6th Ed., New York: Columbia University Press, 1973. By permission of the publisher; Harper and Row for *Comparative Guide to American Colleges*, 8th Ed., by James Cass and Max Birnbaum (page 647), copyright 1977 by the authors. By permission of Harper & Row, Publishers, Inc.; New York Public Library for page 281 of the *Book Catalog*. By permission of the Office of Young Adult Services; New York Times for *New York Times Index* (June 16–30, 1977, page 58), © 1977 by The New York Times Company. Reprinted by permission; Public Affairs Information Service Inc. for 1976 *PAIS Bulletin* (page 633). Reprinted by permission. Charles Scribner's Sons for page 115 of the index to *The Dictionary of the History of Ideas*. Copyright © 1974 Charles Scribner's Sons. Used with permission of the publisher; Siquomb Publishing Corporation for the lyrics from *Big Yellow Taxi*, © 1970 Siquomb Publishing Corp. Used by permission. All rights reserved; Specialized Service and Supply Co. for the catalog cards on page 75. By permission of the Publisher.

The author also wishes to thank the Adwell Company for the photographs of the audiovisual equipment.

TEACHING YOURSELF IN LIBRARIES

CONTENTS

Foreword	vii
Introduction	ix
1. The "Why" and "How" of the Library Media Center	1
2. Being a Well-Informed Citizen	7
3. Health and Science in Your Life	25
4. Your Future: Vocational and College Information	40
5. Living in One World: War and Peace	67
6. Poetry: Music in Words	91
7. Values to Live By	129
8. Getting It Together	148
Test Questions	168
Postscript to the Teacher	171
Index	173

FOREWORD

Because most libraries suffer from a shortage of professional and clerical staff, it is difficult—if not impossible—for libraries to provide the kind of individual attention our patrons need.

This guide, a sort of traveler's aid, for young people is intended in part to alleviate the pressure on librarians by presenting curriculum-oriented units, each of which can be used independently. The suggested titles listed at the end of each chapter may also be useful to librarians as a checklist of titles for possible purchase.

No handbook can replace the expertise of the professionally trained personnel but it can serve as a springboard for encouraging learning by doing on the part of young people. The rationale of this guide is that an individual can go a long way toward solving his or her problems simply by taking some basic research steps and consulting the range of materials that a library is apt to contain.

In preparing this book, I have enjoyed the generous assistance of several librarians who provided me not only with their personal support but also with access to their collections of materials. I should like especially to thank Betty

Schlissel and Mae Willig, librarians at Murry Bergtraum High School, and their principal, Barbara L. Christen; Helen Lansner, librarian at Stuyvesant High School, and her principal, Gaspar Fabbricante; Evi Iglauer and Miriam Pellman, librarians at Hillcrest High School, and their principal, Daniel Salmon; Simpson Sasserath, principal of Norman Thomas High School, and his library staff; Rubin Maloff, principal of Seward Park High School, and his library staff; Benjamin Michelson, principal of Benjamin Cardozo High School, and his library staff; and especially Betty Levy of Francis Lewis High School and Carmel Bernstein of William Cullen Bryant High School, both of whom have been supportive beyond any expression of thanks on my part.

I owe a debt of gratitude also to the three public library systems of my city: Queens Borough Public Library, Brooklyn Public Library, and New York Public Library, at whose Mid-Manhattan branch I spent endless hours, using materials and receiving the advice and good wishes of Lillian Morrison, Coordinator of Young Adult Services, and Emma Cohn, Assistant Coordinator.

One last word: I doubt that this project would have been undertaken at all were it not for the encouragement of Bruce Carrick, Editor of General Publications at The H. W. Wilson Company, and my good friend, Jean Mester, Library Services Specialist at the Wilson Company.

INTRODUCTION

Welcome to the library. Whether you call it a library or a media center, it is also a research laboratory and an entertainment center. Above all, it is yours. Use it!

The plan of this book is not to give you library lessons but rather to suggest ways in which you can learn to solve problems—whether academic or personal—at your own speed and in your own style. Each chapter, instead of constituting a visit to your library, is a gathering together of related ideas and titles on a subject of interest and importance to many people.

Some of the chapter topics are derived from possible school assignments. For that reason you will find advice on how to prepare projects that your teachers may ask of you. Other topics are related to personal, non-academic interests.

The most important thing you can learn from this guide is that you can teach yourself to be a competent user of your school and public libraries and thereby be in a far better position to deal with the many problems and questions that we all face at one time or another.

Humans tend to take for granted things that are just there, like air, water, food—and, maybe, libraries—until those things are threatened with extinction. Joni Mitchell sings a message that is to the point:

They paved paradise and put up a parking lot.
With a pink hotel, a boutique and a swinging hot spot,
Don't it always seem to go
That you don't know what you've got
    Till it's gone.
They paved paradise and put up a parking lot.

They took all the trees and put them in a tree museum
And they charged all the people a dollar and a half
just to see 'em.
Don't it always seem to go
That you don't know what you've got
    Till it's gone
They paved paradise and put up a parking lot.

From "Big Yellow Taxi" in the album entitled
Ladies of the Canyon by Joni Mitchell.

"If a little knowledge is dangerous, where is
the man who has so much as to be out of danger?"

THOMAS HENRY HUXLEY

Chapter 1

THE "WHY" AND "HOW" OF THE LIBRARY MEDIA CENTER

During our youth it often seems that school is only *one* of the many concerns that confront us. We do want to do well in our subjects not just to pass but also to be able to find a job, or go to college—if that is our choice—and perhaps to satisfy a sense of self-esteem.

Other concerns are equally challenging. In this period of physical and emotional change, some of the questions for which we want answers are:

What kind of person am I?

What kind of person do I want to be?

How can I become economically independent?

What should I know about social security? Health insurance? Income taxes? Voting?

How do I develop whatever creative ability I have?

What kind of future is in store for me in the year 2000?

Your education both in school and outside of it should be providing you with possible answers to some of these questions: *There is not always one answer to these questions and the answers may be different for each of us.*

Your classwork and your teachers will be a source of some of the information you need to test out possible solutions to your questions. There is, however, a much broader source of answers.

Libraries, now also called "information centers" and "media centers," contain an enormous range of answers, suggestions, facts, ideas, and examples of how other people have lived, failed, and succeeded. Amid this variety of materials, you are free to pick, dip into, reject, go over again and again, the information that seems to have value for you. The library media center is a springboard for you to test your own developing maturity and independence.

As a younger student you probably learned some guidelines about libraries but you may, perhaps, have been too narrowly involved in some specifics of classification or the card catalog. These details are important but they are only a means to an end, a key to unlocking the answers for which you are searching.

Learning your way around libraries—any kind of library—makes you your own teacher. Since new materials are always being added to this bank of information and pleasure, there is a continuous adding of interest. Today the library media center in your school or your local public library is an amazing resource of print materials (books, pamphlets, newspapers, magazines, catalogs), audiovisual materials (films, recordings, tapes, slides, filmstrips, art prints, transparencies, videotapes), and microforms (newspapers, magazines, and reports reduced in size and transferred to film). People who have had to live on little can tell you that waste is an unforgivable sin. Be smart. Use all of the opportunities available to you: your classroom experience, your teachers, and your libraries.

Some Good Ideas to Help You Make Better Use of Libraries

Know the alphabet. This sounds pretty elementary, but a great many people have trouble using the catalog, the *Readers' Guide to Periodical Literature*, encyclopedias, and other reference tools, because they are not sure of the order of the letters.

Read the directional signs. Almost all libraries clearly designate the areas where, for instance, the reference materials are kept, where the fiction books are located, where biographies are shelved, and where the main non-fiction collection can be found.

Browse around to become acquainted with the arrangement. Getting to know the physical layout of the library will save you time on future visits.

Review what you learned about the card catalog. There are catalog cards that start with the author's name, others that begin with the title of the book, and still others that have the SUBJECT of the book typed across the top in capital letters. Do you know where the call number is on the card in your library? Do you understand the various pieces of information on the card? Figure 1 will refresh your memory. The explanation of the numbered items in the illustration is as follows:

1. Subject heading (always in capital letters);
2. Author's name (last name, first name);
3. Title of the book;

4. Publisher;
5. Date of publication;
6. Number of pages in the book plus other information (here we are told that the book contains illustrations);
7. Call number. (This is needed to find a non-fiction book on the library shelves. A book of fiction generally carries no number and is found in alphabetical order by the author's name.)

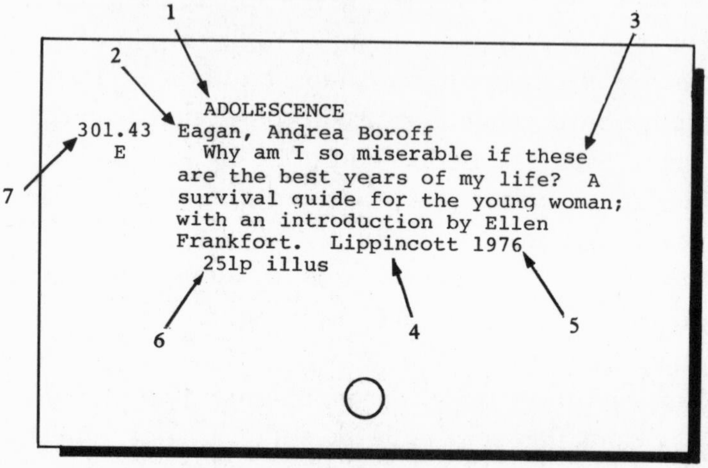

Figure 1. Sample subject catalog card

Learn the different formats of material your library can supply. All libraries have books, pamphlets, magazines, and newspapers. Many others have now added records, films, filmstrips, tapes, pictures, models, videotapes, and microforms. Your library may not have all of these, but it is importtant for you to know which ones it has.

Learn to use the equipment needed for audiovisual materials. In a few minutes you can become a competent user of a filmstrip viewer, an 8mm loop cartridge machine, a microreader, or an overhead projector. They are not any more difficult to use than a record player, a slide projector, or a tape recorder. Careful handling means that the machine will be there for you the next time you need it.

Take careful notes when you do your research. Use the same paper size or index cards so that arranging your notes will be easy when you start to organize your report.

Be patient and persevering. Research is like a treasure hunt: sometimes you have to use clues to get to your goal. The specialists who produce the catalog cards, for example, are locked into certain uniform vocabulary and procedures. It is a test of your ingenuity to see how they have classified your topic. For example, if you wished material on the subject of GOOD BEHAVIOR, what approach would you use? You could try BEHAVIOR, which might lead you, by way of a cross reference, to MORAL SENSE, MORAL EDUCATION or—the most commonly used term—ETHICS. Catalogs, telephone directories, encyclopedias—in fact, most reference resources—do try to help the user by supplying "see" or "see also" references.

Be considerate of your fellow library patrons. Some people can work with the radio going and are able to ignore distracting sounds, but others really need to have reasonable quiet in order to concentrate. If your work in the library requires discussion, find out if there is a section of the library where the sound of voices would not annoy other people. Some media centers today have conference rooms for that very purpose.

Make friends with your librarian (or media specialist, as the newer name is). The person in that position has been trained to help you, knows the resources of the library's collection better than you can hope to and is eager to see that you use these resources to the fullest.

Chapter

2

BEING A WELL-INFORMED CITIZEN

All the topics in this handbook have been chosen because they are so basic to the conduct of your life, present and future. Getting a job or going to college; reaching for beauty in your life; guarding your physical well-being; discovering the values that make it possible to live with yourself—all these important areas are discussed in other chapters.

You might consider this chapter the most important one since it is concerned with such topics as the way you spend the money you earn, your rights and responsibilities as a citizen, and your possible future as the head of a family.

Income and Outgo

When you are a working person, at last, and are anticipating that first paycheck, be prepared to see an amount somewhat smaller than the one stated when you were hired. It helps to know beforehand the reasons for that difference in gross and net salary. In two sound filmstrips, using humorous cartoons, the *Paycheck Puzzle* explains the deductions made in your paycheck and the benefits to which they are applied. Part I is called "Deducting Deductions" and gives information on that mysterious abbreviation on the paycheck called F.I.C.A., which many working people still do not recognize as standing for "Federal Insurance Contributions Act." There is also an explanation of W–2 forms and W– 4 forms, which should be part of any working person's vocabulary. Part II of the film is entitled "Benefiting from Benefits" and points out what sort of assistance is available to the worker in the case of circumstances like unemployment or illness.

This filmstrip sounds useful to a newly employed person. How would you go about finding out if your library has it? What is the basic guide to a library's holdings? Every library maintains some kind of catalog of its resources. Since it is quite usual for people to know only the general topic on which they need information, libraries offer access to their materials by SUBJECT.

For information about what affects your paycheck, the subjects you might consult in the card or book catalog include MONEY, BUDGET, or FINANCE. By scanning the cards under those headings you will come across the most useful subject heading in this case, FINANCE, PERSONAL.

The *Paycheck Puzzle* would be listed if it is in your library. Figures 2 and 3 are additional possibilities:

The two sample catalog cards are subject cards. The top line, typed in capital letters, indicates what the books are about. The catalog would contain two additional cards for each of the above. For Figure 2, cards for Porter, Sylvia as author and for *Sylvia Porter's Money Book*, the title, would enable library patrons knowing such information to find the book. Whichever card one consults, the essential information—the location of the book—is given. In order to obtain

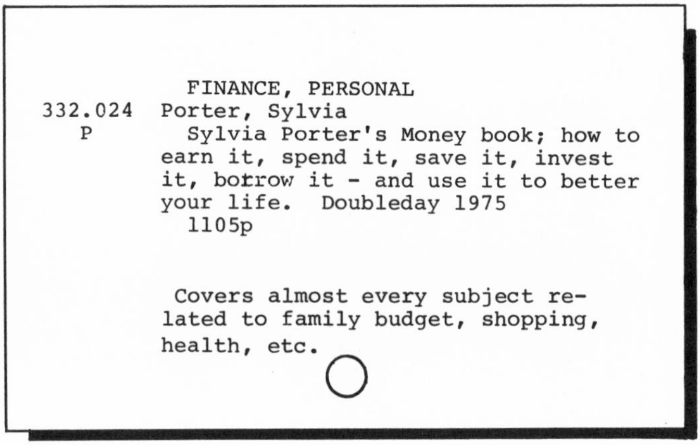

FINANCE, PERSONAL
332.024 Porter, Sylvia
P Sylvia Porter's Money book; how to earn it, spend it, save it, invest it, borrow it - and use it to better your life. Doubleday 1975
1105p

Covers almost every subject related to family budget, shopping, health, etc.

Figure 2. Sample subject catalog card

the actual book we must know where it is shelved. The Dewey decimal classification number 332.024 directs us to the place in the library where books on personal finance are located. Note that under the number in Figure 2, there is the letter P; under the number in Figure 3 there is the letter H. Those letters stand for the initial of the author's last name.

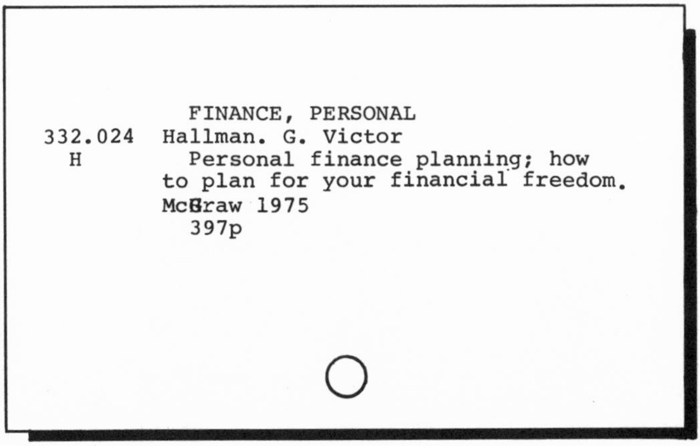

FINANCE, PERSONAL
332.024 Hallman. G. Victor
H Personal finance planning; how to plan for your financial freedom. McGraw 1975
397p

Figure 3. Sample subject catalog card

The catalog card often gives other useful information. Sometimes the length of the book is a consideration for a reader. Here we see that the Porter book is much longer and probably more comprehensive than the book by Victor G. Hallman, since there are over 1000 pages in it.

As you look over materials like those above, other subject headings will occur to you. Two possibilities are CONSUMER EDUCATION and CONSUMER PROTECTION. There are a great many resources available through those headings. Here are some that may interest you:

Elizabeth McGough. *Dollars and Sense: The Teen-Age Consumer's Guide.*
Buyer Beware. 1 filmstrip and cassette.
Mary Beery. *Young Teens and Money.*
How to Buy a Used Car. Film.
Consumer Complaints: The Right Way. Film.

INFORMATION IN PERIODICALS AND PAMPHLETS.

Many magazines carry advice to the consumer on how to spend money wisely and how to determine which is the best product when you are purchasing radios, bicycles, contact lenses, and so forth. Two outstanding titles in the field are *Consumer Reports* and *Consumers' Research Magazine*. Each of these magazines carries its own index in the monthly issues but its articles are also accessible through the index to magazine articles, *Readers' Guide to Periodical Literature.*

In *Readers' Guide*, as with the card catalog, you may find articles listed under the author's name and under the subject but not under the title since magazine articles are generally not remembered that way. For instance, under the subject heading CONSUMER PROTECTION in recent issues of *Readers' Guide*, we find the following examples:

> **Things are getting better faster for consumers. il Changing T 31:17-18 F '77**
>
> Government must assure safe products; interview. E. Peterson. por U.S. News 81:52-3 D 27 '76

If we want to read the articles, what must we do? We have to request the magazines in which the articles appear. In the first entry, "Changing T" is the abbreviated title for *Changing Times*; in the second entry, the magazine you need is *U.S. News and World Report*. Each issue of *Readers' Guide* gives that information at the front in a list of abbreviations used. You note that the first article has no author listed. What about the second entry? The author, Peterson, is the person who has been interviewed for the information. Let us suppose that we choose to read this article. What do we request? We ask for *U.S. News and World Report* for December 27, 1976. It is necessary to include "27" as well as the month because this magazine is a weekly. What do the other parts of the entry mean? The number 81 is the volume number of the magazine; 52-3 tells you the page to which you can turn for the article; "por" indicates that a picture of E(sther) Peterson is included in the article.

> REMINDER: When you make note of a *Readers' Guide* entry be sure to copy the page numbers for yourself because some articles in magazines are not listed separately in the table of contents of that magazine. Without the page numbers you would waste time turning pages to find the article you want.

Here is another *Readers' Guide* entry showing its usefulness for consumer protection.

BICYCLES
10-speed bikes. il Consumer Rep 41:76-85 F '76

What magazine do you need? What issue? How long is the article? What is "il"?

Did you have these answers? The magazine you need is *Consumer Reports* for February 1976 to find an article that is 10 pages long. No author is identified since the article is the work of the staff of the magazine. The abbreviation "il" indicates that there are pictures of the bicycles.

If you were doing more advanced research on topics like investments, banking, and other business subjects, you might wish to read articles in special magazines related to those fields. To find these articles you might also consult *Business Periodicals Index* in the public library; it works like *Readers' Guide* and will give you no trouble if you have used the latter.

Your library's vertical file sometimes called an information file contains important information on many subjects in the form of pamphlets issued by many state and federal agencies as well as private companies and institutions. Also in this file are booklets published by such institutions as the Household Finance Corporation on subjects like money management, installment buying, and consumer guidance. More than 200 free or low-cost booklets from federal agencies are described in a quarterly publication called *Consumer Information Catalog* and that catalog may be in the vertical file or at the desk of your library. Check with the librarian.

Some newspaper articles are difficult to track down. For

this reason you should be aware of a library resource called *Social Issues Resources Series* (SIRS) which periodically gathers a collection of articles on a specific subject from a wide range of newspapers, magazines, and documents. These collections are made available in loose-leaf format, enabling several people to use the contents at one time. In the collection called MONEY, you will find articles on such topics as inflation, property taxes, credit, and incomes. SIRS lists the articles in a table of contents by number and then gives you additional assistance by supplying a subject index so that you can look under INFLATION and find the numbers of the articles in that volume which relate to that topic.

Even a general and basic title like the *World Almanac* can add to your store of information. In the index under the heading CONSUMER, you will find pages listed for information on complaints, consumerism, credit statistics, loan rates, and price indexes.

Security and Unions

The Social Security Act 1935 was intended to provide Americans with a variety of benefits. You might be interested to know something about how that legislation came to be, what it included, what changes have been made since its beginning, and what problems are connected with its application.

As with other topics, an encyclopedia can supply you with an overview of the Social Security Act. For example, in volume 25 of *Encyclopedia Americana* which is organized in alphabetical order, you will find a detailed article on this topic. The index of the encyclopedia will refer you to other articles in other volumes: LABOR LEGISLATION in volume 16 and SOCIAL WELFARE in volume 27.

Very concise explanations of the act can be found in the one-volume *New Columbia Encyclopedia* and in books on economics. In books, too, the index is the guide to the topic you are seeking. You would look in a book's index under SOCIAL SECURITY; you might also find a reference to INSURANCE, SOCIAL. Like a library 's card catalog, a book's index helps you to find this material by way of subject headings and cross-references.

Since there is current debate about the financial strength of the social security system, current information is needed to up-date your knowledge. *Editorial Research Reports* specializes in publishing pamphlets regularly on current issues. These booklets may be in the vertical file of your library; however there will also be bound volumes of *Editorial Research Reports* into which are gathered all the issues for the year. Each bound volume carries an index for the preceding 5-year period. Checking under the subject SOCIAL SECURITY in the 1976 index, for example, we are directed to an issue dated September 20, 1972 on Social Security Financing. The full entry gives the date and the exact location in the volume: September 20, 1972; Vol. II, pp. 707–724.

Also in the vertical file you may find a copy of *Vital Issues* on the social security system. Other pamphlets and clippings will be found in the same folder.

What resources will give even more recent information about social security benefits? You certainly know the answer to that: magazines and newspapers.

Here is an entry on this subject from the *Readers' Guide to Periodical Literature:*

SOCIAL security

In the works: a fairer but costlier social security. U.S. News 82:85-6 Mr 21 '77

U.S. News and World Report carries many articles on problems of an economic nature. Other helpful magazines whose articles are indexed in *Readers' Guide* include *Monthly Labor Review, Scholastic, Reader's Digest*, and *Changing Times*.

In the same way as we found materials about consumerism and social security we can locate information about unions or labor.

> REMINDER: Subject headings used in card catalogs or indexes may not be the ones that come to your mind first. Think of alternatives, see what the library tools themselves may give you in the way of cross-references (UNIONS, see TRADE UNIONS; see also LABOR).

Rights and Responsibilities of Citizens

With the recent lowering of the voting age, the value and the duty resting in the right to vote should be clear to you. The card catalog can bring such materials as these to your attention.

James O'Donnell. *Every Vote Counts: A Teen-Age Guide to the Electoral Process.*

Now You Are A Voter. 4 filmstrips and 2 cassettes that tell about registration, picking a candidate, working in the political world, the election procedure

Municipal Yearbook. An annual compilation of facts about cities including names of mayors and other city officials and an official telephone number

Also important for young citizens is some knowledge of their own rights and the protections to which the law entitles them. The heading CIVIL RIGHTS is one place to start; another, more specific, is YOUTH, with a sub-head CIVIL RIGHTS.

Here are possibilities located through the catalog:

Your Rights and What They Really Mean. 6 filmstrips and 3 cassettes discuss such subjects as bringing suit, experiencing a trial, possible conflicts between the rights of society and the rights of the individual, the balance between privacy and freedom, the meaning of "innocent until proven guilty."

Youth and the Law Series. 6 filmstrips and cassettes entitled Law and the Judge, Law and the Individual, Law and the Police, Law and the Dissenter, Law and the Youthful Offender, Law and the Accuser.

Joseph Newman. *What Everyone Needs to Know About Law.*

Kenneth P. Norwick. *Your Legal Rights*, which touches many bases including landlord-tenant relationships, welfare law, family law, rights of children, and students' rights.

The Rights of Students, the American Civil Liberties Union handbook which describes, among other topics, first amendment rights and due process in addition to specific areas related to school activities (grades, diplomas, etc.).

As a citizen you should feel free to inform your elected representatives in the state legislature and in the Congress about your point of view and to ask for more information about proposed legislation. There are state manuals and special books that contain lists of all the commissions, departments, heads of agencies that direct the activities of your state. For example, the *New York Red Book* carries such information plus biographical sketches of people in the state government. The *Legislative Manual of New York* gives the state's constitution as well as names of mayors, county clerks, and other officials. It is likely that each state has a guidebook that enables the inhabitants of that state to know the names, titles, and addresses of public officials to whom inquiries and complaints may be sent. In the *Monthly Checklist of State Publications* you can look under subject and under your state for this kind of document. You can also ask your state representative to send you the name of the manual which your state publishes with this information.

On the national level the guide that gives you information about senators, congressmen, various departments, committees, members of the press, maps of congressional districts and other useful information is the *Official Congressional Directory for the Use of the U.S. Congress*. One should remember that annuals like the *World Almanac*, the *Information Please Almanac*, and others similar to these also contain some of these governmental facts.

An Eye to the Future

Like everything else, the concept of the family and the attitudes toward love and marriage are subject to change. Reading and thinking about these matters may help you to avoid some problems. There are many pamphlets published by agencies that specialize in family problems and these are likely to be found in the vertical file, or information file, as it is sometimes called.

Also useful is the binder on "Family" in the Social Issues

Resources Series (SIRS) which contains articles on topics, including women and credit, singles and taxes, and marriage. For example, one article in the SIRS collection is entitled "Marriage in the Classroom—They Learn What it's All About," which appeared in a publication called *Parade*, November 4, 1973.

As always, the guide to the library's collection, card or book catalog, will help you find books and audiovisual materials on your subject. For example:

Note that the call numbers (Dewey decimal classification) on the three subject catalog cards in Figures 4, 5, and 6 are the same—301.42. That appears to be an excellent place to look on the shelves for books or other resources on marriage and the family. Do you know what the meaning of the letter under 301.42 is? "W" in Figure 4 is for Wernick, the author of the book; similarly "A" is for Avery. Since one does not usually look under author or producer for audiovisual materials, the title of a filmstrip set or film appears on the main card. In

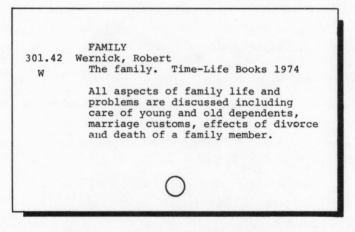

FAMILY
301.42 Wernick, Robert
W The family. Time-Life Books 1974

All aspects of family life and problems are discussed including care of young and old dependents, marriage customs, effects of divorce and death of a family member.

Figure 4. Sample subject catalog card

MARRIAGE
301.42 Avery, Curtis E.
A Love and marriage; a guide for young people. Harcourt 1971
170p illus

Discusses ten important areas of married life

Figure 5. Sample subject catalog card

KIT MARRIAGE
301.42 Love and marriage. Guidance Associates,
L 1969.

2 sound-filmstrips (87, 73 fr), col,
2 cassettes (16, 13 min), guide

Describes problems of couples contemplating marriage and those already married. Difficulties concern money, children, sex, and in-laws.

Figure 6. Sample subject catalog card

Figure 6 "L" is for the first letter of the title of that kit. In the case of specific artists featured on recordings, for example, Joni Mitchell or Placido Domingo, those names *would* be used in the cataloging process since library patrons are particularly interested in the performer.

Other possibilities, found under the subject headings FAMILY and MARRIAGE, might include the following:

What About Marriage? 3 filmstrips and tapes entitled
- I. Til Death Do Us Part (various kinds of marriage)
- II. Romantic Love and Dirty Dishes (Courtly love in the Middle Ages; reality vs romance; liking and loving)
- III. Two Case Studies

David Mace. *Getting Ready for Marriage*, suggests questions that couples should ask themselves before that decision.

Preparation for Parenthood, a kit of slides and cassettes describing the need to understand what makes a "good" parent and how our own memories may affect the kind of parent we will be.

Leontine Young. *The Fractured Family* discusses the changes in family life and the role of grandparents as well as others in the family group.

Mate Selection: Making the Best Choice, 2 filmstrips and cassettes which describe the factors that make for a successful marriage.

Remember always that magazine articles on these subjects can be found through the *Readers' Guide*. Possible subject headings include YOUTH, DATING, FAMILY, MARRIAGE and GENERATION GAP.

You, Your Community, and Your Libraries

In your school the library media center can provide you with information on all the various topics that are described in this book—topics related to your studies, to your future plans, and to your outside interests and problems.

Your public library also extends its information service outside the walls of the library building itself. Not only are there books, films, magazines, newspapers, recordings, art prints, pamphlets, and government documents but there is also information about community activities and agencies that provide advice, assistance, educational opportunities, and entertainment.

In return, there are services and interest that *you* can give to your school and community by participating in clubs, taking an interest in government, and by being a volunteer in some agency that needs willing hands and your special talents. If you want suggestions on how you can be a useful citizen in your school and community you will find programs and success stories in *New Roles for Youth in the School and Community*, a book issued by the National Commission on Resources for Youth. Among the projects undertaken by young people in such communities as Enfield, Connecticut; Philadelphia, Pennsylvania; Ramapo, New York, have been activities connected with health services, tutoring, community manpower, and business undertakings. Sources for further information are also listed in this book.

In his book *Political Economy*, the French philosopher Jean-Jacques Rousseau wrote:

> There can be no patriotism without liberty; no liberty without virtue, no virtue without citizens; create citizens, and you have everything you need; without them, you will have nothing but debased slaves, from the rulers of the State downwards. To form citizens is not the work of a day; and in order to

have men it is necessary to educate them when they are children.

Written in the eighteenth century, this statement is still valid. We, in the twentieth century, would wish to make only one change and that is to add the words "and women" after the word "men" in the last sentence.

SUGGESTED MATERIALS

Avery, Curtis E. and T. B. Johannis. *Love and Marriage*. New York: Harcourt, 1971.

Beery, Mary. *Young Teens and Money*. New York: McGraw-Hill, 1971.

Buyer Beware. 1 filmstrip and cassette. New York: Guidance Associates, 1972.

Business Periodicals Index. New York: Wilson.

Consumer Complaints: The Right Way. Film 11 min color. Los Angeles, CA.: Alfred Higgins Productions, 1976.

Consumer Information Catalog. Pueblo, CO.: Consumer Information Ctr.

Consumer Reports (magazine).

Consumer Research Magazine.

Editorial Research Reports. W. B. Dickinson, ed. Washington, D.C.: Congressional Quarterly, Inc.

Hallman, G. Victor and J. S. Rosenbloom. *Personal Financial Planning*. New York: McGraw-Hill, 1975.

How to Buy A Used Car. Film 16 min color. Mount Vernon, NY: Consumer Report Films, 1976.

Information Please Almanac. New York: Simon and Schuster.

Levine, Alan H. and Eve Cary. *The Rights of Students: The Basic ACLU Guide to a Student's Rights* (American Civil Liberties Union Handbook). New York: Avon, 1976.

Love and Marriage. 2 filmstrips and cassettes. New York: Guidance Associates, 1969.

Mace, David R. *Getting Ready for Marriage*. Nashville, TN.: Abingdon, 1972.

McGough, Elizabeth. *Dollars and Sense: The Teen-age Consumer's Guide*. New York: Morrow, 1975.

Mate Selection: Making the Best Choice. 2 filmstrips with cassettes or discs. Pound Ridge, NY: Human Relations Media Center, 1975.

Municipal Yearbook. Washington, D.C.: International City Management Association.

National Commission on Resources for Youth: New Roles for Youth in the School and the Community. New York: Citation Press, 1974.

New Columbia Encyclopedia. New York: Columbia University, Press, 1975.

Norwick, Kenneth P., ed. *Your Legal Rights: Making the Law Work For You*. Rev. ed. New York: Day, 1975.

Now You Are a Voter. 4 filmstrips and 2 cassettes. Jamaica, NY: Eye Gate.

O'Donnell, James J. *Every Vote Counts: A Teen-age Guide to the Electoral Process*. New York: Messner, 1976.

Official Congressional Directory for the Use of the U.S. Congress. Washington, D.C.: Government Printing Office.

The Paycheck Puzzle. 2 filmstrips and cassettes. New York: Guidance Associates, 1973.

Porter, Sylvia. *Sylvia Porter's Money Book*. New York: Doubleday, 1975.

Preparation for Parenthood. 3 parts—slides and cassettes or recordings. White Plains, NY: Center for Humanities, 1977.

Reader's Digest Almanac. Pleasantville, NY: Reader's Digest Association.

Readers' Guide to Periodical Literature. New York: Wilson.

Social Issues Resources Series. Syracuse, NY: Gaylord Bros.

Vital Issues. Washington, CT: Center for Information on America.

Wernick, Robert. *The Family*. New York: Time-Life, 1975.

What About Marriage? 3 filmstrips and cassettes. Pleasantville, NY: Sunburst Communications.

What Everyone Needs to Know About Law. 4th ed. Joseph Newman, ed. New York: Simon & Schuster, 1975.

World Almanac and Book of Facts. New York: World-Telegram.

Young, Leontine R. *The Fractured Family*. New York: McGraw-Hill, 1973.

Your Rights and What They Really Mean. 6 filmstrips and 3 cassettes. Jamaica, NY: Eye Gate.

Youth and the Law Series. 6 filmstrips and cassettes. Santa Ana, CA: Doubleday Media.

Chapter

3

HEALTH AND SCIENCE IN YOUR LIFE

Science is perhaps the most central factor in the lives of those of us who live in an urban, industrialized society. It is a factor in war and peace, the standard of living, the quality of life, the technology of how information is transmitted, and—most important—our own health and longevity.

Libraries, both school and public, maintain varied resources on the whole gamut of science topics. There are encyclopedias, dictionaries, magazines, books, pamphlets, films, slides, transparencies, and recordings on such subjects as pollution, genetic engineering, energy, health care, nutrition, life in outer space, venereal disease, organ transplants—to name only a few.

Since our health is the keystone to a good life, even beyond monetary success, let us see how the resources of the library can help us to keep ourselves well.

Most handbooks and most teachers recommend making an outline on any topic in which you are doing more than a casual investigation. The following can serve as a fairly simple model of such an outline. The subject is so timely and important that it could readily be the basis for a semester's study in health education or science.

HEALTH—
GETTING IT AND KEEPING IT

I. Factors affecting health
   A. Diet
      1. Elements of good nutrition
      2. Special diets for special problems
   B. Exercise
      1. Basic
      2. Special
   C. Heredity
   D. Environmental influences
II. Methods for maintaining health
   A. Medical check-ups
   B. Safety factors in the environment
   C. Personal hygiene
III. Fighting disease
   A. Heart ailments
   B. Cancer
   C. Illnesses especially related to youth
IV. Health care in the United States
   A. Research
   B. Medical attention in institutions
      1. Average expectation for most people
      2. Current problems related to an aging population
   C. Insurance plans for health protection
V. Innovations in medical treatment
   A. Drug therapy
   B. Transplantation of organs
   C. Genetic engineering

Background Information

Encyclopedias are useful for general coverage of any subject, and on the subject of HEALTH, *World Book Encyclopedia* offers an article in volume "H" directly under the heading HEALTH that includes basic rules for good health. *Collier's*, in its direct access to the subject, gives similar information under the heading HEALTH ORGANIZATIONS. *Encyclopedia Americana*, gives cross-references from HEALTH to such topics as DIET; HEALTH EDUCATION: INDUSTRIAL HEALTH; MENTAL HEALTH; NUTRITION OF MAN; PUBLIC HEALTH; WORLD HEALTH ORGANIZATION; HEALTH INSURANCE.

> REMINDER: Where there is an index volume accompanying a set of encyclopedias, remember that all the information scattered throughout a set on any given topic will be gathered together for you in that index. Use it before turning to individual articles.

Special encyclopedias exist in every field, and for subjects of a scientific nature, when you are looking for very precise, detailed, special facts, you might consult *Van Nostrand's Scientific Encyclopedia* or *McGraw-Hill Encyclopedia of Science and Technology*. The latter title is kept up-to-date with yearbooks that can be consulted for recent scientific developments in your subject. Once you have discovered the classification number for those reference books (probably 503 in the Dewey arrangement), you will come upon other books in the same field.

People In the Field

In your reading you will come across the names of people whose contributions have made an impact on our health and you may want to know something about those leaders. Biographical dictionaries and references that cover all areas will also include many people in the area of health. For example, in *Who's Who in America* there will be information about Dr. Michael Ellis De Bakey (heart specialist) and Dr. Linus Pauling (chemist), and in *Current Biography* very readable accounts of Dr. Lewis Thomas (cell biologist) and Dr. Denton A. Cooley (heart transplant surgeon) have appeared.

As in the case of other kinds of reference books, there are special titles for biographical information about persons in science fields. One example is *Cattell's American Men and Women of Science*, a seven-volume set whose final volume is a classified index by specialty (Veterinary Medicine, Immunology, Genetics, etc.) and by geography. Here you will find thousands of names of scientists that cannot be located in the more general sources and encylopedias. The geographical listings in the index can help you to find information about doctors in your city. Also useful in selecting a specialist for your care is the *Directory of Medical Specialists*. In two volumes, every type of medical attention is listed: surgery, internal medicine, family practice, and so forth. Under these specializations the doctors are listed according to state (subdivided into counties) with brief personal information giving date of birth, place of medical training, diplomas held.

INFORMATION IN DEPTH

Books and audiovisual materials will supply details about health and health care. The subjects in the card or book catalog that are most likely to lead you to the titles you need would include MEDICINE; PUBLIC HEALTH; NUTRITION; DISEASES; PHYSIOLOGY. Cross-references (*see* and *see also*) may direct you to other paths.

Your search in the card catalog then may bring the following to your attention:

In the areas of health and medicine:
Blakiston's Gould Medical Dictionary
Fishbein, *Modern Medical Adviser*
Systems of the Human Body (filmstrips and cassettes)
Trans/vision Book of Health (transparencies included)

Lipkin, *Straight Talk About Your Health Care*
Wagman, *Complete Illustrated Book of Better Health*
Sinacore, *Health: a Quality of Life*
Merck Manual of Diagnosis and Therapy
Busch, *What About VD?*
Langone, *Bombed, Buzzed, Smashed, or . . . Sober*

In the area of nutrition:
Eat, Drink and Be Wary (film)
Nutrition: Foods, Fads, Frauds, Facts (filmstrips and cassettes)

In genetic experimentation:
Fletcher, *The Ethics of Genetic Control*
Genetics: Man the Creator (film)
Goodfield, *Playing God: Genetic Engineering and the Manipulation of Life*
Wade, *The Ultimate Experiment: Man-made Evolution*
Encounters with Tomorrow: Science Fiction and Human Values (filmstrips and cassettes)
The Ethical Challenge: Four Biomedical Case Studies (slides and cassettes)
The Ethnics of Genetic Control (slides and cassettes)

Here is a sample card to show you how you would have found one of the above suggested titles (Figure 7).

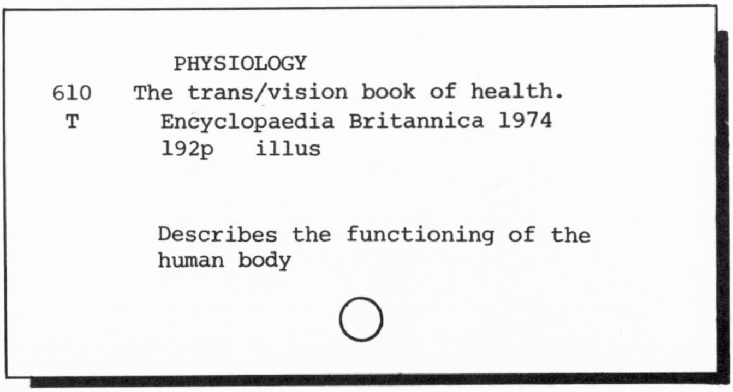
PHYSIOLOGY
610 The trans/vision book of health.
T Encyclopaedia Britannica 1974
192p illus

Describes the functioning of the
human body

Figure 7. Sample subject catalog card

The location of this book (its call number) is 610 in the Dewey arrangement and then within that section in alphabetical order under the letter T. Once you have found that section of the library you will find many other resources covering the same topic. In libraries that interfile all formats of material together, you might even find filmstrips, pamphlet boxes, kits containing slides and filmstrips, records and cassettes, in the same location as the books. In most libraries, however, resources other than the printed materials must be requested at the desk.

If your own special interest is in the field of genetic engineering, you should remember that science fiction writing is a rich resource for themes of that nature. Such titles as Karel Čapek's play *R.U.R.* about robots and Kate Wilhelm's *Where Late the Sweet Birds Sang* (about cloning) will give you food for thought.

Bibliographies

When you prepare a report, oral or written, you should keep a list of materials that you have consulted. This permits you to substantiate your statements in case you are challenged. That list, called a bibliography, will contain all kinds of resources, not just books, and it is arranged alphabetically. The last chapter of this book, "Getting it Together," has more information about making bibliographies. What is important here is that many of the books, filmstrips, encyclopedia articles, and pamphlets that you use also have their own bibliographies at the end so that you have clues to further information if you want it. Libraries often prepare bibliographies on crucial topics, which can ease your search at the start. Some printed bibliographies pertain to very specific fields of knowledge. In the case of science you may wish to look at the *AAAS Science Book List*, which contains over 2,000 titles arranged by Dewey classification, and the *AAAS Science Books and Films*, which four times a year reviews new titles.

The Latest News

In learning about a topic of current importance, we depend on such media as periodicals, newspapers, and radio and television coverage. Some magazines concentrate on health or science. Examples are *Scientific American, Natural History, Science News, Today's Health,* and *Bulletin of the Atomic Scientists*. You might not expect health articles in *Current History, The Progressive,* or *U.S. News and World Report*, yet those magazines also carry information related to this subject. In fact, *Current History* devoted almost its entire May/June 1977 issue to health care in America covering all facets of the problem including the state of health today, federal involvement, health facilities, and prescription drugs.

As an index in a book helps you find a topic in that book, so periodical indexes help you to find out what may have been written on a subject, in a whole range of magazines. There are many magazine indexes and a very special one covering more advanced scientific and technological journals is the *Applied Science and Technology Index*, which you will find only in larger libraries.

The most commonly used periodical index, however, and one which does include science magazines for the general reader is the *Readers' Guide to Periodical Literature*. In 21 paper issues a year and an annual volume over 180 magazines are analyzed. Here for our topic of health and health care, in the May 10, 1977 issue of *Readers' Guide*, which tells you on

MEAD, Margaret
American society and its cities. Current 190:3-9 F '77
Grandparents as educators. il Sat Eve Post 249:54-9 Mr '77
[Monthly column] See issues of Redbook

about

Lecture. New Yorker 53:24-5 Mr 7 '77 *
Margaret Mead at seventy-five. J. Houston. por Sat R 4:6+ F 5 '77 *

MEADOWS
Sunrise, moonrise. S. Shaw. il Nat Wildlife 15:44-7 F '77

MEALS
Marvelous meals for less money. J. Neary. por Parents Mag 52:38-9+ Mr '77
Roast pork with winter vegetables. E. W. Manning. il Farm J 101:56-7 Ja '77
See also
Breakfasts
Buffet meals
Cookery
Diet
Dinners and dining
Lunches
Snacks

MEANY, George
Annual sunbath. K. Bode. New Repub 176:12-14 Mr 12 '77 *
Emancipation from Meany. B. J. Widick. Nation 224:368-72 Mr 26 '77 *
Labor's call on Carter. T. Nicholson and T. Joyce. il por Newsweek 89:60-1 Mr 7 '77 *
Meany draws up his shopping list; with report on Bal Harbour, Fla. executive council meeting by P. Taubman. il por Time 109:43-4 Mr 7 '77 *
Meany faction. C. McWilliams. Nation 224:165 F 12 '77 *
Who speaks for labor? Nation 224:418 Ap 9 '77 *

MEASELL, James S. See Lippert, C. B. jt auth

MEASLES

Preventive inoculation

Measles: an epidemic. J. Seligmann. il Newsweek 89:73 F 21 '77

MEASUREMENT
Missing link: use of paper chains to study measuring. R. Harring. Educ Digest 42:48-9 Ja '77

MEAT
See also
Cookery—Meat

Grading

New beef grades: what do they mean? il Bet Hom & Gard 55:150+ Ap '77

Marketing

Carving out new meat markets. J. Russell. Farm J 101:LK4 Ap '77

MEAT, Frozen
When is a steak not a steak? Consumer Rep 42:64-5 F '77

MEAT industry
Henry G. Parks gives his rules for success. J. Saddler. il pors Ebony 32:100-2+ Mr '77
Packer sees heavy meat output early in '77. Farm J 101:Hog 15 Ja '77
See also
Cattle industry
Monfort of Colorado, Inc

Advertising

BIC is working to sell excess beef on TV; Beef Industry Council. Farm J 101:LK7 Ap '77
Is the checkoff a necessary evil? B. Eftink. Suc Farm 75:no3 B1 F '77
Two vital decisions for cattlemen. W. Kester. il Farm J 101:Beef 28 Ja '77
We need more beef dollars to counter nutrition myths; views of Dr G. V. Mann. Farm J 101:Beef 20+ Ja '77

Export-import problems

Beef management; increased exports could help balance trade. B. Eftink. il Suc Farm 75:no3 A8 F '77

MEAT industry workers
See also
Strikes—United States—Meat industry workers

MEAT loaf, pies, etc. See Cookery—Meat

MECHANICAL banks. See Banks, Coin

MECHANICAL drawing
Careers in art. P. Savino. il Sch Arts 76:11 Ap '77

MECHANICS, Household
Home improvement ideas for the house fixer:
Installing door and window locks. D. Raffel. il House & Gard 149:80 Mr '77
Replacing an electrical switch. D. Raffel. House & Gard 149:68 Ap '77
Housepower clinic; questions and answers (cont) E. Powell. il Pop Sci 210:136+ F '77
McCalls handywoman:
Installing ceramic tile. il McCalls 104:118 F '77
Ladders. il McCalls 104:84 Mr '77
Tips tools & techniques. See issues of Better homes & gardens
See also
Plumbing

MECHANICS, Human. See Human mechanics

MEDALS
See also
Caldecott Medal
Newbery Medal

MEDAWAR, Jean S. See Medawar, P. B. jt auth

MEDAWAR, Sir Peter Brian and Medawar, J. S.
Revising the facts of life; excerpt from The life science: current ideas of biology. Harpers 254:41-8+ F '77

MEDIA centers. See Instructional materials centers

MEDIC Alert bracelets. See Identification tags, bracelets, etc.

MEDICAID

Michigan

Model for fraud; Michigan's Medicaid rip-off. E. E. Chen. Nation 224:242-4 F 26 '77

MEDICAL care
Emergency medicine. H. Perlstadt and L. J. Kozak. il Society 14:41-6 Ja '77
Health economics and preventive care. M. M. Kristein and others. bibl il Science 195:457-62 F 4 '77
Medical-welfare complex; symposium. bibl il Society 14:25-54 Ja '77
See also
Aged—Medical care
Government investigations—Medical care
Mental health care
Poor—Medical care
Prisoners—Medical care

Colombia

Inequality in Colombia. D. K. Zschock. bibl f il Cur Hist 72:68-72+ F '77

MEDICAL care, Cost of
Anatomy of health care costs. E. Marshall. New Repub 176:22-3 Mr 12; 16-19 Mr 19; 11-15 Ap 16 '77
Business looks at health care costs; address, November 18, 1976. J. H. Perkins. Vital Speeches 43:211-15 Ja 15 '77
Curbing the cost of health. Bus W p82 Ap 4 '77
High cost of health. H. Flieger. U.S. News 82:88 F 14 '77
Hot seat; J. Califano of HEW. G. F. Will. Newsweek 89:96 Mr 7 '77
How business can help cut health-care costs. il Nations Bus 65:16-20 F '77
Malpractice and medicine. D. Makofsky. bibl il Society 14:25-9 Ja '77
Uproar over medical bills; with interview with W. J. McNerney. J. Mann. il U.S. News 82:35-40 Mr 28 '77
See also
Hospital care—Cost

MEDICAL care, Rural
Country doctor; work of G. Duckworth in Mound City, Kan. C. Remsberg. il por Fam Health 9:36-9+ Ap '77

MEDICAL care, State
Coming: an overhaul of health programs. il U.S. News 82:76 F 28 '77
See also
Medicaid
Medicare

MEDICAL colleges
See also
Harvard University—Medical School
United States—Uniformed Services University of the Health Sciences, Bethesda, Md.

Admission

Bakke vs. University of California; case of reverse racial discrimination. J. H. Bunzel. Commentary 63:59-64 Mr '77
Reverse discrimination; A. Bakke case. J. K. Footlick. il Newsweek 89:66 Mr 7 '77
White/Caucasian—and rejected; case of A. Bakke. R. Lindsey. il pors N Y Times Mag p42-7+ Ap 3 '77

MEDICAL education
Is a relapse ahead for minority medical education? K. Abarbanel. Educ Digest 42:24-7 Mr '77

MEDICAL electronics
Impact of integrated electronics in medicine. R. L. White and J. D. Meindl. bibl il Science 195:1119-24 Mr 18 '77

MEDICAL ethics
Jackson Pollock's drawings under analysis; question of psychiatric ethics. B. Carter. il Art N 76:58-60 F '77
Karen Ann a year later. E. Keerdoja. Newsweek 89:10 Mr 21 '77

Figure 8. From *Readers' Guide to Periodical Literature* (May 10, 1977)

its cover that it includes indexing for January 15–April 21, 1977, we find several articles that may be useful in our research. Figure 8 shows three articles under MEDICAL CARE but also gives us special information about the cost of this attention under the heading MEDICAL CARE, COST OF. After examining the entries under that heading you may decide the title that seems most promising is the last entry.

Uproar over medical bills; with interview with W. J. McNerney. J. Mann. il U.S. News 82: 35-40 Mr 28 '77

The translation of that entry is that an article entitled "Uproar over Medical Bills" has been written by J. Mann and includes an interview with someone named W. J. McNerny. The article is accompanied by photographs. You can read it in a magazine called *U.S. News and World Report*. At the front of each issue of *Readers' Guide* you are given the full names of magazines cited in the index. You will need the March 28, 1977 issue of that magazine and will turn directly to page 35 for the article. The number 82 before the colon is a volume number and may not be important in a library that does not bind its magazines into annual volumes.

> REMINDER: The page numbers for a magazine article in a *Readers' Guide* entry are *after* the colon.

If you know how to use the *Readers' Guide* you will have no trouble using the *Applied Science and Technology Index* or *General Science Index*, which is intended for the nonspecialist science reader and indexes periodicals that cover such fields as earth sciences; food and nutrition; medicine and health; environment and conservation; genetics; astronomy.

Once you have decided which article or articles you want, the next step is to obtain the magazines. Some libraries may leave their magazines on the open shelves. Most libraries, in order to maintain them in proper chronological order, will house the magazines in a special place and will ask you to fill out a request slip for each separate magazine that you need.

Other Sources of Information

Some of the information you want may be statistical—figures for how many people are hospitalized each year for example, and for how many of them are covered by insurance, or for the mortality rates among different groups of people. Annual almanacs such as *The World Almanac, Information Please Almanac*, and the *Readers's Digest Almanac* are treasure-houses of such facts and figures. Another collection of statistical information is in the government-printed *Statistical Abstract of the United States*, also issued annually, which contains figures and tables on social, political, economic, and other aspects of American life.

Pamphlets and Other Vertical File Materials

The U.S. government is a very active publishing source, and the vertical file or information file in the library you use will contain pamphlets from hundreds of government agencies filed under subjects similar to those in the card catalog or in *Readers' Guide*. One helpful guide to a wider range of government documents than your library is likely to have is Leidy's *Popular Guide to Government Publications*. Under the heading HEALTH you can find such listings as "Qué Es Diabetes?" or "Your Medicare Handbook," each followed by the stock number by which it can be ordered. The guide is arranged under broad headings, but the index will help you to the appropriate one for your particular topic. At the back of the book are the addresses of government printing office bookstores where you can buy these valuable publications and also addresses of libraries which keep fairly complete files of these documents.

Besides government documents, your vertical file will contain newspaper clippings, other pamphlet material, and perhaps pictures. Organizations connected with hospitals or medical research often print and distribute releases that give you factual and statistical information about health and health care.

Collections of Articles

One useful series that tries to bring together information from many sources—newspapers, magazines, special journals, and government documents—is called SIRS (Social Issues Resources Series). Among the subjects SIRS has covered in its collection are, POLLUTION, DRUGS, HEALTH, and MENTAL HEALTH, all of which have some relevance to the topic under discussion in this chapter.

In the volume entitled *Health*, for example, there are 60 reprints from such varying sources as *AFL/CIO American Federationist*, *Harvard Magazine*, and the Washington *Post*, sources not easily found through the usual channels of our search. Typical articles in this volume on health include "What Ails Medicare"; "Preventing Cancer"; "Do You Know Your Rights as a Patient?" and "The Malpractice Blow-up." There is a subject index in each volume to help you locate articles that bear on your special interest.

Another library resource that gathers not only reprints of

current magazine articles but also excerpts from books and speeches is the *Reference Shelf*. A recent title in that series pertaining to the subject of health is *Medical Care in the United States*, which includes information on health care, national health insurance, and the responsibilities of doctors. Pro and con points of view on controversial issues often emerge in the timely articles. Other significant titles recently issued in the series are *The Ocean Environment*, *The Death Penalty*, and *The World Food Crisis*.

TOMORROW'S SCIENCE

It is obvious that the results of scientific experiments, continuing research, and new technology can make today's news obsolete. Your library remains the most important source of materials that document these changes and can be examined at leisure. While it is true that television and radio are more current than any other media, their reports may be too brief and delivered so quickly that you do not have time to absorb the details of what you are hearing. After you have heard a TV talk-show discussion, for example, on the ramifications of a national health insurance bill, you can pursue the topic in depth by consulting magazines and newspapers via such indexes as the New York *Times Index, Facts on File, Editorial Research Reports*, and *Readers' Guide to Periodical Literature*.

Learning never stops. To continue to learn is to be alive.

SUGGESTED MATERIALS

Applied Science and Technology Index. New York: Wilson.

Blakiston's Gould Medical Dictionary. 3rd ed. New York: McGraw-Hill, 1972.

Busch, Phyllis S. *What About VD?* New York: Four Winds Press, 1976.

Căpek, Karel. *R.U.R.* New York: Washington Square Press.

Cattell's American Men and Women of Science. 13th ed. New York: Bowker, 1976.

Current Biography. New York: Wilson.

Current History. Philadelphia, PA: Current History, Inc.

Deason, Hilary J. *The AAAS Science Book List*. 3rd ed. Washington, D.C.: American Association for the Advancement of Science, 1970.

Directory of Medical Specialists. Chicago, IL: Marquis.

Eat, Drink and Be Wary. Film 19 min color. Los Angeles, CA: Churchill, 1974.

Encounters with Tomorrow: Science Fiction and Human Values. 6 filmstrips with cassettes or discs. New York: Harper, 1976.

Encyclopedia Americana. New York: Americana Corp.

The Ethical Challenge: Four Biomedical Case Studies. 2 carousels of slides with cassettes or discs. White Plains, NY: Center for Humanities.

The Ethics of Genetic Control. 2 carousels of slides with cassettes or discs. White Plains, NY: Center for Humanities.

Fishbein, Morris, ed. *Modern Home Medical Adviser: Your Health and How to Preserve It*. New York: Doubleday, 1969.

Fletcher, Joseph F. *The Ethics of Genetic Control*. New York: Doubleday, 1974.

General Science Index. New York: Wilson.

Genetics: Man the Creator. Film 22 min color. Toronto, Canada: Document Associates, 1971.

Goodfield, June. *Playing God: Genetic Engineering and the Manipulation of Life*. New York: Random, 1977.

Information Please Almanac. New York: Simon and Schuster.

Langone, John. *Bombed, Buzzed, Smashed, or . . . Sober: A Book About Alcohol*. Boston: Little, Brown, 1976.

Leidy, W. Philip, comp. *A Popular Guide to Government Publications*. 4th ed. New York: Columbia University Press, 1976.

Lipkin, Mack. *Straight Talk About Your Health Care*. New York: Harper, 1977.

McGraw-Hill Encyclopedia of Science and Technology. 4th ed. New York: McGraw-Hill, 1977. Yearbooks.

Merck Manual of Diagnosis and Therapy. 12th ed. Rahway, NJ: Merck and Co., 1972.

Natural History. New York: American Museum of Natural History.

Nutrition: Foods, Fads, Frauds, Facts. 3 filmstrips and cassettes. New York: Guidance Associates.

Progressive. Madison, WI: Progressive, Inc.

Reader's Digest Almanac. Pleasantville, NY: Reader's Digest Association.

Readers' Guide to Periodical Literature. New York: Wilson.

Reference Shelf series. New York: Wilson.

Science and Public Affairs (Bulletin of the Atomic Scientists). Chicago, IL: Educational Foundation for Nuclear Science, Inc.

Science News. Washington, D.C.: Science Service, Inc.

Scientific American. New York: Scientific American, Inc.

Sinacore, John S. *Health: A Quality of Life*. 2nd ed. New York: Macmillan, 1974.

Social Issues Resources Series (SIRS). Syracuse, NY: Gaylord Brothers.

Systems of the Human Body. 6 filmstrips and 3 cassettes. Baldwin, NY: Bear Films.

Today's Health Magazine. Chicago, IL: American Medical Association.

The Trans/vision Book of Health. Chicago, IL: Encyclopaedia Britannica, 1974.

U.S. Bureau of the Census. *Statistical Abstract of the United States*. Annual. Washington, D.C.: Government Printing Office.

U.S. News & World Report. Washington, D.C.: U.S. News & World Report, Inc.

Van Nostrand's Scientific Encyclopedia. 5th ed. New York: Van Nostrand Reinhold, 1976.

Wade, Nicholas. *The Ultimate Experiment: Man-Made Evolution*. New York: Walker, 1977.

Wagman, Richard J., ed. *Complete Illustrated Book of Better Health*. Chicago, IL: J. G. Ferguson, 1973.

Who's Who in America. Chicago, IL: Marquis.

Wilhelm, Kate. *Where Last the Sweet Birds Sang*. New York: Harper, 1976.

World Almanac and Book of Facts. New York: Newspaper Enterprise Association, Inc.

World Book Encyclopedia. Chicago, IL: Field Enterprises.

Chapter

4

YOUR FUTURE: VOCATIONAL AND COLLEGE INFORMATION

Most of us in our growing-up period have dreams about what we would like to be. Some of these are just dreams, not very realistic or capable of attainment, a bit like Walter Mitty's secret life. If you cannot carry a tune, a future in opera is not a wise choice, no matter how much you like the idea of it.

In the past some aspirations appeared unlikely because of the attitude of a society that had certain conceptions about which careers were suitable for women and which were reserved for men only. The old attitude has not changed completely, but women have now broken many of the barriers that kept them out of engineering, medicine, the military, and the trucking industry, to name a few formerly male-only job areas.

Now in your school years you are closer to making crucial decisions about your future. There are a number of alternatives, and sometimes there are certain restrictions.

To work or to go to college may be philosophical alternatives for a few but a more painful problem for many. Aside from the scholastic requirements for pursuing higher education, many young people must face a financial hurdle. Some families need the earning power of a young person to supplement the parents' income.

College education has often been equated, improperly, many think, with a way of earning more money. College can be the path to financial success but only if your choice leads to one of the profit-making professions, for example, business, medicine, or law. Teaching, librarianship, and social work, for instance, all require college and graduate study but do not lead to wealth. Clearly, then, the choice of a college education should be made for other reasons than material ones. College education should open challenging areas to one's intellect; it ought to provide resources that make for an interesting life as an adult.

Because some people feel that college and its benefits have been oversold, there have been many books describing worthwhile alternatives. Examples are Sarah Splaver's *Your Career if You're Not Going to College*, Caroline Bird's *The Case Against College*, and one title that discusses interrupting the college years, Judi Kesselman's *Stopping Out: A Guide to Leaving College and Getting Back in*.

If money is the prime factor in your decision about the future, there are many fields of endeavor that do not require college and graduate education. Some of these are vocations learned through apprenticeship, such as the plumbing and electrical trades, in which financial return can be quite good. Bird's book lists alternatives in vocational training, apprenticeships, arts and crafts, jobs that are mainly physical and outdoors.

Stopping Out describes the external degree program, giving details on how it works in 12 different states. It is in this very kind of self-learning activity that the library becomes your personal university.

It should be pointed out that the decision you make now does not have to be for the rest of your life. Surveys have been made that indicate that many people change their direction during their 30s and 40s. In fact, many college students change their minds about major studies during their college years.

How do you find out which route to take? You must, first of all, try to understand yourself. Being what your best friend is or what your parents hope you will be may be right for you—or it may be like putting on a straitjacket. Some of us have strong inclinations toward specific activities and just as strong aversions to others. Some people have so many interests and abilities that they are absolutely immobilized about making choices. There are agencies and counseling institutions that can help you. Many libraries now maintain special files called "Community Resources" or "Human Resources."

In a tray so labeled you can look under a heading like VOCATIONAL GUIDANCE and find listed there such community agencies as the local YMCA or local Youth Boards that are available to you for consultation. You may find specific information identifying local artisans, businessmen, or other persons who have indicated a willingness to come to schools and speak about their work, or have extended to students invitations to visit their shops and learn, at first hand, the operations involved in taxidermy, sculpting, or carpentry.

A valuable kit of slides and cassette tapes or recordings, *Self Fulfillment: Becoming the Person You Want to Be*, is full of information about the many alternatives open to young people in school, at work, and in their free time.

This kind of overview is also available to you in an encyclopedia that specializes in that kind of information. One such example is the *Encyclopedia of Careers and Vocational Guidance*. This two-volume reference, now in its third edition, not only gives general information about preparing for the world of work but also describes hundreds of vocational areas, analyzing them in terms of the nature of the work, employment outlook, opportunities for experience, earnings, advancement, work conditions, and lists other sources of information.

The vocations are arranged under broad headings, for example, PROFESSIONAL, MANAGERIAL AND TECHNICAL OCCUPATIONS; CLERICAL OCCUPATIONS; SALES OCCUPATIONS; SERVICE OCCUPATIONS. If you are interested in some area without having decided just exactly what aspect appeals most, this allows you to get an overall view. If, on the other hand, you are specifically interested in the airline industry and would like to consider being a flight attendant, how would you locate that information from among those broad categories? Just as you locate a topic like "Continental Congress" in your American history text: you would consult the index, which is arranged in alphabetical order.

Using reference resources sometimes requires some imagination. Flight attendants may be so listed but also be identified as AIRLINE PERSONNEL or STEWARDS AND STEWARDESSES. When one approach is not successful, you must try alternatives or synonyms for your topic, although reference books often help you by supplying cross-references to the correct subject heading.

Is there any drawback to using the information in a title like the *Encyclopedia of Careers and Vocational Guidance*? It is the same problem that exists in all subjects that are constantly changing. One must be careful to use the latest edition and, in fact, to note when that latest edition was published.

In an effort to be as current as possible in a field of change and fluctuation, the *Occupational Outlook Handbook* is published every two years by the United States Department of Labor, Bureau of Labor Statistics. This guide describes in detail over 800 occupations.

Realizing that even a regularly published title like the handbook, coming out every two years, will need updating in that interval, the Department of Labor also publishes the *Occupational Outlook Quarterly*, which brings more current information.

Another series designed for young people in search of the latest information about job opportunities and related educational requirements is *Current Career and Occupational Literature* by Leonard H. Goodman. It is published at two-year intervals and contains references to hundreds of pamphlets and books (free or inexpensive) grouped under many different job titles.

Two other titles worth examining are *Lovejoy's Career and Vocational School Guide* and Lederer's *Guide to Career Education*, which describes "200 Good Occupations That Do Not Require College Degrees."

Pamphlets and Documents

The United States Government Printing Office is one of the most prolific publishers, and government documents are a very valuable source of information on almost every subject from automation to zoology. A few libraries are designated as depositories and receive copies of a vast number of documents; most libraries buy only those documents that they think are useful for their library patrons. School libraries can check the *Monthly Catalog of Government Publications* to purchase titles in science, health, vocations, etc. Those leaflets, documents, brochures are generally found in your library's vertical file or information file. Many libraries try to make vocational information more accessible by putting all those that pertain to careers in a separate file called "Vocational Guidance."

Your information in the Vocational File related to airline flight attendant might not be in the drawer marked A. Where else would you look, then? AIRLINE WORKERS is a possibility or STEWARDS/STEWARDESSES.

In the folder labeled AIRLINE FLIGHT ATTENDANTS, a representative collection of material might include:

a Career Brief, published by Careers, Inc. (Largo, FL)
a booklet from Chronicle Guidance Publications (Moravia, NY)
promotional leaflets from airlines like Delta, American, Eastern
a booklet from an air career school
a reprint from *Mademoiselle* magazine
a reprint from *Manpower* magazine, official monthly journal of Manpower Administration, U.S. Department of Labor

These folders are kept as current as possible, with older materials being discarded and newer clippings, leaflets, government documents, and so forth being added.

Newspaper items and television programs are other sources of career information, as are magazine articles. You have probably used *Readers' Guide to Periodical Literature* before; here is another instance of its usefulness. Under the heading OCCUPATIONS the following entries appeared in the March 25, 1977 *Readers' Guide*:

Best job bets for 1985. Sr Schol 109:5 F 10 '77
100 best careers for the future. il Ebony 32:33-6+ Mr '77

1. Which is the longer of these two articles?
2. What does + stand for?
3. What magazine is "Sr Schol"?
4. Why does the date in the first entry include the number "10"?
5. What does "109" in the first entry stand for?

Check your answers against these:

1. The second article is the longer because it covers pages 33 through 36 and more, while the first article is listed as being contained on page 5.

2. The sign "+" means that the article is continued farther on in the magazine.

3. "Sr Schol" stands for *Senior Scholastic*. That abbreviation and the sign in the answer above are both explained in the list of abbreviations at the front of each issue of *Readers' Guide*.

4. Magazines that have more than one issue a month must include the *day* as well as the month and year. Other examples besides *Senior Scholastic* would be *Time, Newsweek, New Yorker*.

5. "109" stands for the volume of the magazine. The number *before* the colon (:) is a volume number: the number *after* the colon tells you the page or pages.

Many special magazines in the field of business and industry are published and to find that kind of article, you can use

AUGUST 1975–JULY 1976 885

VIOLENCE and television—*Continued*

JWT's Johnston says violent TV should get sponsors' axe. Broadcasting 90:33-4 Je 14 '76
Lear blames network execs for TV violence. C. Wingis. Adv Age 47:2+ My 3 '76
NPR is scene of blasts at commercials and children. Broadcasting 89:29 Ag 4 '75
No let-up on some fronts in attacks on TV violence. Broadcasting 89:20-1 D 22 '75
Others back TV violence gripes, but group action seen doubtful. M. Christopher. Adv Age 45[46]2+ D 1 '75
Plan to stem TV violence gaining fans: Knowlton. M. Christopher. Adv Age 47:8 Mr 22 '76
Public pressure mounts on TV violence, execs says. M. Christopher. Adv Age 47:1+ F 16 '76
Strong words from Knowlton on program violence. Broadcasting 89:28 N 24 '75
Study of violence effect on TV ads gains support. Adv Age 46:3+ D 8 '75
Two major studies for ABC-TV cite the many factors when assessing effect of TV violence on young. Broadcasting 90:109-11 Mr 22 '76
Use government report, TV violence foes urged. Adv Age 46:46 O 27 '75
Violence count finds decline in family time, nowhere else. Broadcasting 90:22+ Ap 5 '76
See also
Television broadcasting—Family viewing programs

VIOLENCE in labor disputes
ABC presses Davis-Bacon and violence issues. Eng N 196:10 Mr 4 '76
Hobbs act amendment would curb jobsite violence, crime. Air Cond Heat & Refrig N 137:4 Mr 15 '76
Mountaineer mine wars: an analysis of the West Virginia mine wars of 1912-1913 and 1920-1921. H. N. Wheeler. Bus Hist R 50:69-91 Spr '76
NABET on strike against NBC over manning new technology. Broadcasting 90:24 Ap 5 '76
Open shop work triggers violence and hardship. Eng N 196:10 F 12 '76
Rampage! [Washington Post] R. H. Green and M. F. Chazin. il Inland Ptr/Am Lith 176:39-41 N '75

VIRGIN ISLANDS
Shipping: closing a loophole in the Jones act. il Bus W p36-7 Ap 19 '76

VIRGINIA
See also
Norfolk
also subhead Virginia under the following subjects
Dams
Hydroelectric plants
Real estate business
Roads

VIRGINIA Chemicals Inc.
Virginia Chemicals reports record sales and earnings. Air Cond Heat & Refrig N 138:25 My 17 '76

VIRGINIA Electric & Power Company
Legal joust expands; contractor, sued by utility, charges faulty A-plant design. Eng N 196:13 Ap 29 '76
Virginia utility faced with possible nuclear fine. Pub Util 95:16 Je 19 '75

VIRUSES
See also
Antiviral agents

VISAS. See Passports

VISITORS
Fund raiser for local HBAs: a busman's holiday for visiting builders. il H & Home 48:10 D '75

VISITORS, Foreign. See Foreign visitors

VISUAL aids
How color visuals are created in daylight without chemicals. il Am Mgt 36:48-50 S '75
See also
Audio-visual materials

VISUAL aids in selling. See Salesmanship—Audio-visual aids

VISUAL instructions. See Audio-visual instruction

VITAL statistics
Cramped quarters yield space for the year 2000 [Alabama Division of Vital Statistics] il Adm Mgt 37:48-50 Ap '76
Key-to-disk speeds New York city vital statistics. il Infosystems 23:60+ My '76
See also
Birth rate
Census
Death—Causes
Fertility
Longevity
Mortality
Population—Statistics

VITAMINS
Ascorbic acid supplies high; purchases beginning to rise. Chem Mktg Rep 207:20 Je 30 '75
Chemical profile; ascorbic acid. Chem Mktg Rep 208:9 D 29 '75
FDA will make another attempt to revise vitamin regulations. Chem Mktg Rep 207:3+ Je 2 '75
Ford's decision on vitamin rider awaited. Chem Mktg Rep 209:3+ Ap 19 '76
Nutritional approach to marketing expands with vitamin C enriched tomato juice [Del Monte] il Food Process 36:31 N '75
Proxmire liberates vitamins. il Bus W p36 Mr 29 '76
Riboflavin, thiamine steady; supplies high, demand good. Chem Mktg Rep 208:25 Jl 14 '75
Vitamin C demand depressed; US producers see an upswing. Chem Mktg Rep 208:20 D 1 '75
Vitamin C is accused as a threat to DNA; charge sharply denied. Chem Mktg Rep 209:4+ My 24 '76
Vitamin E demand is down despite previous optimism. Chem Mktg Rep 208:19 Ag 11 '75
Vitamin regulations. R. L. Cherry. Chem Mktg Rep 208:9 D 22 '75
Vitamins: the latest in cosmetics that do something. Chem Mktg Rep 207:29 Je 23 '75

VITICULTURE
Fresh look at California vineyards. J. Madrick. Bus W p78 Je 14 '76

VIVA (periodical)
Viva covers up for its supermarket sales bid. B. Donath. Adv Age 47:80 My 10 '76

VOCATIONAL education
As I see it [interview with D. Rakoff] Forbes 117:64-6 F 15 '76
Consumer demand for professional and vocational education. H. Stillwell. Pub W 208:41-3 O 13 '75
Education for work. S. Lusterman. Conf Bd Rec 13:39-44 My '76
Fast-buck gimmicks mar career schools' record. Am Federationist 82:23 Ag '75.
Here's where you can get new office help. B. I. Blackstone. Office 83:132+ Ja '76
Labor's stake in vocational education. R. Oswald. Am Federationist 82:21-2+ Ag '75
See also
Deaf—Education
Employees, Training of
Occupational training

Russia

Development of vocational training in the USSR in response to scientific and technological progress. G. Bogatov. il Int Labour R 112:467-82 D '75

VOCATIONAL guidance
Notes from the job underground [career consultants and the executive job seeker] L. Smith. Duns R 106:46-8+ Ag '75
Positive view of self [guidance counselors] Pers J 55:104 Mr '76
See also
Counseling
Professions

VOCATIONAL rehabilitation
Effect of financing disabled beneficiary rehabilitation. R. Treitel. Soc Sec Bull 38:16-28 N '75
Employment process for rehabilitants: two studies of the hiring of emotional rehabilitants. C. A. Burden and R. Faulk. Pers J 54:529-31 O '75
Evaluating vocational rehabilitation programs for the disabled: national long-term follow-up study. J. Greenblum. Soc Sec Bull 38:3-12 O '75
It's not your usual programming class [California rehabilitation program] E. K. Yasaki. il Datamation 21:113+ D '75
See also
Handicapped—Employment

Great Britain

Disabled professional: his place at work. M. Kettle. il Pers Mgt 7:31-4 N '75
Handicapped—but doing a good job. il Pers Mgt 7:11+ N '75

Great Britain

Putting injured employees to work. D. Clutterbuck. il Int Mgt 31:27 Mr '76

VOICE
See also
Automatic speech recognition
Speech

VOICE analysis
CIA-tied technique adapted by agency for ad copy research. B. Donath. Adv Age 45[46] 3+ D 1 '75

VOICE of America. See Radio broadcasting—Government programs

VOICE-response systems. See Automatic speech recognition

Figure 9. From *Business Periodicals Index* (August 1975–July 1976)

the *Business Periodicals Index*, which resembles the *Readers' Guide* but indexes a different group of periodicals, all specializing in the field of business. Some of those are *Advertising Age, Bankers Monthly, The Economist, Journal of Taxation* and the *International Labour Review.* Figure 9 shows the kind of articles that appear under the subject heading VOCATIONAL EDUCATION in *Business Periodicals Index*—probably too specialized for your personal needs.

EXTENDING YOUR INFORMATION

Magazine articles can be very up-to-date, but they are not as likely to give you as much information as a book. The card or book catalog will direct you to titles if you look under the subject headings OCCUPATIONS; VOCATIONAL GUIDANCE or specific career titles like ENGINEERING AS A PROFESSION; NURSES AND NURSING; SALESMEN AND SALESMANSHIP.

The catalog card in Figure 10 describes a book of interest to women in the world of work. The title, *Saturday's Child*, written by Suzanne Seed can be found in the non-fiction section of the library where the 331s are shelved. Other titles

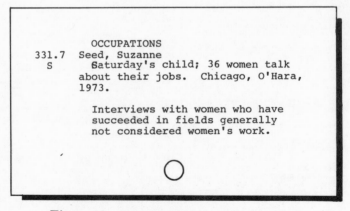

```
           OCCUPATIONS
331.7   Seed, Suzanne
  S       Saturday's child; 36 women talk
        about their jobs.  Chicago, O'Hara,
        1973.

          Interviews with women who have
          succeeded in fields generally
          not considered women's work.
```

Figure 10. Sample subject catalog card

will be discovered either by thumbing through the catalog or by browsing through the 331 section of the library. Some other books that are helpful in a variety of ways are:

Gordon G. Barnewall. *Your Future as a Job Applicant.*
Mark Boesch. *Careers in the Outdoors*. Forestry, soil science, and outdoor recreation among others
John Keefe. *The Teenager and the Interview*. Applications, summer jobs, college admissions, employment laws
Ruth Lemback. *Teenage Jobs*. For the immediate future
Charlotte Lobb. *Exploring Careers Through Volunteerism*. Suggestions for volunteer activities in many popular occupations
Joyce Slayton Mitchell. *I Can Be Anything*. Careers and colleges for young women, including how many women there are in various fields of work
William C. Ronco. *Jobs: How People Create Their Own.*

Another kind of book often gives information about a profession or calling—the biography or autobiography. You may know the name of a person in a field whose biography you can read, or you could select a person to read about by looking through Margaret Nicholsen's *People in Books: A Selective Guide to Biographical Literature Arranged by Vocations and Other Fields of Reader Interest*. The sample page in Figure 11 shows you how to find a biography or autobiography of someone who has been identified with a particular vocation, from engineering and sports to journalism and hotel management. The first volume published in 1969 has been continued by the 1977 publication of the First Supplement.

Some recent biographies that might be in your school or public library are:

HORSEMEN

American—20th century—*Continued*

Mesannie Wilkins

Wilkins, Mesannie and Sawyer, Mina Titus. Last of the Saddle Tramps. Prentice-Hall 1967 BKL A

English—20th century

William Holt

Holt, William. Ride a White Horse. Dutton 1967 BKL A

Lillie Langtry (Emily Charlotte [Le Breton] Langtry), 1852-1929

Gerson, Noel Bertram. Because I Loved Him: The Life and Loves of Lillie Langtry. Morrow 1971 BKL A

HORTICULTURISTS

American—19th century

Luther Burbank, 1849-1926

Beaty, John Y. Luther Burbank: Plant Magician. Messner 1943 ESLC—JH

American—20th century

Luther Burbank, 1849-1926

Beaty, John Y. Luther Burbank: Plant Magician. Messner 1943 ESLC—JH

Kraft, Ken and Kraft, Pat. Luther Burbank: The Wizard and the Man. Meredith 1967 BKL A&Y

COLLECTIONS

Bolton, Sarah (Knowles). Famous Men of Science; rev. by Barbara Lovett Cline. Crowell 1960; first published 1889 BESL—ESLC—JH

Hylander, Clarence J. American Scientists. Macmillan 1962; first published 1935 ESLC(5-6)

Hylander, Clarence J. American Scientists: Pioneer Teachers and Specialists. Macmillan 1968; first published 1935 ESLC(6-8)—JH—SH

HOTEL OWNERS AND MANAGERS

American—20th century

Jennie (Grossinger) Grossinger, 1892-1972

Pomerantz, Joel. Jennie and the Story of Grossinger's. Grosset 1970 BKL A—PLC

Conrad Nicholson Hilton, 1887-

COLLECTIONS

Lavine, Sigmund A. Famous Industrialists. Dodd 1961 (Famous Biographies for Young People) ESLC(6-8)—JH

Nation's Business. Lessons of Leadership: 21 Top Executives Speak Out on Creating, Developing and Managing Success. Doubleday 1968 SH

Russian—20th century

Boris Lissanevitch

Peissel, Michel. Tiger for Breakfast: The Story of Boris of Kathmandu. Dutton 1966 SH

HUMANITARIANS

See Philanthropists; Red Cross Workers; Social Workers

HUMORISTS

See also Cartoonists

American

COLLECTIONS

Allen, Everett S. Famous American Humorous Poets. Dodd 1968 (Famous Biographies for Young People) JH

Benét, Laura. Famous American Humorists. Dodd 1959 (Famous Biographies for Young People) JH

Ade; Benchley; Day; Field; Hale; Lardner; Leacock; Marquis; Nash; Shute; C. O. Skinner; Stockton; Streeter; Tarkington; Thurber; Twain; and others

American—19th century

Samuel Langhorne Clemens, 1835-1910

Allen, Jerry. The Adventures of Mark Twain. Little 1954 PLC

Baetzhold, Howard G. Mark Twain and John Bull: The British Connection. Ind. Univ. 1970 BKL A

Blair, Walter. Mark Twain & Huck Finn. Univ. of Calif. 1960 SH

Blair, Walter, ed. Mark Twain's Hannibal: Huck & Tom. Univ. of Calif. 1969 BKL A

Brooks, Van Wyck. The Ordeal of Mark Twain. Meridian 1955; first published 1920 SH

Cox, James Melville. Mark Twain: The Fate of Humor. Princeton Univ. 1966 BKL A—PLC

Daugherty, Charles Michael. Samuel Clemens. Crowell 1970 (A Crowell Biography) BKL C(2-5)—ESLC(1-5)

De Voto, Bernard Augustine. Mark Twain's America. Houghton 1951; first published 1932 PLC

Eaton, Jeanette. America's Own Mark Twain. Morrow 1958 ESLC—JH

Ganzel, Dewey. Mark Twain Abroad: The Cruise of the Quaker City. Univ. of Chicago 1968 BKL A

Geismar, Maxwell David. Mark Twain: An American Prophet. Houghton 1970 BKL A

Gordon, Edwin. Mark Twain. Crowell-Collier 1966 (America in the Making) BKL C&Y(7-10)—JH

Kaplan, Justin, ed. Mark Twain: A Profile. Hill & Wang 1967 (American Profiles) BKL A—PLC

Kaplan, Justin. Mr. Clemens and Mark Twain: A Biography. Simon & Schuster 1966 PLC—SH

Lorch, Fred W. The Trouble Begins at Eight: Mark Twain's Lecture Tours. Iowa State Univ. 1968 BKL A

McNeer, May Yonge. America's Mark Twain. Houghton 1962 BESL—CC—ESLC

Miers, Earl Schenck. Mark Twain on the Mississippi. World 1957 JH

Figure 11. From *People in Books (First Supplement)*

Bill Bradley. *Life on the Run* (basketball)
Margot Fonteyn. *Autobiography* (ballet)
Muhammad Ali. *The Greatest* (boxing)
Arthur Ashe. *Arthur Ashe, Portrait in Motion* (tennis)
Lynn M. Osen. *Women in Mathematics*

You will also find many newer titles by browsing in local bookstores which probably also arrange their stock so that biographies may be shelved together.

Brief biographical information about people in many fields of work is available in *Current Biography*, which carries on the inside front cover of every issue a list of the professions included in the issue.

More library media centers in the past years have been adding audiovisual resources to their collections and there are some excellent materials in this format for career and vocational information. For example, when you look through the catalog tray in which VOCATIONAL GUIDANCE is filed, the following card may be found:

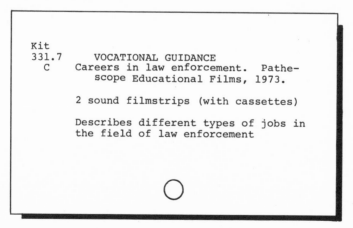

```
Kit
331.7      VOCATIONAL GUIDANCE
  C     Careers in law enforcement.  Pathe-
           scope Educational Films, 1973.

        2 sound filmstrips (with cassettes)

        Describes different types of jobs in
        the field of law enforcement
```

Figure 12. Sample subject catalog card for audiovisual material

As with books, the number in the upper left-hand corner of the card gives you the location of the material. In some libraries you may find this kit shelved with all other materials having the same number. In other centers, where it is not possible to shelve audiovisual materials with books because of the variation in size of formats, you will ask the librarian at the desk to get you this material. Perhaps you will be able to borrow the kit, along with a filmstrip viewer and cassette player; otherwise you will be directed to that part of the library media center where the equipment is kept out throughout the day for use by patrons.

Some libraries prepare special bibliographies of audiovisual resources that you can consult for the titles and location numbers of such materials as these:

Jobs in Health Service.
8 filmstrips and 8 cassettes which describe the work of the dental assistant, dental laboratory technician, medical laboratory assistant, medical photographer, nurse's aide, optical technician, optometric assistant, radiology technician.

The Essence of Accounting.
6 filmstrips and 3 cassettes designed to introduce the student to the purposes and elements of accounting and its general terminology.

Choosing the Kind of Job You Want.
2 filmstrips and 2 cassettes (plus other instructional materials) which are part of a series on Career Directions using interviews with various people, many of them young, to describe various kinds of jobs, their advantages and disadvantages. Also useful in this connection are the other three titles in the series: *Deciding on Your Career, Entering the Job Market*, and *Staying With It and Getting Ahead.*

There are many technician-level and semiprofessional jobs that do require some post-high school training, for example those in the areas of health and public services. *Occupational Education*, edited by Max Russell, contains useful information on where to go for further technical and professional education:

1. A list of occupational schools of the United States arranged alphabetically by states and then by schools within those states.
2. An alphabetical list of curricula and programs of instruction with the names and locations of the schools giving training in that area.
3. Lists of business schools, two-year institutions, accredited home study schools, accredited medical and dental programs, Veterans Administration-approved schools, nursing schools, and sources of financial aid.

College Questions

The titles by Splaver and Bird discussed at the beginning of this chapter direct themselves to the question of *whether* college should be your choice. Important in that decision is a clear understanding of what the purposes of a college education are.

If you have decided that going to college is the necessary prerequisite for the future you have chosen, there remain these problems to answer:

1. Are there geographical considerations?
2. Do you and your family prefer you to be at home and commute to school?
3. Are you qualified according to the admissions requirements of the college(s) you wish to attend?

4. How much will college cost and how will you meet those expenses?

A number of directories are available that give information on these points:

History of the school
Statement of the school's philosophy
Profile of entering freshmen in terms of academic standing
Number of faculty
Number of students
Size of library
Student campus life
Degree requirements
Admissions requirements
Financial costs and aid

One such guide is the *Comparative Guide to American Colleges* by James Cass and Max Birnbaum. Unlike most other college directories, this one is alphabetically arranged by name of college. In order to supply the geographical information that you may want, there is a state index as well as a religious index and a selectivity index. The last-mentioned index indicates how selective a school is, that is, how difficult, comparatively, it is to gain admission. The sample page shown in Figure 13 illustrates the amount of detail given under the various categories listed above.

In most directories the main section is arranged alphabetically *by state* with the colleges and universities listed alphabetically under each state. These are some good examples:

American Universities and Colleges (revised every four years) gives background on higher education, admis-

commute. Sexes segregated in coed dormitories by floor. There are 14 fraternities, 9 sororities on campus which about 30% of men, 32% of women join; 5% of men live in fraternities; sororities provide no residence facilities. About 10% of students leave campus on weekends.

ANNUAL COSTS. Tuition and fees, $3,300; room and board, $1,700; estimated $300 other, exclusive of travel. About 25% of students receive financial aid; average amount of assistance, $2,561. University reports some scholarships awarded on the basis of academic merit alone; nongovernmental loans available to middle-income students.

Newcomb College

New Orleans, Louisiana 70118

1,501 W (full-time) Independent, 1886
71 W (part-time)

The coordinate women's liberal arts college of Tulane, the H. Sophie Newcomb Memorial College maintains its own faculty, curriculum, and extracurricular activities. At the same time, it is an integral part of the university, and its students participate in all aspects of university life. The college occupies part of the university's 100-acre main campus in a residential area of New Orleans.

ADMISSION is very selective. About 81% of applicants accepted, 42% of these actually enroll; 53% of freshmen graduate in top fifth of high school class, 79% in top two-fifths. Average freshman SAT scores: 521 verbal, 531 mathematical; 80% of freshmen score above 500 on verbal, 22% above 600; 89% score above 500 on mathematical, 25% above 600. *Required:* SAT or ACT; ACH, interview recommended. *Nonacademic factors* considered of moderate importance in admissions: alumnae daughters, diverse student body, special talents. *Entrance programs:* early decision, early admission, midyear admission, advanced placement, deferred admission. *Apply* by February 1. *Transfers* welcome; 151 accepted 1976–77.

ACADEMIC ENVIRONMENT. Unit curriculum requires completion of 32 academic units, each equivalent to 4 semester hours. Normal load is 4 units per semester. Continuing emphasis on interdepartmental seminars, interdisciplinary majors, and colloquia. Women's studies courses in several departments. Administration reports 30–40% of courses required for graduation are elective; distribution requirements fairly numerous: 2 credits in each of 3 broad groupings (social sciences, humanities, natural sciences), plus 5 other credits outside major. *Degrees:* AB, BS, BFA. *Majors offered* include usual arts and sciences, anthropology, theater; coordinate major in Latin American studies.

Class attendance required. *Pass/fail option* in all courses. About 58% of students entering as freshmen graduate eventually; 15% of freshmen do not return for sophomore year. *Special programs:* independent study, study abroad, honors, undergraduate research, 3-year degree, individualized majors, combined degree programs in law, medicine, business administration, student-initiated colloquia. *Calendar:* semester. *Miscellaneous:* Phi Beta Kappa.

GRADUATES CAREER DATA. *Full-time graduate study* pursued immediately after graduation by 20% of students; 2% enter medical school; less than 1% enter dental school; 6% enter law school. *Careers in business and industry* pursued by 20% of graduates.

FACULTY. About 83% of senior faculty, 75% of assistant professors hold doctorate.

STUDENT BODY. College seeks a national student body; 63% of students from South, 16% North Central, 13% Middle Atlantic. *Minority group students:* special financial, academic, and social provisions including tutoring, Black Student Union.

CAMPUS LIFE. Newcomb shares social and cultural life of the university; also initiates and maintains student activities of its own. The Women's Center will provides career counseling. Freshmen required to live on campus. Drinking permitted for those of legal age; cars allowed. Intervisitation hours vary with dormitories.

About 69% of women live in traditional dormitories; 10% in coed dormitories; rest live in off-campus housing or commute. Sexes segregated in coed dormitories by floor. There are 9 sororities on campus which about 32% of women join; they provide no residence facilities. About 10% of students leave campus on weekends.

ANNUAL COSTS. Tuition and fees, $3,300; room and board, $1,700; estimated $300 other, exclusive of travel. About 25% of students receive financial aid; average amount of assistance, $2,561. College reports some scholarships awarded on the basis of academic merit alone; nongovernmental loans available to middle-income students.

UNIVERSITY OF TULSA

Tulsa, Oklahoma 74104

1,901 M, 1,477 W (full-time) Independent, 1894
695 M, 562 W (part-time)
6,309 total graduate and undergraduate

An independent institution, located in a city of 500,000, formerly affiliated with the United Presbyterian Church.

ADMISSION is selective. About 85% of applicants accepted, 64% of these actually enroll. Average freshman scores: SAT, 488 M, 491 W verbal, 544 M, 495 W mathematical; 46% of freshmen score above 500 on verbal, 15% above 600; 59% score above 500 on mathematical, 29% above 600; ACT, 23.3 M, 21.3 W composite, 23.2 M, 20.1 W mathematical. *Required:* SAT or ACT. *Entrance programs:* early admission, midyear admission, advanced placement, deferred admission. *Apply:* rolling admissions. *Transfers* welcome; 690 accepted 1976–77.

ACADEMIC ENVIRONMENT. Administration reports continuing efforts to revise degree requirements to permit increased freedom of course selection "within a fixed credit requirement in specific fields of learning." *Undergraduate studies* offered by colleges of Arts and Sciences, Business Administration, Education, Engineering and Physical Sciences, Nursing. *Majors offered* in Arts and Sciences in addition to usual studies include anthropology, mass media news, library science, medical record administration, medical technology, telecommunications, theater, urban studies. *Undergraduate degrees conferred* (874): 19% were in business and management, 17% in education, 13% in social

Figure 13. From *Comparative Guide to American Colleges* (1977)

sions and problems, as well as the listing of institutions.

The College Blue Book (15th edition) is in 3 volumes: U.S. Colleges: Narrative Descriptions; U.S. Colleges: Tabular Data; Degrees Offered by Colleges and Subjects. The first volume is the one you will find most useful, arranged by state and with a map accompanying each state for locating the institutions listed.

Barron's Profiles of American Colleges (10th edition) is in two volumes with Volume 1 giving the college information and Volume 2 offering information about curriculum specialties. The introductory section contains comparisons on the relative competitive aspects of colleges, ranging from "most competitive" to "noncompetitive." Brief update information is also available on new programs and on trends and changes.

Lovejoy's College Guide is divided into 3 sections. In the first part there is much information on how to choose a college, when to apply, entrance examinations, expenses, financial help, etc. Section 2, entitled "Career Curricula and Special Programs," is an alphabetical list of careers with the names of the schools best suited for pursuing those. The third section gives brief descriptions of the colleges, arranged by state. Some rather unusual lists in *Lovejoy* also name schools that offer cooperative education (work/study), correspondence schools and external curricula, colleges with facilities for handicapped students, honors programs, etc.

The usual classification number (Dewey) for shelving books of this kind is 378.73, and browsing in that area will enable you to examine, compare, and decide which directory is best for your purposes by checking the table of contents and discovering the special features of each.

Obviously, the most complete information about any one college will be contained in its own catalog, which can run to one hundred or more pages. Your high school media center, your public library, and your high school college adviser all probably maintain a current file of college catalogs, at least those most frequently requested. In them you will find not only all the data given in more abbreviated form in the directories listed above but also detailed information about the courses of study offered, kinds of degrees given, scholarships available, teaching staff, how the institution is governed, and sometimes even pictures of the college and its environs.

TWO-YEAR INSTITUTIONS

Since the 1950s there has been a great increase in the number of two-year and community colleges. For reasons having to do with scholarship, finances, and the amount of time available to a young person for higher education after finishing high school, many students have found the answer to their needs in these institutions, which offer such degrees as Associate in Arts. There are directories that also give information for these institutions.

Barron's Guide to the Two-Year Colleges is in two volumes. Volume 1 gives descriptions of junior colleges, community colleges, technical-vocational institutes, business schools, and 4-year colleges which have 2-year programs. Volume 2 is the Occupational Program Selector.

Cass and Birnbaum's *Comparative Guide to Two-Year Colleges and Career Programs* includes information on non-residential institutions and offers an alphabetical index of programs, ranging from "Accounting

Technologies" to "Welding Technologies" with the names of schools where those careers can be pursued. For example, if your interest is in a vocation related to recreational activities, under the heading "Recreation Leadership" you will find 38 states listed and under each the school(s) offering pertinent courses. This directory is arranged by state and there is a religious index.

Unusual Choices

The interest shown by high school students in "alternative" or "free" schools is reflected also in directories giving information about non-traditional education at the post-secondary level.

One directory, *Guide to External and Continuing Education*, is arranged by state. *Guide to Alternative Colleges and Universities: A Comprehensive Listing of Over 250 Innovative Programs* is arranged alphabetically by school and has a geographical index. Colleges like Antioch, Bennington, and Goddard have long been known for their open structure but this book describes unusual programs offered by such institutions as Brooklyn College. The range of alternative plans includes not only campus-based learning but also on-the-job learning in occupations like mining and fishing; learning at "free" universities; and foreign educational programs, including World Campus Afloat.

Another unusual directory is John Coyne's *This Way Out: A Guide to Alternatives to Traditional College Education in the United States, Europe and the Third World*. Information given includes a directory of experimental colleges and a study/travel guide to education abroad.

MEETING COLLEGE COSTS

In a filmstrip/cassette kit entitled *How Can I Pay for College* you learn how three students go about making plans for meeting their college expenses. The four filmstrips in the kit—"Available Help to Pay for College"; "Making the System Respond"; "Maximizing Your Assets"; and "Doing it by Day-Hopping"—show what you, your family, your school, and your college adviser should know about how to obtain loans, scholarships, and part-time work to pay college costs. In this filmstrip you follow the students until their acceptance at New York University, Pace University, and Yale. Just as the three schools are different from each other, so are the families and neighborhoods from which the students in the filmstrip come.

The Barron's Educational Series includes two guides to financial aid for college and for two-year institutions. *Barron's Handbook of American College Financial Aid* is arranged by state with the colleges listed alphabetically under each. Information in tabular form is given (Figure 14) about the kinds of forms and statement required (for example, the Parents' Confidential Statement or Student's Financial Statement), what grants or loans are available, who is eligible, and the person to whom to write at the college or university. *Barron's Handbook of Junior and Community College Financial Aid* gives the same kind of information for these institutions.

Official College Entrance Examination Board Guide to Financial Aid for Students and Parents offers background on what kind of aid is available, the kinds of forms that must be completed (with samples included) and chapters on such specific sources as the Basic Educational Opportunity Grant

Name of Institution Bridgewater State College

Public X **Private** ___

Financial Aid Corresponding Address
(of Person Responsible For Financial Aid)

David A. Morwick
Director of Financial Aid
Bridgewater State College
Bridgewater, Massachusetts 02324

		Application Required					Available to				
		PCS or SFS	ACT	Coll. Form	Other	Appl. Date*	Fr.	Soph.	Jr.	Sr.	Transfer
Grants Available	Nursing Scholarship										
	Ed. Opportunity Grant	X				4/1	All students				
	L.E.E.P.										
	College Work-Study Program	X				4/1	All students				
	Campus Part-time Work										
	Off-campus Part-time Work										
	State Grants										
	Instit. Scholarships or Grants										
	Commun./Jr. College Graduates										
Loans Available	National Direct Student Loan	X				4/1	All students				
	United Student Aid Funds										
	Guaranteed Loan Program				X	open	All students				
	L.E.E.P.										
	College or Univ. Loans										
	Deferred Tuition Payment Plan										
	Commun./Jr. College Graduates										
	Nursing Student Loan Program										

Name of Institution Clark University

Public ___ **Private** X

Financial Aid Corresponding Address
(of Person Responsible For Financial Aid)

Robert M. Kidd
Director of Financial Aid
Clark University
950 Main Street
Worcester, Massachusetts 01610

		Application Required					Available to				
		PCS or SFS	ACT	Coll. Form	Other	Appl. Date*	Fr.	Soph.	Jr.	Sr.	Transfer
Grants Available	Nursing Scholarship										
	Ed. Opportunity Grant	X				2/1	X	X	X	X	ltd.
	L.E.E.P.										
	College Work-Study Program	X				2/1	All students				
	Campus Part-time Work										
	Off-campus Part-time Work										
	State Grants										
	Instit. Scholarships or Grants	X				2/1	X	X	X	X	ltd.
	Commun./Jr. College Graduates										
Loans Available	National Direct Student Loan	X				2/1	X	X	X	X	ltd.
	United Student Aid Funds										
	Guaranteed Loan Program				X	open	All students				
	L.E.E.P.										
	College or Univ. Loans			X		2/1	X	X	X	X	ltd.
	Deferred Tuition Payment Plan				X		All students				
	Commun./Jr. College Graduates										
	Nursing Student Loan Program										

Name of Institution College of the Holy Cross

Public ___ **Private** X

Financial Aid Corresponding Address
(of Person Responsible For Financial Aid)

Director of Financial Aid
College of the Holy Cross
Worcester, Massachusetts 06110

		Application Required					Available to				
		PCS or SFS	ACT	Coll. Form	Other	Appl. Date*	Fr.	Soph.	Jr.	Sr.	Transfer
Grants Available	Nursing Scholarship										
	Ed. Opportunity Grant	X		X			X	X	X	X	
	L.E.E.P.										
	College Work-Study Program	X		X		2/1	All students				
	Campus Part-time Work	X		X		2/1	All students				
	Off-campus Part-time Work										
	State Grants	X		X		2/1	All students				
	Instit. Scholarships or Grants	X		X		2/1	X	X	X	X	
	Commun./Jr. College Graduates										
Loans Available	National Direct Student Loan	X		X		2/1	All students				
	United Student Aid Funds	X		X		open	All students				
	Guaranteed Loan Program	X		X		open	All students				
	L.E.E.P.										
	College or Univ. Loans										
	Deferred Tuition Payment Plan										
	Commun./Jr. College Graduates										
	Nursing Student Loan Program										

*Application Deadline Date

197

Figure 14. From *Barron's Handbook of American College Financial Aid*

Program, Guaranteed Student Loan Program, Special-Purpose Programs, State Resources, Local Resources. Under State Resources, for example, the list for New York includes: Higher Education Opportunity Program; New York Tuition Assistance Program; New York State Regents College and Nursing Scholarships; Children of Veterans Awards; War Veterans Scholarships; Educational Opportunity Programs; College Discovery; SEEK. For each entry there is a description of the grant or scholarship, a statement of who is eligible, and an address to which you can write for more information and an application.

Financial Aids for Higher Education 76–77 Catalog gives information about the college entrance examination tests (Preliminary Scholastic Aptitude Test, Scholastic Aptitude Test, National Merit Scholarship Qualifying Test, American College Testing Program), kinds of financial statements that may be needed, and an alphabetical list of programs offering financial aid.

The vertical file will contain brochures, announcements, and lists of financial aid programs available from national corporations, fraternal organizations, labor unions, and other agencies that offer this kind of assistance. Government documents like *Springboard to Education After High School: Five Federal Financial Programs* may also be filed there.

Ready or Not?

Long before you have made definite decisions about choosing a specific college, you will be preparing to take examinations like the Preliminary Scholastic Aptitude Test (PSAT), the Scholastic Aptitude Test (SAT), College Entrance Examination Board achievement tests, and National Merit Scholarship exams.

There are books containing sample tests as well as lessons on improving vocabulary, mathematical skills, and reading comprehension. Your library will probably have these titles or similar ones:

Barron's How to Prepare for the American College Testing Program

Scholastic Aptitude Test (SAT) for College Entrance

The College Boards Examination: Complete Preparation for the Scholastic Aptitude Test (SAT/PSAT/NMSQT (verbal and mathematical sections)

Scoring High on College Entrance Examinations. 3 cassettes which tell you how to train for the task

Individual titles useful in preparation for the achievement tests in specific subjects like physics, biology, or English are also available. Young people today, accustomed to owning their own paperbacks, spend more time in bookstores and will find, in the larger stores, whole sections devoted to handbooks that help to prepare for entrance into college or career. You may wish to buy your own copy and write out the answers to sample examinations or you can recommend that the titles be purchased by your school or public library if it does not already own them.

Your preparation for higher education or employment begins much further back than the taking of these special examinations. The school record you have formed tells your prospective employer or college admissions officer something important about your school work, your character, and your contribution to the group of which you are a member. We all differ from each other in special talents. Some of us excel in mathematics, science, or foreign language; others are outstanding in music, dance, sports, or creative writing.

There are, however, areas in which we can all be more alike. Regular attendance, regular use of the resources of your school and public libraries, honest preparation of work assigned, to the best of *your* ability—these are all within the capabilities of every student. As with most undertakings, the more you give to an activity, the more return you can expect. That is as true of your academic responsibilities as it is of your basketball practice.

SUGGESTED MATERIALS

Ali, Muhammad. *The Greatest, My Own Story*. New York: Random, 1975.

American Universities and Colleges. 11th ed. Washington, D.C.: American Council on Education, 1973.

Ashe, Arthur and Frank Deford. *Arthur Ashe, Portrait in Motion*. Boston, MA: Houghton, 1975.

Barnewall, Gordon G. *Your Future as a Job Applicant*. New York: Arco, 1976.

Barron's Guide to the Two-Year Colleges. Woodbury, NY: Barron's Educational Series, 1975.

Barron's How to Prepare for the American College Testing Program. Woodbury, NY: Barron's Educational Series, 1976.

Barron's Profiles of American Colleges. 10th ed. Woodbury, NY: Barron's Educational Series, 1976.

Bird, Caroline. *The Case Against College*. New York: McKay, 1975.

Blaze, Wayne and others. *Guide to Alternative Colleges and Universities: A Comprehensive Listing of Over 250 Innovative Programs*. Boston, MA: Beacon, 1974.

Boesch, Mark. *Careers in the Outdoors*. New York: Dutton, 1975.

Bradley, Bill. *Life on the Run*. New York: Quadrangle/New York Times Book, 1976.

Business Periodicals Index. New York: Wilson.

Career Directions: Planning for Career Decisions. 2 filmstrips and cassettes or discs. Washington, D.C.: Visual Education Corp.; Changing Times Education Service, 1974.

Cass, James and Max Birnbaum. *Comparative Guide to American Colleges*. 8th ed. New York: Harper, 1977.

Cass, James and Max Birnbaum. *Comparative Guide to Two-Year Colleges and Career Programs*. New York: Harper, 1976.

Choosing the Kind of Job You Want. 2 filmstrips and 2 cassettes. Princton, NJ: Visual Education Corp.

College Blue Book. 15th ed. New York: Macmillan, 1975.

Coyne, John and Tom Hebert. *This Way Out: A Guide to Alternatives to Traditional College Education in the U.S., Europe and the Third World*. New York: Dutton, 1972.

Encyclopedia of Careers and Vocational Guidance. William E. Hopke, ed. Garden City, NY: Doubleday, 1975.

The Essence of Accounting. 6 filmstrips and 3 cassettes. Jamaica, NY: Eye Gate.

Fonteyn, Margot. *Margot Fonteyn: Autobiography*. New York: Knopf, 1976.

Goodman, Leonard H. *Current Career and Occupational Literature:* 1973–1977. New York: Wilson, 1978.

Gruber, Edward C. and Morris Bramson. *Scholastic Aptitude Test*. New York: Monarch, 1973.

Guide to External and Continuing Education. Moravia, NY: Chronicle Guidance Pub., 1976.

How Can I Pay For College? 4 filmstrips and 2 cassettes. Jamaica, NY: Eye Gate.

Jobs in Health Services. 8 filmstrips and 8 cassettes. Chicago, IL: Coronet Instructional Films, 1971.

Keefe, John. *The Teenager and the Interview*. New York: Richards Rosen, 1971.

Keeslar, Oreon. *Financial Aids for Higher Education 76–77 Catalog*. 7th ed. Dubuque, IA: William C. Brown, 1976.

Kesselman, Judi R. *Stopping Out: A Guide to Leaving College and Getting Back In*. New York: Evans, 1976.

Lederer, Muriel. *The Guide to Career Education*. New York: Quadrangle/New York Times Book, 1976.

Lembeck, Ruth. *Teenage Jobs*. New York: McKay, 1971.

Lobb, Charlotte. *Exploring Careers Through Volunteerism*. New York: Richards Rosen, 1976.

Lovejoy, Clarence E. *Lovejoy's Career and Vocational School Guide*. New York: Simon and Schuster, 1973.

Lovejoy, Clarence E. *Lovejoy's College Guide*. New York: Simon and Schuster, 1976.

McDonough, Martin and Alvin J. Hansen. *The College Boards Examination: Complete Preparation for the Scholastic Aptitude Test* (SAT/PSAT/NMSQT—verbal and mathematical sections). New ed. New York: Arco, 1972.

Mitchell, Joyce Slayton. *I Can Be Anything; Careers and Colleges for Young Women*. New York: College Entrance Examination Board, 1975.

Nicholsen, Margaret E. *People in Books: A Selective Guide to Biographical Literature Arranged By Vocations and Other Fields of Reader Interest*. New York: Wilson, 1969. *Supplement*. 1977.

Occupational Outlook Handbook. Division of Manpower and Occupational Outlook. Washington, D.C.: Government Printing Office.

Osen, Lynn M. *Women in Mathematics*. Massachusetts Institute of Technology, 1974.

Proia, Nicholas C. and Vincent M. DiGaspari. *Barron's Handbook of American College Financial Aid*. Woodbury, NY: Barron's Educational Series, 1977.

Proia, Nicholas C. and Vincent M. DiGaspari. *Barron's Handbook of Junior and Community College Financial Aid*. Woodbury, NY: Barron's Educational Series, 1977.

Readers' Guide to Periodical Literature. New York: Wilson.

Ronco, William C. *Jobs: How People Create Their Own*. Boston, MA: Beacon, 1977.

Russell, Max M., ed. *Occupational Education*. New York: CCM Information Corp., 1972.

Scoring High on College Entrance Examinations. 3 cassettes. Port Chester, NY: Multi Dimensional Communications.

Seed, Suzanne. *Saturday's Child*. Chicago, IL. 1973.

Self-Fulfillment: Becoming the Person You Want to Be. 3 sets of slides and cassettes or discs. White Plains, NY: Center for Humanities, 1976.

Splaver, Sarah. *Your Career if You're Not Going to College*. New York: Messner, 1971.

Springboard to Education After High School: Five Federal Aid Programs. (Government document) #OE 77–17911, Washington, D.C.: Government Printing Office.

Suchar, Elizabeth and others. *Official College Entrance Examination Board Guide to Financial Aid for Students and Parents*. New York: Monarch, 1975.

U.S. Superintendent of Documents. *Monthly Catalog of Government Publications*. Washington, D.C.: Government Printing Office.

Chapter 5

LIVING IN ONE WORLD: WAR AND PEACE

In a world that has become very small because of the speed of travel and communication, the issues of war and peace are close to all of us regardless of how far away a troubled area is. At this time in the history of earth, political leaders and experienced observers are in general agreement that the Middle East is the most politically volatile area of the world and, consequently, the most important to understand.

Geography

What is meant by the term Middle East? Exactly where is it? Locating it geographically is a first step. For that kind of information we may look in a geographical dictionary. *Webster's New Geographical Dictionary* is arranged like any word dictionary you have used. There are about 47,000 place names, both current and historical, and some maps. Other useful features are a glossary of geographical terms and a list of map symbols. Finding Middle East in its alphabetical place we learn that it is "an extensive region comprising the countries of SW Asia and NE Africa; term formerly also included Afghanistan, Pakistan, India and Burma; an indefinite and unofficial term; the U.S. Department of State does not officially employ it."

The Columbia–Lippincott Gazetteer of the World is a similar but larger reference work. Gazetteer means geographical dictionary or index. This volume contains over 130,000 names with many cross-references and gives a great deal of detailed information. For example, under MIDDLE EAST, Columbia–Lippincott not only locates the area but also lists all the nations covered by that umbrella term. It reminds the reader that "In America the term Near East is often used as a synonym for the Middle East and is the term used by the U.S. Department of State." (Keep in mind, however, that the latest edition of the *Columbia–Lippincott*—1952, with a 1961 supplement—is now older than the latest edition of *Webster's*.) Large dictionaries like *The American Heritage Dictionary of the English Language*, *Random House Dictionary of the English Language*, and *Funk and Wagnalls Standard College Dictionary* all give a limited amount of geographical information. *Webster's Third New International Dictionary of the English Language*, however, does not include any geographical information.

Locating our area in words must be extended to locating it in its relationship to a broader area, seeing it with its boundaries and size and shape. This is possible by finding it on a map. Many libraries maintain map files in which individual maps are kept by region. (There is, for example, a single map issued by The Hammond Company entitled "Middle East Crisis Map.") All libraries have collections of maps bound as books that are called atlases. These range from not very large to oversized. An example of the smaller variety is *Goode's*

World Atlas, a collection of physical, economic, and political maps that includes such specialized features as a "world portrait map" and a "natural vegetation map."

Among the larger atlases are the *Hammond Ambassador World Atlas, Rand McNally Cosmopolitan World Atlas*, and *The New York Times Atlas of the World.* The extra kinds of information given in various atlases range from the inclusion of postal zip numbers to maps showing the world's food, energy, and mineral resources or the prevailing weather pattern in a certain region of the earth. A look at the table of contents of the atlas will tell you of these special features.

In every instance, an atlas will have an index so that you can locate a place name immediately. For example, in discussions on the Middle East, the Gaza Strip is frequently mentioned. The index entry in the *Rand McNally Cosmopolitan World Atlas* will have this listing: "Gaza Strip, Isr. occ., Asia C6 32." The translation is: Israeli-occupied land, found on a map of Asia, page 32, within the area of C6, which can be found by using the map's grid system, as in the diagram below:

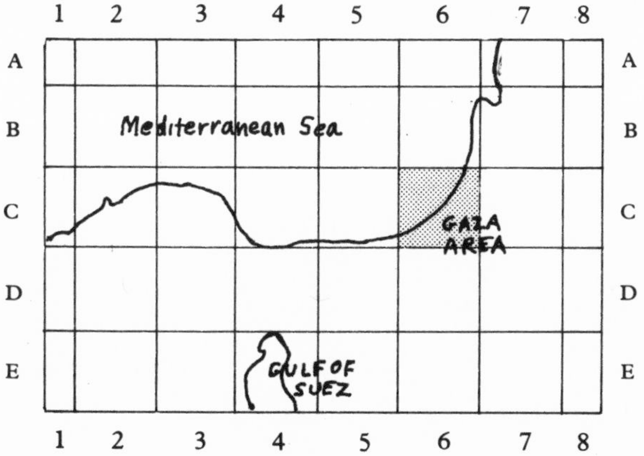

Figure 15. From *Rand McNally Cosmopolitan World Atlas*

It has already been pointed out that maps may be physical, economic, or political in their representation. Some atlases specialize in one kind of information. One example is the *Oxford Economic Atlas of the World* in which there are maps showing such information as precipitation, soil classification, and raw materials. Since the Organization of Petroleum Exporting Countries (OPEC) is a major factor in the Middle East situation, the maps in this atlas indicating the areas where crude oil is produced and those where it is refined are useful. Also included in this atlas are statistical charts for countries with economic information which is not easily accessible elsewhere.

History

Geography is only one aspect of what is needed to understand current events. The history, customs, and other unique characteristics of a country enable us to see better why certain events take place or why the people of a certain country behave as they do. Encyclopedias are a good starting point and offer a little background or quite a good deal, depending on which one you use. *World Book* has a five-page article on the Middle East with cross-references to articles on Israel, Jordan, etc. *Encyclopedia Americana* gives a 34-page article with a chronology of events from the years 622 to 1976. Included is information on the history, the people, their cultural life, and recent developments. *Collier's* gives approximately the same information in an article that is just a bit shorter.

A specialized encyclopedia is the five-volume *Worldmark Encyclopedia of Nations* consisting of the following: United Nations; Africa; Americas; Asia and Australia; Europe.

While the information included is what one expects in any encyclopedia article, that is, history, geography, climate, economy, religion, culture, education, etc., it is the style of the presentation that makes this reference easy to use.

A special reference title is the *Area Handbook Series*, published by United States Army and prepared by individual experts under the direction of the Foreign Area Studies Department of the American University in Washington, D.C. Each volume covers one country, and for some of those countries it is the only available source of information in English. There are volumes for the United Arab Republic (Egypt), Syria, Saudi Arabia, and Israel. Basic data are given briefly at the beginning of each volume and then much detail follows on the social, historical, cultural, and economic background of the people.

YEARBOOKS AND ALMANACS

Since encyclopedias cannot be revised at very frequent intervals, most of them are kept up-to-date by the publication of yearbooks or annuals. *Britannica*, the *Americana, World Book*, and *Collier's*, for example, will add recent events that have taken place in the Middle East in their yearbooks.

A vast amount of annual and statistical information is found in almanacs like *The World Almanac*, *Information Please Almanac*, and the *Reader's Digest Almanac*. These almanacs also contain longer articles on recent happenings in the world.

The Statesman's Yearbook, a British publication, is a very special kind of annual. It is divided into four sections covering the United Nations and other international organizations (NATO, SEATO, the Arab League, World Council of Churches, International Trade Unionism, etc.); the British Commonwealth; the United States; the other countries of the world. Information of every kind is included: constitution and government, flag and national anthem, area and population, education, religion, finance, defense, court system, important industries, weights and measures, and the names of diplomatic representatives to and from Great Britain, and to and from the United States.

Leaders in the Picture

In reading and discussions you will encounter the names of the heads of state or ambassadors or other people at the forefront of international negotiations, and you may wish to know something about them. *Current Biography*, a magazine that comes out eleven times a year, tries to cover who is news at the moment. Each monthly issue has an index that includes all names in the year's previous issues; a hard-cover Yearbook cumulates each year's sketches and indexes the names listed in previous yearbooks of the decade; finally, there is a separate index volume covering the years 1940–1970 so that at most only three alphabetical lists have to be consulted to find any name you are researching.

Who's Who (an annual biographical dictionary covering British persons) and *Who's Who in America* (issued biennially) list outstanding *living* people and would be useful for information about diplomats and politicians like Cyrus Vance (in the American volume) or James Callaghan (in the British one).

Such leaders as Anwar Sadat of Egypt, King Hussein of

Inst. 68-73; Vice-Pres. Chair. A.A.A.S., Physics Section 70-71; Dir. Argonne Nat. Laboratory 73-; Visiting Prof., Princeton Univ. 55-56, Univ. of Paris 59-60; mem. Nat. Acad. of Sciences, Chair. Physics Section 77-; Fellow, American Acad. of Arts and Sciences; Guggenheim Fellowship 59-60; Hon. D.Sc. (Purdue Univ.) 67.
Leisure interest: sailing.
Publs. *Nuclear Theory* 53; numerous articles in scientific journals.
Argonne National Laboratory, 9700 South Cass Avenue, Argonne, Ill. 60439; Home: 5490 South Shore Drive, Chicago, Ill. 60615, U.S.A.
Telephone: 312-739-7711, ext. 4567 (Office); 312-752-2077 (Home).

Sa'd, Farid Ali, B.SC.; Jordanian business executive and politician; b. 1908, Umm el Fahm, Palestine; *s.* of Ali Sa'd and Almaza Ownallah; *m.* Khadijeh Yousef Khalidi 1943; one *s.* three *d.*; ed. American Univ. of Beirut.
Teacher 28-35; District Gov., Palestine Govt. 35-43; Dir. Arab Bank in Haifa 43-48; mem. Board of Dirs. Jordan Tobacco Co. 49-55, Pres. 55-; Minister of Finance 72-73; mem. Board of Trustees, American Univ. of Beirut, Univ. of Jordan.
Leisure interests: sports, mainly walking.
Jordan Tobacco and Cigarette Co. Ltd., P.O. Box 59, Amman, Jordan.
Telephone: 36345.

Sadeghi, Reza; Iranian politician; b. 1917, Sabzevar; ed. Karaj Agricultural Coll., Syracuse Univ., N.Y.
With Ministry of Agriculture 39, Procurement Officer, Section Head; with Crown Lands and Rural Estates 40; Asst. Dir. Forestry Agency; Head of Karkheh Devt. Authority; Head of Agriculture Div., Plan Org.; Under-Sec., Ministry of Agriculture; Head of Agricultural Bank of Iran; Gov.-Gen. Khuzistan 73; Minister of Co-operatives and Rural Affairs 73-76; Founder-mem. Iran Novin Party.
c/o Ministry of Co-operatives and Rural Affairs, Teheran, Iran.

Sadat, Col. Mohamed Anwar El-; Egyptian army officer and politician; b. 25 Dec. 1918, Tala Dist., Menufia Governorate; *s.* of Mohamed El-Sadat; *m.* Jihan Sadat; one *s.* three *d.* (also three *d.* by previous marriage); ed. Military Coll.
Commissioned 38; fmr. Gen. Sec. Islamic Congress; participated in Officers' coup 52; Editor *Al Jumhuriya* and *Al Tahrir* 55-56; Minister of State 55-56; Vice-Chair. Nat. Assembly 57-60, Chair. 60-68; Gen. Sec. Egyptian Nat. Union 57-61; Chair. Afro-Asian Solidarity Council 61; Speaker U.A.R. Nat. Assembly 61-69; mem. Presidential Council 62-64; Vice-Pres. of Egypt 64-66, 69-70; interim Pres. of Egypt Sept.-Oct. 70, Pres. Oct. 70-, Prime Minister 73-74; proclaimed Military Gov.-Gen. March 73; Pres. Council Fed. of Arab Repubs. 71-; Chair. Arab Socialist Union 70-; mem. Higher Council on Nuclear Energy 75-; Sinai Medal 74.
The Presidency, Cairo, Egypt.

Sadawi, A. M. Suhail Al; Libyan oil executive; b. 1928, Beirut; ed. American Univ. of Beirut.
With Gulf Oil Corpn., Libya 58-61; Int. Labour Office, Geneva 62-63; Head, Gen. Econ. Section, Org. of Petroleum Exporting Countries (OPEC) 63; participated in negotiations for amendment of Libyan Petroleum Law 65; mem. Pricing Comm., Libya 67, Chair. 68; Asst. Under Sec., Libyan Ministry of Petroleum 68; Deputy Dir. Gen. Libyan Nat. Petroleum Corpn. 68; Sec.-Gen. Org. of Arab Petroleum Exporting Countries 70-73.
Arab Economists Petroleum Affairs (Consultants), P.O. Box 8840, Beirut, Lebanon.
Telephone: 352319.

Sadek, Gen. Mohammed Ahmed; Egyptian army officer; ed. Frunze Military Academy, U.S.S.R.
Served in Egyptian army, World War II, Palestine War 48, Suez Campaign 56; Mil. Attaché, Egyptian Embassy to Fed. Repub. of Germany 64; Dir. of Studies, Mil. Acad., Cairo 65-67; Dir. of Information, Army Intelligence Dept. 67; Chief of Staff of the Army Sept. 69; Minister of War and Mil. Production May 71-72; Deputy Premier for Nat. Defence Jan.-Oct. 72; mem. Supreme Council of the Armed Forces.
Ministry of War, Cairo, Egypt.

Sadiq, Issa, PH.D.; Iranian educationist; b. 1894, Teheran; *m.* Badry Heravi 1925; two *s.* two *d.*; ed. Univs. of Paris, Cambridge (England), and Columbia (New York).
Directed various depts. Ministry of Educ. 19-30; mem. Nat. Constituent Assembly 25, 49, 67; Pres. and Prof. Nat. Teachers' Coll.; Dean of Faculties of Arts and Science, Teheran Univ. 32-41, Prof. 32-72, Prof. Emer. 72-; Chancellor of Univ. 41; Minister of Educ. 41, 43-45, 47, 60-61; Vice-Pres. Persian Acad. 37-70; mem. Board of Governors, Nat. Bank of Persia 37-52; Senator for Teheran 49-52, 54-60, 63-67, 67-71, 75-; Pres. Persia-America Relations Soc. 49-53; founding mem. Nat. Soc. for Physical Educ. 33-54, Soc. for Preservation of Nat. Heritage 44-, Nat. Soc. for Protection of Children 53-; mem. High Educ. Council 34-41, 51-58, 72-, Royal Cultural Council 62-, Higher Council Nat. Org. for the Protection of Historical Monuments 65-, mem. Acad. of Iran language 70-, mem. Higher Council of Culture and Art 72-76, 77-.
Leisure interests: walking in the country, reading.
Publs. *Principles of Education*, *New Methods in Education*, *History of Education*, *Modern Persia and her Educational System* (in English), *A Year in America*, *The March of Education in Persia and the West*, *A Brief Course in the History of Education in Iran*, *A History of Education in Europe*, *History of Education in Persia from the Earliest Time till Today*, *Forty Lectures*, *Memoirs* (autobiography, 3 vols.); trans. *Past and Future of Persian Art* (by A. V. Pope); eleven essays, etc.
316 Avenue Hedayat, Valiabad, Teheran; and The Senate, Teheran, Iran.
Telephone: 318266.

Sadler, Donald Harry, O.B.E., M.A.; British astronomer; b. 22 Aug. 1908, Dewsbury, Yorkshire; *s.* of James W. Sadler and Gertrude Needham; *m.* Flora Munro McBain 1954; ed. Trinity Coll., Cambridge.
Entered H.M. Nautical Almanac Office 30, Deputy Superintendent 33, Superintendent 36-71; Sec. Royal Astronomical Society 39-47; Pres. Inst. of Navigation 53-55; Gen. Sec. Int. Astronomical Union 58-64; Vice-Pres. Council of Fed. of Astronomical and Geophysical Services 66-68, Pres. 68-70; Pres. Royal Astronomical Soc. 67-69; retd. 72.
Leisure interests: bridge, chess.
8 Collington Rise, Bexhill-on-Sea, Sussex, England.
Telephone: Cooden 3572.

Sadli, Mohammad, M.SC., PH.D.; Indonesian politician; b. 10 June 1922; *m.* Saparinah Subali 1954; ed. Univs. of Gadjah Mada and Indonesia, Massachusetts Inst. of Technology, Univ. of California (Berkeley) and Harvard Univ.
Lecturer, later Prof. of Econs., Univ. of Indonesia 57-, Army Staff Coll. 58-65, Navy Staff Coll. 58-65; Dir. Inst. of Econ. and Social Research, Faculty of Econs., Univ. of Indonesia 57-63; Asst. to Pres., Univ. of Indonesia 63-64; mem. Gov. Council, UN Asian Inst. of Devt. and Planning 63-64; Chair. Indonesian Economists Assen. 66-72; Chair. Tech. Cttee. for Foreign Investment 67-73; Minister of Manpower 71-73, of Mines 73-; Chair. Board of Govt. Commrs. PERTA-

Figure 16. From *International Who's Who* (1977–78)

Jordan, Menachem Begin of Israel are to be found in the annual *International Who's Who*. Information in any of the *Who's Who* biographical dictionaries is abbreviated. The sample page of the *International Who's Who* illustrates this with the sketch of Sadat in Figure 16. When you compare it with an entry in *Current Biography* you can see the difference in style and in the amount of information.

BOOKS AND NON-BOOKS

Books and audiovisual resources will be discovered as you look in the card catalog under such subject headings as MIDDLE EAST (which will probably direct you to NEAR EAST), ISRAEL, and ISRAELI-ARAB CONFLICT (which may have a reference to JEWISH-ARAB RELATIONS). Here are just a few of the sort of materials that you may locate:

The New Israelis: A report on the first generation born in Israel by David Schoenbrun. In addition to the interviews, the book contains some results of a survey of national opinion on such topics as relations with the Arabs, security, and the economic situation.

Israel Is Born. A recording of actual events and voices of important people during the volatile years 1947 through 1951. You hear David Ben Gurion, Ralph Bunche, Mohammad F. Jamali, Abba Eban, Arab-Jewish debate on partition, the vote in the U.N., sounds of the warfare in Israel, etc.

Eyes on the Arab World. A kit consisting of 4 filmstrips and 4 cassettes, plus the teacher's guide and 3 pamphlets. The 4 programs are entitled: The Mark of History; Oil: Key to World Power; From Nomad to City Dweller; Contrasting Societies—Yemen and Kuwait. (See Figure 17.)

Kit
915.3
E Eyes on the Arab world; by JoAnne Buggey and
June Tyler. EMC, SS 215000.

Contents: 4 sound-filmstrips, col, 4 records, 12", 33 1/3 rpm, or 4 cassettes, titles: The mark of history (109 fr). Oil: key to world power (100 fr). From nomad to city dweller (93 fr). Contrasting societies: Yemen and Kuwait (84 fr). 3 paperback books by Doreen Ingrams, titles: -cont.
1305-SS215000

Kit -2-
915.3
E Eyes on the Arab world...

Tents to city sidewalks, Mosques and minarets, New ways for ancient lands. Political map. Teacher's guide w/duplicating masters, activity sheets, quizzes/answers.
1 Arab countries-Social life and customs
2 Civilization, Arab 3 Kuwait 4 Oil industry and trade 5 Yemen I Auths. II 7 title anals.

1305-SS215000

Kit
915.3 OIL INDUSTRY AND TRADE
E Eyes on the Arab world; by Jo Anne Buggey and
June Tyler. EMC, SS 215000.

For complete contents, see main entry.

1305-SS215000

Figure 17. Sample main entry for audiovisual kit (catalog card)
Sample subject catalog card (bottom)

Jerusalem, Key to Peace by Evan M. Wilson. The background of the crisis, the role of the United Nations, the conflict of June 1967, the problem of the Holy Places. The appendix contains information related to basic documents, including the McMahon correspondence, the Balfour Declaration, and the Sykes-Picot agreement.

The Arab World (The Reference Shelf). Gives history, geography, political factors, the Arab-Israeli conflict, the relationship between the Arab countries and the United States and Russia.

Other Printed Resources

For a topic like the crisis in the Middle East, the vertical file will contain a wide range of pamphlet materials, some of them presenting a very specific point of view, as in the *Palestine Digest*, published by the League of Arab States, *Questions and Answers on Middle East Problems*, issued by the American Jewish Committee, or *Answers and Questions: The Palestinian Issue*, which comes from the Information Division of the Ministry for Foreign Affairs, Jerusalem. Under the subject heading MIDDLE EAST or NEAR EAST the vertical file will probably contain hearings before subcommittees of Congress, clippings from newspapers like the *Wall Street Journal*, pamphlets from the Middle East Institute or the United States Military Academy, and other related materials. When you are dealing with material on any controversial subject, *note the source of the publication* in order to evaluate intelligently the information and point of view being offered. That, of course, is good advice in judging *any* source of information—books, films, tapes, verbal recordings. You have probably heard the saying about there being three sides to any question; yours, mine, and the truth.

KEEPING UP-TO-DATE

A topic as current and vital as the Middle East situation and its impact on world peace will receive constant attention in all the media. There are aids to keeping track of on-going events.

Facts on File is a weekly digest of the news of the world issued in loose–leaf form and bound together in an annual volume. Its indexes help you to locate the information you want, giving the date of the event, the page number, and even the location on that page. For example, looking in an issue of *Facts on File* under MENACHEM BEGIN about his election to office in Israel (Figure 18), we find through its index the following listing: "6-21, 474G1, C2." This tells us that the event occurred on June 21 and that the report about it is in *Facts on File* (G1 and C2 simply indicate where on page 474 you will find mention of Begin's election).

Editorial Research Reports is another source of information on topics that are likely to be major issues of the day. The kinds of subjects selected include SOLAR ENERGY, JOB HEALTH AND SAFETY, NUCLEAR WASTE DISPOSAL, and, of course, MIDDLE EAST PROBLEMS. Four times a month a report of about 6,000 words is published in pamphlet form. The pamphlets are bound into two annual volumes, each carrying indexes that refer to the five preceding years of reports. In the past three years reports have been listed under such subject headings as ARAB DISUNITY, THE PALESTINIAN QUESTION, and MIDDLE EAST DIPLOMACY. The index gives the date of the issue as well as the volume number and page.

8 BALANCE— **FACTS ON FILE INDEX**

Portugal Jan-Feb deficit rptd 4-2, 330E3
Bonn, Japan OK deficit move 5-7—5-8, 357G2
'76 Swiss surplus rptd 5-12, 489E3
Peru '76 deficit rptd 5-17, 427C3
US asks Japan, W Ger, Swiss, Dutch deficit move; notes US shift 5-25, 437D3
BIS warns US re deficit 6-12, 502D1
US 1st ¼ deficit record, '76, 4th ¼ revised 6-22, 501G3
Deficit Aid—*See also lending agencies (e.g., IMF, WORLD Bank Group)*
Arab monetary fund created 4-18, 318A1
7-natn summit backs fund 5-7—5-8, 357B1
Intl bankers conf in Tokyo 5-22—5-25, 437D3
BALDWIN, Alfred
Claims vs Nixon funds rptd 5-6, 482G2
BALDWIN, Roger
FBI ACLU surveillance rptd 6-19, 481G1
BALDWIN Co., D. H.
FRB bars S&L ownership 2-22, 155E1
BAL Harbor, Fla.—*See FLORIDA*
BALIDAWA, Charles
Defects to UK 3-13, 308D2
BALL, George
Vs science research curbs 2-22, 184F1
BALTIMORE, Md.—*See MARYLAND*
BALTIMORE Evening Sun (newspaper)
Trust suit setld 5-26, 504A2
BALZANO, Michael P.
Brown succeeds 2-25, 148C3
BANANA, Rev. Canaan
Arrested 1-25, 50B1
BANASZAK, Pete
Raiders win Super Bowl 1-9, 24E3, F3
BANCAL Tri-State Corp.
Bars British takeover 3-1, 155A2
BANDA, Hastings Kamuzu
2 sentenced in plot 2-14, 309E2
BANDA, Zengani
Dismissed as Zambia power min 4-24, 490B2
BANDARANAIKE, Sirimavo (Sri Lanka prime minister)
Warns emergency rule 1-25, 68B3
Ends parlt 2-12, foes score 2-15, 137E3
Subasinghe quits Cabt, Freedom Party 3-1, 183G1
Defectors form new party 4-10, 309D3
BANGLADESH (formerly East Pakistan)—*See also COMMONWEALTH of Nations, NONALIGNED Nations Movement*
UN Assemb member 3F3
OPEC allocates loan funds 1-10, 12A3
Sweden budgets aid 1-10, 23B1
India Ganges talks collapse 1-23, 64D1
Mushtaque sentenced 2-26, 183C1
Mushtaque acquitted of 2d chrg 3-10, 309G1
Tornado kills 900 4-1, 312E2
Pres Sayem quits, Rahman sworn 4-21, 309F1
Nixon reminisces 5-12, 386B2
Martial law policies approved 5-29, 451D2
BANGOR Punta Corp.
Chris-Craft damages voided 2-23, 150A2
Smith & Wesson
'66-75 Latin arms sales rptd 4-8, 415G2
BANKAMERICA Corp.
Bank of America National Trust & Savings Association
IBEC loan cancelled 1-26, 123E2
BANKERS Trust New York Corp.
Bankers Trust Co. (N.Y.)
On Sovt-bloc Western debt 2-13, 335F3
BANK for International Settlements (BIS)
UK sterling balances accord 1-10, 20C2; Callaghan to supervise 1-21, 44E2
Sovt-bloc Westn debt rptd 2-23, 335D3, F3
Warns US re paymts, trade gaps 6-12, 502D1
BANKS (& Banking)—*See also CREDIT, MONETARY Developments; also bank, country names*
Saxe pleads guilty 1-17, sentncd 2-11, 140E1
GAO scores fed regulators 1-31, 154E3
Record '76 savings inflow rptd 2-1, 155G1
NYC debt repaymt dvpts 2-8—3-11, 193C1-G3
Franklin, Hamilton auditors sued 2-9, 2-11, 155A3, C3
FRB bars bank S&L ownership 2-22, 155D1
NYC banks chrgd re job bias 2-23, 279G1
Chemical Bank indicted 2-24, 155C2
Bank of Calif takeover rejected 3-1, 156A2
Problem bank list rptd up 3-11, 194C2
'73-76, bank failures cited 3-11, 194F2
Ill bank withdraws farmland fund plan 3-11, 195A1
Security Natl double jeopardy bar upheld 3-28, 276F3
Carter drops tax rebate plan 4-14, 271F1
Interest Rates
Belgium discount rates cut 1-5, 24F1; 2-16, 199F3
Dutch discount rate cut 1-6, 24C2
Canada cuts bank, prime rates 2-1, 97G2
'76 US bank loans abroad rptd up 2-17, 145F2
Lower rate, mergers linked 2-18, 274C2
Japan discount rate cut 3-12, 3-16, 201C2
Ceiling powers cleared 4-5, 273A2; Carter signs 4-19, 380E3
Tax rebate plan dropped, rate dips 4-14, 271B2
Japan discount rate cut 4-18, 329G3
Belgium discount rate cut 5-5, 466E1
Dutch discount rate lowered 5-6, 412G1
Canada bank, prime rates cut 5-9, 5-10, 372E2
Low US rates, forgn investmt rise linked 5-11, 5-25, 385C3
Oct '74-May '77 prime rate graph 407A1
Prime raised, fed funds rate cited 5-13, 5-30, 407D1
International Developments—*See also 'Interest Rates' above*
'76 Swiss credits rptd 1-4, 48F2
UK gets $1.5 bln consortium loan 1-24, 99G1
Quebec bars forgn control 1-25, 81G3
Bank of Amer group cancels IBEC loan 1-26, 123D2
Australia SRD rate raised 2-2, 113C2
Sovt-bloc Western debt rptd 2-13—4-13, 335C3
'76 US bank lending record 2-17, 145E2
S Africa small bank aid set 2-22, 160E3
'76 US bank interventn rptd 3-2, 188E3
Swiss bank closed 3-2, 489D3
Riviera bank robber escapes 3-10, 288E2
FRB asks OPEC lending role 3-10; IMF debt managing role rptd 3-28, 362E3-363D1
Iran, Pak, Turkey sign pact 3-12, 190C2
'76, 4th ¼ bank lending rptd 3-23, 234G1
Jamaica to natlize Barclays 3-23, 257A2, D2
'66-75 Latin arms purchases rptd 4-8, 415E2
Argentina Graiver guerrilla fund scandal 4-11—4-23, 345A2; 4-23—5-4, 371G1
US loans to Indonesia rptd risky 4-18, 392G2
Chase curbs S Africa loans 4-19, 350C2
3 Swiss officers arrested 4-24, 350F2-B3
Geneva pvt bank fails 5-9, 489B3
Tokyo monetary conf 5-22—5-25, 437B3
Forgn lending rptd up, US '76 loans 6-5, 438B1
BANQUE pour L'Amerique du Sud (Brussels)
Argentina Graiver scandal breaks 4-11, 345C2
BANTAM Books Inc.—*See under AMERICAN Financial Corp.*
BANZER Suarez, Gen. Hugo (Bolivia president)
Sees Todman 5-16, 414F2
BAPTISTS
Carter Ga church bars black member 1-9, 53C2
Carter joins DC church 1-23, 53C2
Sovt dissident rptd jailed 4-4, 314E2
Coll prof chrgs divorce bias 5-2, 472C1
BARAK, Aharon
Ofer probe dropped 1-9, 21D1
BARAKAT, Daud
On Israel electn 5-19, 401B3
BARAZZUTTI, Corrado
Loses Monte Carlo WCT 4-10, wins Charlotte 4-24, 430G2, A3
BARBADOS—*See also COMMONWEALTH of Nations, IDB, OAS*
UN Assemb member 3F3
Cuba details Angola war role, US interventn 1-9, 19G1
'75-76 trade, paymts table 3-11, 189A2 + C2
'61-75 GDP variatn table 5-30, 439A1
Belize independnc backed 6-16, 494G2
BARCAK, Andrej
Norway cancels visit 1-20, 99C3
BARCLAYS Bank Ltd.
Jamaica to natlize unit 2-23, 257D2
BARD, Brig. Gen. John C.
W Point apptmt cited 1-5, 41E1
BARDELLA, Claudio
Asks return to democracy 2-18, 281C2
BARK, L. Dean
On drought affects 2-21, 183C2
BARKER, Bernard L.
Nixon com to pay $50,000 2-22, 157G2
BARKER, Sue
Loses Bloomington Va Slims 1-30, 104A1
Va Slims tourn results 2-27, 3-6, 3-27, 431C1, F1
BARNES, Wiley
Hiring defended 3-23, 3-25, 236D1
BARNETT, Robert
Rpts problem bank list up 3-11, 194D2
BARNUM, John W.
Replaced in Transport post 2-10, 148D3
BARNWELL, S.C.—*See SOUTH Carolina*
BAR-On, Hanan
Assured on Carter Mideast views 3-9, 165G2
BAROOAH, Dev Kant
Quits as Cong Party pres 4-13, 392B2
BARRANTES Lingan, Alfonso
Arrest rptd 3-11, 241F2
BARRE, Maj. Gen. Mohamed Siad (Somali president)
Sees Young 2-5, 105D1
Sees Castro 3-12—3-14, 249C2
At Red Sea summit 3-22—3-23, 208F2
Sees Podgorny 4-2, 248C1
Rejcts Africa Horn federatn 5-18, 428E2
BARRE, Raymond
Defends Daoud release 1-13, 27B2
Inflatn curbs effective 1-26, unions protest 1-26—2-1, 159D2
On S Africa A-bomb capacity 2-17, 160C2
Urges Chirac-Giscard unity 3-20, 221B2
Names new Cabinet 3-30, 239C1
Econ plan protested 4-18, 4-26, Assemb OKs 4-28, 328B3, F3
On steel industry aid 4-19, 391D2
Viet premr visits 4-25—4-28, 329A1
OKs A-plant 5-12, scored 5-30, 450B1
Unions strike vs wage curbs 5-24, 486D2
BARRETT, Edith
Dies 2-22, 164C2
BARRETT, Edward J.
Dies 4-4, 356F2
BARRYMORE, Ethel (1879-1959)
Daughter dies 5-22, 452F2
BARSHAI, Rudolf
Emigrates to Israel 1-30, 117G1
BARTH, Dale
EPA backs DNA controls 3-8, 184B3
BARTLETT, Sen. Dewey (R, Okla.)
Warsaw Pact rpt released 1-24, 70A2
BARUA Castaneda, Luis
Quits as econ min 5-13, 427C2
BASEBALL
Carter call-in on US Cuba games 3-5, 171F1
US OKs Cuba games, Kuhn balks 3-8, 181C1
FCC pay-TV rules voided 3-25, appeal set 4-14, 376F2
Cuba-US all-star plans cited 4-11, 283B2
Obituaries
Wrigley, Philip 4-12, 356G3
Player & Executive Developments
Jets to remain at Shea 2-18, 163D3
Finley, Kuhn clash over player sales 2-18—4-8; Finley loses suit 3-17, 310A3
Randle slugs Ranger mgr 3-28, suspended 4-5, 310E3 +
Mets-Jets dispute settled 5-26, 491A2
BASES, Military—*See DEFENSE under U.S. GOVERNMENT; also country names*
BASHIR, Mohammed al-
Killed in air crash 2-9, 87D1
BASKETBALL
Awards & Honors
SD team Cuba games OKd 3-5, 181C1
NCAA Div II, III titles 3-19, 262D2
St Bonaventure wins NIT title, Sanders named MVP 3-20, 262E2
5 named to Hall of Fame 5-2, 490E3
Collegiate
NCAA conv 1-10—1-12, 104A2
Tex Southn wins NAIA tourn 3-12, 262F2
Marquette wins NCAA title, Lee named MVP 3-28, 262E1
SD team in Cuba 4-4—4-8, 282B3
Professional
NBA final standings, table 4-10, 331B3
NBA referees strike 4-10—4-25, 331G3
NBA playoffs 5-22—6-5; Portland wins title, Walton named MVP 6-5, 490G2
BASKETBALL Association, National (NBA)—*See BASKETBALL*
BASKETBALL Referees, National Association of (NABR)
NBA strike 4-10—4-25, 332A1
BASU, Jyoti
West Bengal chief min 6-21, 488A1
West Bengal chief min 6-21, 488A1
BATEMAN, Raymond H.
Wins primary for gov 6-7, 446D3
BAUDOUIN, King (Belgium)
Asks Tindemans to form govt 4-22, 326A3
Bars Tindemans resignatn 6-2, swears Cabt 6-3, 465E3
BAUXITE—*See ALUMINUM & Bauxite*
BAYARDO Bengoa, Fernando
Uruguay justice min 1-27, 351G2
BAYLOR, Elgin
In Basketball HOF 5-2, 490F3
BAYLOR University (Waco, Tex.)
Green in NFL draft 5-3, 353B3
BAY of Pigs—*See 'U.S.' under CUBA*
BAYONA Jimenez, Rafael
Assassinated 2-13, 255B1
BAZELON, Judge David L.
Vs FCC obscenity order 3-16, 216A1
BBC—*See BRITISH Broadcasting Corp.*
BEALE, Edith Bouvier
Dies 2-5, 164C2
BEAM Distilling Co., James B.—*See AMERICAN Brands Inc.*
BEAME, Mayor Abraham D. (N.Y.)
Debt repaymt talks 2-8—3-9, plan OKd 3-10; US loan released 3-11, 193B1-D3
Jets to remain at Shea 2-18, 163D3
Carter visits 3-17, 191B1
Revokes NY Airways landing rights 5-16, 412C3
BEAN, Andy
Wins Doral Open 3-13, 311A2
BEATRICE Foods
Discounts, overbilling rptd 3-14, 233C2
BEAUFORT Sea
Canada OKs oil search 6-1, 425E3
BEAUTIFUL Swimmers: Watermen, Crabs, and the Chesapeake Bay (book)
Wins Pulitzer Prize 4-18, 356E2
BECERRIL, Carlos
Escalera KOs 5-16, 395D1
BECHTEL Corp.
Settles Arab boycott suit 1-10, 78B2-A3
BECKS, Michael Steven
Flees to Brazil 2-9, 144E3
BECVAR, Rudolph
Sentenced 3-31, 380B2
BEDARD, Marc-Andre
On Levesque auto mishap 2-25, 159C1
BEEF—*See MEAT*
BEEL, Louis J. M.
Dies 2-11, 164C2
BEER—*See ALCOHOLIC Beverages*
BEETHOVEN, Ludwig van (1770-1827)
China lifts ban 3-26, 449D3
BEG, Mirza Hameedullah
Opposed as chief justice 1-25; named 1-28, sworn 1-29, ct boycotted 1-31, 71A3
BEGIN, Menahem (Israel premier)
Facts on 377D2
Likud wins electns 5-17, Peres rejcts unity bid 5-19, 377A1
Assures US, Arabs on peace; affirms occupatn policy 5-17, 377B2
PLO, Arab reactn to Likud victory 5-18—5-24, 401B3
Asks more W Bank setlmts 5-19; scores US peace plan, PLO role 5-22, 401F2
Hospitalized 5-23, 401D2
Seeks DMC coalitn 5-24, 401B2
Carter sees moderation 5-26, 417A2
Delays Dayan appointment 5-29, 450A2
Aide in US 6-2, 440C2
Named to form govt 6-7, 450C2
Gives Agudat Israel concessns 6-9, 474A3
Likud adopts forgn policy plank 6-17, 474F2
NRP, Agudat Israel join Likud 6-19; presents Cabt to pres 6-20; wins parlt confidence vote, becomes premr 6-21, 474G1
OKs Viet refugee asylum 6-21, 497A2
Denies 'ultimatum' 6-23, 495B3
US worried re views 6-27, 495G2
BEGUN, Iosif
Detained 2-28, 3-10, US protests 3-1, 226D2, D3
Sentenced 6-1, 436E2
BEJARES, Gen. Hernan
Chrgs Christian Dem 'plot' 3-11, 219C3
BEKER Industries Inc.
Rpts payments 1-4, 94D2
BELGIUM—*See also EUROPEAN Community, IDB, IEA, NATO, OECD*
Budget vote splits coalitn 3-3, RW mins ousted 3-4, gen electn called 3-9, 199B2
Electn results 4-17; Tindemans named caretaker premr 4-22, asks 'grand coalitn' 4-27, 326D2
Brussels hotel fire kills 15 5-22, 429B3
Federatn plan OKd 5-24; FDF stalls govt formatn 6-2, Cabt sworn 6-3, 465E3
Economy & Labor
Bank discount rate cut 1-5, 24F1
'76 factory wage study rptd 1-28, 158B3
Franc devaluatn rejctd 2-3, 199D3
Dec '75-76 inflatn rate rptd 2-7, 87A2
Austerity program set 2-13, unions strike 2-24—3-9, 199F2
Bank discount rate cut again 2-16, 199F3
'76 econ growth rate rptd 2-22, 146C2
Jan jobless rate rptd 2-28, 199A3
Unemploymt at 9% 4-18, 326C3
Bank discount rate cut 5-5, 466E1
Foreign Relations (misc.)
UN Assemb member 3F3
'76 Eur snake loan, forgn reserves cited 1-5, 24G1
In UK sterling balance pact 1-10, 20C2
'76 Eur Cncl pact vs terrorism cited 9G2
Mobutu visits 1-17—1-24, 199G3
In 14-natn sulphur-dioxide pact 1-19, 109B3
Exporters seek franc devaluatn 1-20, rejctd 2-3, 199D3
ICFTU S Africa boycott fails 1-21, 67B3
Air Canada to end svc 1-28, 43D2
Benin coup attempt detailed 2-1, 96F1
IMF SDR defined 87G2
ESA flight set 2-16, 170C3
Brazil mil aid request seen 3-7, 168B1
Zaire gets arms 3-17, 207D3
USSR sentences natl 3-25, 314B3
Saltars captured arms displayed 3-28, 337B2

Figure 18. From *Facts on File* (1977)

Editorial Research Reports is organized to begin with an overview of the topic (its importance, the major issues involved), continue with an in-depth examination that includes background and development, and conclude with a discussion of possible future developments. Many libraries file the weekly pamphlets in the vertical file, unless they maintain separate pamphlet collections or keep the reports by date as they do magazines.

For the serious researcher, *Public Affairs Information Service Bulletin* (P.A.I.S.) is an index that covers "books, pamphlets, government publications, reports of public and private agencies, and periodical articles related to economic and social conditions, public administration, and international relations." This weekly index is expensive and it is likely that you will have to consult it in a public library rather than in your school media center if you wish to use it. There is an annual bound volume. Under MIDDLE EAST you are referred to NEAR EAST the official term (Figure 19). Other related subject headings, include ISRAEL, PALESTINE LIBERATION ORGANIZATION, and PALESTINIAN ARABS.

Magazines and Newspapers

It is obvious that problems of a current nature will receive attention in the mass media. The newspapers report from day to day the events and meetings that are taking place and obstacles that stand in the way of settlements. There are thousands of newspapers in the nation, although most cities, like New York or Los Angeles, seem to have only a few available. It is desirable to read the account of an event in more than one newspaper (or weekly news magazine) in order

NAVAL bases
Absurdities of Diego Garcia [and the United States strategic plans for its development as a naval base]. Edgar P. Young. Labour Mo 57:376-8 Ag '75
Report from the Pentagon: why U.S. is building an Indian ocean base [on Diego Garcia]. map U S News 79:60 S 8 '75
US adds to bases in Indian ocean area: Diego Garcia is the latest, but not necessarily the last, of the US bases in the Indian ocean area. Robert Manning. il African Development p 39 S '75
† United States. House. Com. on armed services. Special subcom. to inspect facilities at Berbera, Somalia. Report, July 15, 1975. '75 ii+11p (94th Cong., 1st sess.) (H.A.S.C. no. 94-19)
Question of whether Russia is building a naval base in Somalia.
† United States. Senate. Com. on armed services. Soviet military capability in Berbera, Somalia: report, July, 1975, of Senator [Dewey F.] Bartlett. '75 iii+29p il maps (Com. print)
NAVAL officers. See Officers, Military and naval
NAVAL power. See Sea power
NAVAL petroleum reserves. See Petroleum industry—Naval reserves
NAVAL ships. See Ships, Naval
NAVIES
See also
Ships, Naval
Submarines, Atomic-powered
also subhead Navy under individual countries, e.g. Russia—Navy
Conference on the problems of naval armaments. Sea power in the 1970s. George H. Quester, ed. '75 vii+248p tables (Univ. pr. of Cambridge, Mass. ser.) (LC 73-88666) (ISBN 0-8046-7088-9) $15—Kennikat
Published by Dunnellen publishing company.
Papers prepared for the conference sponsored by the Program on peace studies. Cornell university, and held at Ithaca, N.Y., Apr., 1972.
NAVIGATION
See also
Radar aids to navigation
Satellites, Artificial—Navigation uses
NAVIGATION rights. See Straits—Navigation rights
NE WIN (Maung Shu Maung), 1911
Burma: lining up against [President] Ne Win. William Mattern. il Far Eastern Econ R 89:27-8 Jl 11 '75
NEAR EAST
See also
Air transport—Near East
Arab league
Arab states
Atomic weapons
Building—Near East
Communication systems
Cotton industry—Near East
Directories—Banking
Employment in foreign countries—Recruitment
Export marketing
Germany (Federal Republic)—Commerce—Near East
Guerrillas—Near East
Investments, Foreign—Near Eastern
Iron and steel industry—Near East
Korea Republic—Commerce—Near East
Manpower utilization—Near East
Market statistics—Near East
Military market
Money—Near East
Petroleum chemicals
Petroleum industry—Near East
Ports—Near East
Production—Near East
Railroads—Near East
Russia—Foreign relations—Near East
Shipping—Near East
Syria—Foreign relations—Near East
United Nations—Near East
United States—Foreign relations—Near East
United States—Military assistance program—Near East
Urbanization—Near East
Chronology: May 16, 1975-August 15, 1975. Middle East J 29:434-50 Autumn '75 (cont. q.)
Isenberg, Irwin, ed. The Arab world. '76 180p bibl (Ref. shelf v. 48, no. 2) (LC 76-8872) (ISBN 0-8242-0596-0) pa $5.25—Wilson
Middle East and South Asia, 1975. Ray L. Cleveland. '75 iv+91p il table maps (World today ser.) (9th ed.) pa $2.25 with order—Stryker-Post
† Stanford research inst. The Middle East and North Africa. '75 56p bibl tables map pa Membership; nonmembers 50c
Reviews economic and political conditions of particular interest to foreign investors.
Super powers in the Middle East—backstage. Jon Kimche. Midstream 21:7-13 Je/Jl '75
The U.S. and Israel: proposals to avert another Middle East war. Mark A. Bruzonsky. Internat Problems 14:30-44 Fall '75

Commerce
Great Britain
British and European trade with the Middle East. Richmond Beaumont. table Asian Affairs 63:138-48 Je '76

Russia
Moscow and the Middle East: ever more ground to make up, by Naomi Sakr; Soviet Union: imports from the Middle East; Soviet Union: exports to the Middle East. tables Middle East Econ Dig 20:3-4+, 28-9 Ag 6 '76

Defenses
See also
Central treaty organization

Economic conditions
The Middle East comes alive. N. D. Modak. Can Banker 83:22-4 Ja/F '76
Perspectives on the Middle East [based on address]. L. Dean Brown. Conference Bd Rec 13:38-40 F '76

Economic development
Ambitious development programs put pressure on cement supplies [in Near East countries]. Atef Sultan. tables Middle East Econ Dig 20:3+ My 28 '76
Development administration in the Arab Middle East. Delwin A. Roy. tables Internat R Admin Sciences 41:135-48 no 2 '75
Easy come, easy go: oil nations discover ways to spend money, but profits are elusive. Ray Vicker. Wall St J 186:1+ O 17 '75
† Kuwait fund for Arab econ. development. The Middle East's economic aspirations and the United States [address]. Abdlatif Y. Al-Hamad. S '75 11p—P.O. Box 2931, Kuwait
Plow-back: the use of Arab money; in 1974 the Arab world and Iran invested some $62 billion—in its own future. Bertrand P. Boucher and Harbans Singh. il tables Aramco World M 26:22-5 S/O '75
Running dry: Mideast spurs projects to help area after oil disappears. Ray Vicker. Wall St J 187:1+ My 5 '76
† United Nations. Econ. comm. for western Asia. Studies on development problems in countries of western Asia, 1974. '75 vi+141p tables (Sales no. E. 75.II.C.2) (ST/ECWA/1) pa $7—U.N. agent

Finance
† Kuwait fund for Arab econ. development. Towards closer economic cooperation in the Middle East: financial aspects [conference paper]. Abdlatif Y. Al-Hamad. O '75 15p tables—P.O. Box 2931, Kuwait

Labor aspects
Help wanted: foreign workers flow into Mideast oil states as job market booms; modernization drive brings global search for labor. Ray Vicker. Wall St J 188:1+ Jl 22 '76

Finance
Desert gold: a bankers' guide to the Middle East [24-page section]. il map Bankers' M (London) 220:7+ Je '76
Partial contents: The Middle East: land of oil and money, by Anthony McDermott; Arab funds in Euro markets, by E. R. Shaw; Beirut: phoenix or dodo? by Anthony McDermott; No oil, no disadvantage: a study of Jordan, by Anthony Kiely.

Foreign relations
New Zealand
New Zealand and the Middle East [address]. J. V. Scott. N Z For Affairs R 26:11-15 Ja '76

Russia
Becker, Abraham S. Moscow and the Middle East settlement: a role for Soviet guarantees? [symposium presentation]. O '75 11p (P-5532) $1.50—Rand corp.
Freedman, Robert O. Soviet policy toward the Middle East since 1970. '75 ix+198p bibl (Praeger special studies in internat. politics and govt.) (LC 74-31504) (ISBN 0-275-05920-0) $16.50; (ISBN 0-275-89170-4) pa $5.95—Praeger
Horelick, Arnold L. Moscow's new "time of troubles" in the Middle East: Soviet options for staying in the game [symposium presentation]. N '75 13p (P-5542) $1.50—Rand corp.

Figure 19. From *Public Affairs Information Service Bulletin* (1976)

to get some perspective on an issue, particularly a controversial one like the Middle East or the Panama Canal. Reading the editorial page can alert you to the stand that a newspaper has taken on political or international issues.

The New York *Times* maintains an index that can help you to locate information that has appeared in its pages. In addition to providing the date of the newspaper and the page and column location of an article, the index itself actually carries abbreviated accounts of the news. For the Sunday edition with its many parts the index also identifies the section by number. Figure 20 shows a page from a semi-monthly issue of the New York *Times Index* (at the end of the year a bound, cumulated volume is published). Now let us look under the heading MIDDLE EAST, subhead ISRAELI-ARAB CONFLICT to see how much information is included in the entry. Read to the end of the June 16 item and you note Je 16, 22:5. You are using the June 16–30, 1977 index so, if you want to read the entire account in the paper, request the *Times* for June 16, 1977. You will probably be given a roll of microfilm covering that date and, having found the June 16th edition, you will turn to page 22, column 5 on that page. The index, then, gives the date first (Je 16) followed by the page (22) and ending with the column (5). As in all reference resources, any abbreviations used in the index will be explained in a list of abbreviations.

Magazines, appearing weekly, semi-monthly, monthly and quarterly, are able to prepare articles that examine a subject in greater depth than newspapers since they do not have to face daily deadlines. Among magazines there is a choice of thousands. Some magazines concentrate on one area of interest: there are sports magazines, poetry magazines, music journals, comics, business titles, science and technology

- 58 -

Labor
Gov Carey approves amendment to Public Health Law exempting med technicians from liability for injury or death when they deliver free emergency med assistance (S), Je 30,IV,16:1

MEDITERRANEAN Area. See also country names
Malta Prime Min Dom Mintoff to open internatl conf in Malta on June 20 that has 1 of its major themes elimination of all foreign mil bases and fleets in Mediterranean area; conf is organized by Secretariat for Socialist Parties in the Mediterranean, orgn based in Libya (S), Je 20,30:6

MEDVEDOW, Leon A (Town Clerk). See also New Haven (Conn), Je 26

MEEHAN, M J, & Co. See also Williams, Blair S, & Co, Je 30

MEHAU, Larry. See also Crime—Hawaii, Je 30

MEIER, Richard, & Associates. See also Mental Deficiency, Je 16

MEILE, Thomas A. See also United States Trust Co (NYC), Je 26

MEINHOF, Ulrike (?-1976). See also West Ger—Pol, Je 19

MEIR, Golda
Illus with Anne Bancroft, who will play leading role in Bway play on Meir's life, Je 23,3:2

MELE, Olga. See also Public Service, American Institute of, Je 24

MELIA, Aloysius J (Justice). See also Nursing Homes, Je 24

MELSTON, Ken. See also Roads—NYS, Je 19

MEN. See also Colls—US—Teachers, Je 18. Educ—Conn, Je 19. Social Security (US), Je 28. Sweeteners, Artificial, Je 18,26

MENCKEN, Henry Lewis (1880-1956). See also Books—Book Trade—US, Je 24

MEND (Massive Econ Neighborhood Development) (Orgn). See also NYC—Econ Conditions—Antipoverty, Je 30

MENDELSOHN, Robert. See also US—Interior Dept, Je 30

MENDELVICH, Lev I (Amb). See also Arms Control, Je 22

MENES, Yves. See also Cooking, Je 28

MENGISTU Haile Mariam (Lt Col). See also Ethiopia, Je 26

MENNEN-Greatbatch Electronics Inc. See also Med—US, Je 25

MENSTRUATION
Mrs Tom Lockhart, mother of daughter attending Amherst, Ohio, jhs, protests procedure by which her daughter could be excused from taking shower in gym class during menstrual period; procedure required her to shout 'M' after calling her name while teacher was taking role; Educ Bd now requires note instead (S), Je 26,32:3

MENTAL Deficiency and Defectives. See also Handicapped (for inclusion)
NY City Club cites Bronx Development Center for annual Bard Award for Excellence in Architecture and Urban Design; center was developed by Facilities Development Corp and designed by Richard Meir & Assocs (M), Je 16,II,22:1
Residents of NYC and suburban communities oppose opening of hostels for mentally retarded children and adults; NYS seeks to remove patients from large insts such as Willowbrook but is having difficulty finding sites; project in Metro North houses, E Harlem, described; illus; legal opposition by Freeport and N Hempstead revd (M), Je 18,21:1
Charles and Emily Kingsley, White Plains, NY, describe rewards they derive from decision to raise Down's Syndrome son, 3, at home in normal environment; illus; couple also works with orgns helping other such families (M), Je 19,XXII,1:1
Little Neck, Queens, home for retarded children opens 2 yrs after neighbors began ct zoning fight to stop it; Revs Robert E Johnson and Ronald Petroski offer prayers; home to house 8 children (S), Je 26,33:1

MENTAL Health and Disorders. See also Prisons (for insts for criminally insane). Types of crimes, eg, Murders (for individual insanity cases, pleas and tests connected with crime), Sex Crimes (for individual insanity cases, pleas and tests connected with crime)
Dr Thomas Szasz criticizes role of Dutch psychiatrist Dr Dick Mulder in negotiating with S Moluccan terrorists, Je 19,IV,16:4

Netherlands
Dr Thomas Szasz criticizes role of Dutch psychiatrist Dr Dick Mulder in negotiating with S Moluccan terrorists, Je 19,IV,16:4

New Jersey
Psychiatrist Dr Abraham Chaplan, who has offices in NYC and NJ, is indicted on charges of stealing $500,000 in Medicaid payments between '73 and '77; is accused of billing Medicaid for psychotherapy sessions not held and billing NYC med assistance program for 45-min sessions that lasted 5-10 mins (S), Je 17,II,22:6
NJ officials acknowledge that mental hosp patients have been mistreated physically and medically; agree to abide by order of Superior Ct Judge Robert Muir Jr to protect med, personal and human rights of 1,100 patients at Greystone Park Psychiatric Hosp, Morris Plains, and to set up plan to insure such protection; settlement was reached with State Public Advocate Stanley C Van Ness; Human Services Dept officials agree to observe standards contained in Muir order; Van Ness agrees to drop his '74 suit against Greystone and dept; Asst Public Advocate Judith A Yaskin says dept has agreed to ask State Civil Service Comm to upgrade qualifications of employees at mental health insts; dept mental health dir Dr Michail Rotov says problems remain; agreement outlined; comments by Human Services Asst Comr David Einhorn and Human Services Comr Ann Klein; Van Ness por (M), Je 30,II,19:4

New York City
Ed on NYS Investigation Comm rept of mistreatments and deaths at Bronx Psychiatric Center, Je 16,22:1
Psychiatrist Dr Abraham Chaplan, who has offices in NYC and NJ, is indicted on charges of stealing $500,000 in Medicaid payments between '73 and '77; is accused of billing Medicaid for psychotherapy sessions not held and billing NYC med assistance program for 45-min sessions that lasted 5-10 mins (S), Je 17,II,22:6

New York State
NYS auditors making post-midnight spot checks in wards of Pilgrim, Kings Park and Central Islip Psychiatric Centers (Suffolk County, NY) find 22 employees asleep and 7 others who appear to be dozing when they all should have been watching over sleeping patients; there were no indications that any patients missed medication or suffered because of inattention; insts' officials concede difficulties of policing staffs of dormitory wards; Central Islip dir James Ramseul and Kings Park deputy dir Dr John Pitrelli comment (M), Je 26,14:3

United States
Rosalyn Carter illus in San Francisco, where she attended all-day hearings of Pres Comm on Mental Health, Je 22,14:6

MENTAL Tests. See also Educ—NYC—Grading of Students, Je 30. Educ—NYC—Teachers, Je 25. Educ—US—Sectarian Schools, Je 25

MENTES, Jorge. See also East Ger—Pol, Je 19

MENTMORE Towers (GB). See also Household Equipment and Furnishings, Je 16. Rosebery (Lord) (Neil Archibald Primrose) (1847-1929), Je 16,24

MENZA, Alexander J (Sen). See also Auto Ins—NJ, Je 29. Prisons—NJ, Je 22

MERCANTILE National Bank (Dallas, Tex). See also Teamsters, Je 18

MERCEDES-Benz Division of Daimler-Benz AG. See also Autos—Intl Trade, Je 26. Taxicabs—NYC, Je 22

MERCHANDISING Centers. See Expositions. Retail Stores

MERCHANT Marine. Use Ships

MERCHANTS Insurance Group. See also Auto Ins—NJ, Je 16

MERCY Missions
USCG transports crewman Peznichenko M Sergeevich from Soviet Trawler near Ore coast to nearby hosp because of severe ulcer (S), Je 30,7:2

MERGERS, Acquisitions and Divestitures. See co, indus and orgn names

MERKLE, Walter (Detective). See also Stamps—US, Je 19

MERLINO, Joseph P (Sen). See also Public Utilities, Je 21

MERMELSTEIN, Joshua. See also TV—Amateur Radio, Je 17

MEROLA, Mario (Dist Atty). See also Govt Employees—Ethics, Je 24. NYC—Pol—Ethics, Je 24. US—Govt Employees—Ethics, Je 24. Welfare (US)—NYC, Je 24

MERRILL Lynch International Bank Ltd
To expand commercial banking operations outside US (S), Je 21,52:4

MERRILL Lynch Pierce Fenner & Smith Inc. See also Stocks (Genl)—US—Margin Trading, Je 22,26

MESA Tribune (Ariz)
Cox Enterprises purchases Mesa, Ariz, Tribune, Sun Valley Spur shopping guide, and Blythe, Calif, Palo Verte Valley Times; sale is announced by R W Calverti and Garner Anthony (S), Je 22,14:5

MESHEL, Yeruham. See also Israel—Econ Conditions, Je 23. Israel—Pol, Je 23

MESSER, Thomas M. See also Art—Shows, Je 24

METAL Poisoning. See metal and mineral names

METALS and Minerals. See also co, metal, mineral and product names

METEOROLOGY. Use Weather

METEORS and Meterorites. See Space—Meteors

METERS. See also Elec Light—US, Je 16. Water—NYC Met Area, Je 21

METHAPYRILENE (Antihistamine). See also Cancer, Je 22. Sedatives, Je 22,24

METRIC Conversion Act of 1975. See also Metric System, Je 25

METRIC System
Natl Weather Service plans to use dual Fahrenheit/Celsius temperature readings during June '78 and switch completely to Celsius scale after June (S), Je 19,IV,7:5; Fed Hwy Adm dir William M Cox says Govt, faced with overwhelming public opposition, will abandon plan to convert natl hwy signs to metric system; conversion, under Metric Conversion Act of '75, is voluntary (S), Je 25,II:6

METRO-Goldwyn-Mayer Inc. See also Motion Pictures—Retrospective Shows, Je 24

METROPOLITAN Areas. Use Urban Areas

METROPOLITAN Museum of Art (NYC). See also Art, Je 24. Art—Shows, Je 19,26
City Club of NY Bard Award for Excellence in Architecture and Urban Design won by 5th Av plaza and east front of Met Museum, designed by Kevin Roche, John Dinkeloo and Assocs (S), Je 16,II,22:1
Philippe de Montebello, vice dir for curatorial and educ affairs, has been named acting dir, effective July 1; Met pres Douglas Dillon notes that apptmt is interim 1 and that museum is still looking for dir although Montebello may be named; por (M), Je 23,III,24:1; Leah Shanks Gordon article on possible successors to Thomas P F Hoving, dir of Met Museum; trustees are looking for 2 heads for museum and propose to hire professional mgr as pres; he will assume administrative duties; 6 museum trustees who make up search com are Richard Perkins, Roswell Gilpatrick, Norbert Schimmel, Richard Paget, Clara Weber and Douglas Dillon; pors of those being considered for adm post--James M Hester, Nelson Rockefeller, Robert O Anderson, Joshua Taylor, Sir John Pope-Hennessy and Jean Sutherland Boggs; drawing (L), Je 26,VI,p13; analysis of changes wrought on Met Museum under directorship of Thomas Hoving, who is being succeeded by acting dir Philippe de Montebello; illus (M), Je 30,III,18:1

METROPOLITAN Opera Assn. See Opera—Met Opera

METROPOLITAN Regional Council. See also Credit (Genl)—US—Consumer Credit, Je 22

METZENBAUM, Howard M (Sen). See also Atomic Energy—US—Elec Light, Je 25,28

MEXICO
Las Delicias desert scene described; some villagers comments; illus (L), Je 24,2:3

MEXICO, Gulf of. See also Gas—US—Offshore, Je 24. Oil—US—Offshore, Je 24

MEXLETTER-Mexican Business and Investment Service. See also Stocks (Genl)—US—Violations, Mexletter

MEYER, Rauer H (Dir). See also Data Processing, Je 24. USSR—Armament etc, Je 24

MEYER, Robert N Jr. See also Commodities (General), Je 18. Soybeans, Je 23

MEYNER, Helen S (Repr). See also Women—US, Je 20

MIAMI, University of. See also Cancer, Je 17

MICHENER, James A. See also Travel—Israel, Je 21

MICHIGAN, Lake. See also Ships—Great Lakes. Water Pollution—Sewage, Je 17,19, Je 21,22

MICROWAVES. See also USSR—Foreign Diplomatic Corps, Je 28

MIDDLE East. See also country names
Syrian Pres Assad, in int with Arabic magazine Al Mostakbal, charges that US engineered 'massacre' in Lebanon after it failed to perpetuate conflict between Egypt and Syria that began after Egypt concluded '75 Sinai accord with Israel (S), Je 26,6:1
Article on improved relations between Sudan and US discusses realignment of power throughout northeastern Africa, where Arab states are attempting to extend their dominion over Red Sea while USSR is striving to spread its influence inland from Somalia (M), Je 27,3:1
Iraq and France reaffirm importance of warmer relations between Arab states and Eur community following 2-day visit by French Prime Min Raymond Barre (S), Je 27,10:3

Israeli-Arab Conflict
June 16: secret trial of 2 W Gers, Brigitte Schultz and Thomas Reuter, held by Israel in connection with alleged attempt to shoot down El Al plane with Strella missile in Jan '76 is reptdly postponed indefinitely; 2 Gers are being held with 3 Arabs (S), Je 16,10:3; lr from Rabbi Walter S Wurzburger, pres of Rabbinical Council of Amer, says UN Sec Gen Kurt Waldheim's reaction to recent Israeli elections was more damaging to cause of peace than even hysterical outbursts of some Arab spokesmen; says US Jewry supports Menahem Begin as head of Israeli Govt; scores public declarations by Carter on specific issues in advance of actual peace negotiations, Je 16,22:3; lr from J Peter Brunswick, public relations manager for El Al Airlines, says June 8 editorial on Uganda Pres Amin stated that Dora Bloch, hostage taken at Entebbe Airport, was aboard El Al plane; notes it was Air France jet that was hijacked; ed regrets error, Je 16, 22:5; **June 17:** Pres Carter, stung by criticism of his Middle East policy by US Jews, has sought in recent days to improve his standing in Israel and to ease apprehension among Israel's supporters; Adm source says more than 90% of mail recd on Middle East this wk has been critical of Carter's stand, particularly his call for Palestinian homeland and on need for Israeli withdrawal from occupied lands; Carter aides say he remains committed to Israel's security and survival; Sen Richard Stone says he was assured by Menahem Begin that forthcoming govt will be flexible in negotiations on all fronts, including West Bank, news conf; proposes that Arab and Israeli officials begin face-to-face talks at low levels; many supporters of Israel believe Zbigniew Brzezinski, Carter's adviser on natl security affairs, is willing to have direct confrontation with Israel in effort to make progress toward settlement; White House aides deny Brzezinski holds anti-Israel views; Carter receives Ashkenazic Chief Rabbi of Israel Shlomo Goren; session, attended by Brzezinski and Amb Simcha Dinitz, seen aimed at sending message to Israel; Goren says Carter told him that he does not want to see Palestinian homeland established as separate ind state but rather established through Jordan; illus of Carter with Goren and Dinitz (M), Je 17,3:1; US delegate James Leonard walks out of African-sponsored UN meeting in protest against exclusion of Israel; meeting, commem shooting 1 yr ago of black

Figure 20. From New York *Times Index* (June 16–30, 1977)

magazines. There are also periodicals that feature articles on current problems or short stories or poetry and book reviews in each issue.

For discussion of the Middle East crisis there are several magazines that are likely sources of information. Some may be familiar to you: *Newsweek, Time, Harper*'s, *Reader's Digest, The Atlantic Monthly,* New York *Times Magazine, Senior Scholastic, U.S. News and World Report.* Others may be unknown to you but are important resources for political and international topics. Among these are *Vital Speeches of the Day* (which publishes important addresses by public figures), *Foreign Affairs, Current History, Saturday Review* and *The Progressive.*

From among all these possibilities the best way to begin a search is by means of the *Readers' Guide to Periodical Literature.* This is an index to approximately 180 magazines of fairly popular appeal in a wide range of interests. All of the titles named above, for example are included. (Remember that this is an *index* to the magazines; having found what you want, you must then request the magazine itself.)

Readers' Guide is published monthly in February, July, and August and semi-monthly the rest of the year. During the year there are four cumulated issues (interfiled alphabetical lists) and a bound annual volume. Whether you are using a current paper issue or a bound volume, the date is clearly stated on the cover so that you know exactly what period of time is included in that particular issue.

If we examine the May 10, 1977 issue of *Readers' Guide* for articles on the Middle East, we find that some related subjects are suggested and also that there are subdivisions of the main

MICROPROCESSORS
Microprocessors. J. Free. il Pop Sci 210:90-3 Mr '77
Smart instruments: microprocessors not the whole story. A. L. Robinson. Science 195:1315-18+ Mr 25 '77

MICROSCOPES and microscopy
See also
Electron microscopes and microscopy
X Ray microscopes and microscopy

MICROSURGERY
Preventing strokes: surgical bypass of the internal carotid artery. Newsweek 89:79 Ja 31 '77

MICROTUS. See Mice

MICROWAVE cookery
Microwave kitchen. H. McCully. See issues of House beautiful

MICROWAVE Cooking Products Division. See Litton Industries, Inc

MICROWAVE ovens
Home works: what's cooking with today's ranges—from conventional to de luxe. il Redbook 148:130+ Mr '77
Microwaving—20 years after the revolution. N. Craig. House B 119:104+ Ap '77

Manufacture
See also
Litton Industries, Inc

MIDAS-International Corporation
Midas touch. il por Time 109:43 Mr 14 '77

MIDDLE age

Anecdotes, facetiae, satire, etc.
How do you know when you're 40? J. Viorst. il N Y Times Mag p66-7 F 6 '77
Menopause that refreshes. G. Nachman. por Newsweek 89:19 Ap 18 '77

MIDDLE Ages
See also
Troubadours

MIDDLE EAST
See also
Suez Canal
Syria
United Nations—Armed Forces—Forces in the Middle East
United Nations Relief and Works Agency for Palestine Refugees in the Near East

Antiquities
See also
Bible—Antiquities

Description and travel
Anecdotes, facetiae, satire, etc.
Follow me, Cy., New Repub 176:47 Mr 26 '77

Economic conditions
Profitless confrontation in the Mideast. America 136:90 F 5 '77

Foreign relations
United States
See United States—Foreign relations—Middle East

History
See also
Israel-Arab War, 1948-1949

Politics and government
For U.S. a race against time in the Mideast. il por map U.S. News 82:19-20 F 28 '77
1977: year of opportunity in the Middle East? address, December 8, 1976. T. F. Eagleton. Vital Speeches 43:201-4 Ja 15 '77

MIDDLE EASTERN dancing. See Dancing, Middle Eastern

MIDDLE WESTERN States
See also
Agriculture—Middle Western States
Reclamation of land—Middle Western States

MIDDLEBROOK, David
David Middlebrook. il Ceram Mo 25:54-5 Mr '77 *

MIDDLETON, Thomas H.
Light refractions. See issues of Saturday review

MIDNIGHT ride of. . .Who? drama. See Majeski, B.

MID-OCEAN Dynamics Experiment. See Oceanographic research

MIDWAY Airport. See Chicago—Airports

MIES VAN DER ROHE, Ludwig
Enduring splendor of Mies van der Rohe. A. L. Huxtable. il por N Y Times Mag p70-1+ F 27 '77 *
Prince and the puritan; exhibition of furniture at the Museum of Modern Art. D. Davis. il Newsweek 89:77-77A Mr 28 '77 *

MIG airplanes. See Airplanes, Military—Russia

MIGNONETTES
It's dowdy, it's weedy, but also it's fragrant. Sunset 158:266 Ap '77

MIGRANT labor
See also
United Farm Workers

MIGRATION, Internal
Look where America is growing fastest: rural settings. L. Palmer. il Farm J 101:52-4+ Ja '77
Mobility. C. Fischer and A. Stueve. Society 14:8-10 Ja '77
Population redistribution, migration, and residential preferences. G. F. De Jong and R. R. Sell. bibl f il Ann Am Acad 429:130-44 Ja '77
Slowdown for strip cities: reversal of century-old trend. il maps U.S. News 82:39-42 Mr 7 '77

History
Farmers' frontier; excerpt from The American farm: a photographic history. M. Conrat and R. Conrat. il Am West 14:22-33 Mr '77

MILAN, Italy

La Scala
See Opera—Italy

MILANOV, Zinka
Most beautiful voice in the world; interview, ed by R. Jacobson. il Opera N 41:8+ Ap 9 '77

MILES, Benny
How an elementary teacher does it. Todays Educ 66:76-7 Ja '77

MILES, Charles
Indian relics. See issues of Hobbies

MILES, Dick
Table tennis (cont) il Sports Illus 46:73-4+ Ap 18 '77

MILESKO-PYTEL, Diana
Changing the specifications for engineers. il Am Educ 13:27-31 Ja '77

MILETI, Dennis S.
Forecast: future shock. il Time 109:83 Ja 24 '77 *

MILGO Electronic Corporation-Racal Electronics Ltd merger. See Electronic industries—Acquisitions and mergers

MILHAUD, Darius
La mère coupable. il Opera N 41:26-8 Mr 5 '77 *

MILITARY architecture
See also
Navy yards and naval stations

MILITARY art and science
See also
War games

MILITARY assistance

Africa, Southern
How a Ugandan bishop views Africa's upheaval; excerpts from interview. F. Kivengere. por U.S. News 82:30 Ap 4 '77

MILITARY assistance, American
Aid, human rights link reappraised. Aviation W 106:18 Ap 11 '77
Military aid, human rights face study. K. Johnsen. Aviation W 106:59 F 7 '77
Proliferating arms industry: America exports its know-how. M. T. Klare. Nation 224:173-8 F 12 '77

Ethiopia
Fifteen-year war: Ethiopia, Eritrea & U.S. policy. D. Connell. il map Nation 224:337-40 Mr 19 '77

Far East
U.S. economic and security assistance programs in East Asia; statement, March 10, 1977. R. C. Holbrooke. Dept State Bull 76:322-6 Ap 4 '77

Israel
Staunch friends at arms length. il Time 109:30-1 Ja 31 '77

MILITARY assistance, Cuban

Africa
Castro in Africa—challenge to Carter? U.S. News 82:32 Mr 28 '77
Cubans, Cubans everywhere. il map Time 109:33-4 Mr 28 '77
Cubans in Africa. G. A. Geyer. New Repub 176:11-13 Ap 2 '77

MILITARY avionics. See Avionics

MILITARY bases
Military bases on Guam declared incompatible with Charter purposes. UN Chron 14:35-9 Ja '77
See also
Navy yards and naval stations

MILITARY budget. See United States—Defense, Department of—Appropriations and expenditures

MILITARY cemeteries. See National cemeteries

MILITARY communications satellites. See Communications satellites—Military use

MILITARY desertion. See United States—Armed Forces—Desertion

MILITARY education
See also
Military schools
United States Military Academy, West Point

Figure 21. From *Readers' Guide to Periodical Literature* (May 10, 1977)

topic. As we look down the entries on page 239 (Figure 21), we may decide that the specific subdivision that is most appropriate to our research is POLITICS AND GOVERNMENT. Of the two articles listed, the first one, "For U.S., a race against time in the Mideast," gives more than written text. Note the abbreviations—"il" "por"—and the word "map." All abbreviations are spelled out in the front of every issue of the *Readers' Guide* but you may already know that "il" means "illustration" and "por" means "portrait." Thus we have an article with pictures *and* a map. The article can be read in *U.S. News and World Report*, volume 82, page 19 to 20 of the February 28, 1977 issue.

Look at the second entry under MIDDLE EAST—POLITICS AND GOVERNMENT:

1. In what magazine does it appear?
2. What issue?
3. What does "address" mean here?
4. What is "Dec. 8, 1976"?
5. Who is the author?

If you would like to check your answers, they should have been as follows:

1. *Vital Speeches (of the Day)*
2. January 15, 1977 (volume 43, pages 201 to 204)
3. "Address" means a speech.
4. The date on which the speech was made.
5. Eagleton was the person who made the speech (therefore, the author of this article). If you wanted to know something about this person, you could check in *Who's Who in America* or *Current Biography*; or it is also likely that the magazine will identify him in a note.

> REMINDER: Libraries usually keep back issues of magazines in special areas and will expect you to make out a request slip for the issue you want. Public libraries generally bind their magazines and in that case the volume number—the number before the colon in the *Readers' Guide* entry—is very helpful to them in locating the right issue. School libraries vary.

For the person who wishes to pursue his magazine research more deeply, there are specialized periodicals like *Middle East Journal*, *New Middle East*, and *World Politics*. Magazines like these are too specialized to be indexed in *Readers' Guide*, but there are other more specialized indexes. For this subject and the magazines just mentioned, there is the *Social Sciences Index* and a glance at the list of titles included in that index will show how special they are. You will probably discover the names of magazines you might find useful in connection with other interests or research you have in mind. Only schools with large budgets are likely to have this index but your public library may have it. What is important for you to keep in mind is that *Readers' Guide*, while the most widely used, is only one of a number and that there are specialized indexes for periodicals in subject areas like art, music, science, medicine, and humanities, to name a few others.

AND MORE

Since this guide has tried to show you how varied are the sources of information, we have not limited ourselves strictly to the resources found within libraries, although these are a very rich mine, indeed. We do live in a multi-media world and for that reason we must take into account television and radio programs—some of which are available in your libraries.

Television carries regular daily newscasts, but they tend, often, to be superficial and over-dramatized. There are, however, excellent reports-in-depth from time to time like "Sixty Minutes," or documentaries on public broadcasting reflecting competent research. Your television program guide can help you to be more selective about your viewing and alert you to upcoming programs that may be of interest to you.

Museums can be regarded as a kind of extension of libraries; you can learn a great deal from exhibits in your local museums. For the topic of the Middle East, dioramas of life among rural and city inhabitants of the Middle East may help reveal the nature of certain political and social conflicts. Knowing about the history, cultural heritage, artifacts of a people can sometimes bring you to a better understanding of their aspirations.

All the resources mentioned in this chapter are simply a few logical suggestions just as the visible tip is the merest indication of the size of an iceberg. If you know your way around your school and public libraries—where the reference section is, where the vertical file or information file is located, where the periodical indexes are shelves—you can apply the same research technique to any other subject related to world conditions, whether that topic is Ireland, Eritrea, India, Rhodesia—or pollution, poverty, and population.

In any case, a final element must be noted: your own evaluation of what you are reading, hearing, seeing. The source of your information may make a difference. Which magazine are you citing? Do you know its point of view? Who is the author of the book you are reading? What are the author's qualifications for presenting this material? Is the film you viewed meant to be factual or provocative, critical or persuasive?

Clearly, you are in a better position to come to some sound conclusions as a well-informed citizen if you use many sources, from many different points of view, rather than depending on only one.

SUGGESTED MATERIALS

American Heritage Dictionary of the English Language. Boston, MA: Houghton Mifflin, 1969.

Atlantic Monthly (periodical). Boston, MA: Atlantic Monthly Co.

Collier's Encyclopedia. New York: Crowell-Collier.

Columbia-Lippincott Gazetteer of the World. New York: Columbia University Press, 1962.

Current Biography. New York: Wilson.

Current History (periodical). Philadelphia, PA: Current History, Inc.

Editorial Research Reports. Washington, D.C.: Congressional Quarterly.

Encyclopedia Americana. New York: Americana Corp.

Encyclopedia Britannica. Chicago, IL: Encyclopedia Britannica.

Eyes on the Arab World. 4 filmstrips and cassettes. St. Paul, MN: EMC Corp.

Facts on File: A Weekly Digest of World Events with Cumulative Index. New York: Facts on File.

Foreign Affairs (periodical). New York: Council on Foreign Relations.

Funk and Wagnalls Standard College Dictionary. New York: Funk, 1977.

Goode's World Atlas. 13th ed. Chicago, IL: Rand McNally, 1970.

Hammond Ambassador World Atlas. Maplewood, NJ: Hammond, 1971.

Harper's (periodical). New York: Harper's Magazine, Inc.

Information Please Almanac. New York: Simon and Schuster.

International Who's Who. London, England: Europa Publications. Annual.

Isenberg, Irwin, ed. *The Arab World.* Reference Shelf Series (Vol. 48, No. 2). New York: Wilson, 1976.

Israel Is Born. Recording. Caedmon TC 1014.

The Middle East: Facing a New World Order. 6 filmstrips and cassettes. Chicago, IL: Society for Visual Education, 1976.

Middle East Journal (periodical). Washington, D.C.: Middle East Institute.

New Middle East (periodical). London: New Middle East Publishing Co.

The New York Times Atlas of the World. New York: Quadrangle/New York Times Book, 1975.

New York Times Magazine (periodical). New York: New York Times Co.

Newsweek (periodical). New York: Newsweek, Inc.

Nyrop, Richard F. and others. *Area Handbook on Syria.* Washington, D.C.: Government Printing Office, 1971.

Oxford Economic Atlas of the World. 4th ed. New York: Oxford University Press, 1972.

Progressive (periodical). Madison, WI: Progressive, Inc.

Public Affairs Information Service Bulletin. New York: Public Affairs Information Service.

Rand McNally Cosmopolitan World Atlas. Chicago, IL: Rand McNally, 1971.

Random House Dictionary of the English Language. New York: Random, 1966.

Reader's Digest (periodical). Pleasantville, NY: Reader's Digest Association.

Reader's Digest Almanac. Pleasantville, NY: Reader's Digest Association.

Readers' Guide to Periodical Literature. New York: Wilson.

Saturday Review (periodical). New York: Saturday Review, Inc.

Schoenbrun, David and Lucy Szekely. *The New Israelis*. New York: Atheneum, 1973.

Senior Scholastic (periodical). New York: Senior Scholastic Magazines, Inc.

Smith, Harvey H. *Area Handbook on U.A.R.* (Egypt). Washington, D.C.: Government Printing Office, 1970.

Smith, Harvey H. and others. *Area Handbook on Israel*. Washington, D.C.: Government Printing Office, 1970.

Social Sciences Index. New York: Wilson.

Statesman's Year-book. New York: St. Martin's Press.

Time (periodical). New York: Time, Inc.

U.S. News & World Report (periodical). Washington, D.C.: U.S. News & World Report, Inc.

Vital Speeches of the Day (periodical). Southold, NY: City News Publishing Co.

Walpole, Norman C. *Area Handbook on Saudi Arabia*. Washington, D.C.: Government Printing Office, 1971.

Webster's New Geographical Dictionary: A Dictionary of Names of Places, with Geographical and Historical Information and Pronunciations. Springfield, MA: G. & C. Merriam, 1972.

Webster's Third New International Dictionary of the English Language. Springfield, MA: G. & C. Merriam, 1961.

Who's Who. New York: St. Martin's Press.

Who's Who in America. Chicago, IL: Marquis.

Wilson, Evan M. *Jerusalem, Key to Peace*. Washington, D.C.: Middle East Institute, 1970.

World Almanac. New York: World-Telegram.

World Book Encyclopedia. Chicago, IL: Field Enterprises.

World Politics (periodical). Princeton, NJ: Princeton University Press.

Worldmark Encyclopedia of the Nations. 4th ed. New York: Worldmark Press and Harper, 1971.

Chapter 6

POETRY: MUSIC IN WORDS

Poems have been written in praise of love, in despair over death, in amusement over the foolish antics of humankind, in celebration of great events. Poems can be ponderous, long, obscure, avant-garde or classical. They are also amorous, humorous, and brief. There is something for every taste.

Because a message can be compressed into a few lines of a poem, many young people, especially those whose hearts and minds are filled with some specific emotion or problem, have tried their own hands at writing poetry. School publications often include examples of this creative writing; sometimes such efforts have even found their way into print via regular book publishers. Many more young people have written poems but have kept them concealed as private communications with themselves.

As with most pursuits, if we wish to improve our technique, whether it is tennis or writing, the way to begin is to study the experts. The school library media center or public library can start you along the way to enjoying poetry and, if you wish, even writing it. Unless you are already interested in a particular writer or a specific type of poetry, a good beginning is to leaf through an anthology. An example of an anthology that allows you to range through a variety of poetic styles and subjects is the *New Oxford Book of American Verse*, which begins with Anne Bradstreet, who wrote poetry in the seventeenth century, and includes writers through the succeeding years up to the twentieth century, including Delmore Schwartz, Sylvia Plath, Karl Shapiro, and Robert Lowell. In recent times, women poets have received much attention; a current anthology, *Alone Amid All This Noise*, contains an historical selection of poems by women starting with the great Greek poet Sappho and concluding with Jane Katz.

Some poetry books represent the works of only one poet: Stevie Smith's *Collected Poems* includes verse dealing with death and the macabre, biting in style. Also appealing to young adults are the poems of Sylvia Plath, whose novel *The Bell Jar* you may already know. One of Plath's poetry collections is entitled *Ariel*, which like the rest of her poetry reflects the complex young woman she was.

Love poems have been popular since the beginning of recorded messages. D. J. Klemer's *Modern Love Poems* is a collection from the works of many poets. One of the most famous volumes of love poetry is Elizabeth Barrett Browning's *Sonnets from the Portuguese*, love-lyrics for her husband-to-be, Robert Browning, whose pet name for his wife was "the Portuguese."

Poems about war, poems by black poets, poems about sports—these abound. Here are some titles that you might enjoy:

Langston Hughes, ed. *New Negro Poets: U.S.A.*

Arnold Adoff, ed. *Poetry of Black America.*

M. C. Livingston, ed. *O Frabjous Day; Poetry for Holidays and Special Occasions.*

Richard Eberhart, ed. *War and the Poet.*

Lillian Morrison. *The Sidewalk Racer (and Other Poems of Sports and Motion).*

Richard Peck, ed. *Pictures That Storm Inside My Head.*

Let us not forget poems that make us laugh: there are volumes of poetry by Edward Lear and Ogden Nash—to name two of the best known humorous poets—and there is the *Fireside Book of Humorous Poetry*, edited by William Cole. In this last title one can find poems under such headings as "Bores and Boobs," "Edibles, Potables and Smokeables," and "Playful and Tricky."

One could go on endlessly listing the types of poetry anthologies. You get the idea however: there is a book of poetry to suit every taste and every kind of reader.

A fact, often overlooked, is that song lyrics also constitute a kind of poetry. Rock music has produced many songs whose lyrics have been compared in content and feeling with the poetry of some very famous writers. In a book called *Grandfather Rock: The New Poetry and the Old*, David Morse has analyzed such themes as "Spaces," "Death," and "Loneliness and Love," which have supplied material for both the modern balladeer and the classical poet. He compares, for example, Bob Dylan's "New Morning" with Robert Browning's "Song"; Joni Mitchell's "Cactus Tree" with a sonnet of William Shakespeare; Leonard Cohen's "Suzanne" with Matthew Arnold's "Dover Beach." On your own, you could try to match up some of your favorite lyrics—by the Beatles or Simon and Garfunkle or anyone else—with poems written years or even centuries ago by poets like Byron, Shakespeare, and Whitman.

Finding Your Poetry

Many of us enjoy just looking through shops, browsing around until something catches our eye. This is not a bad way to find a book of poems you might like to read. If you remember your experiences in the school library you will recall that there is a system that organizes the books for the convenience of the reader. Putting things together by their subject is a sensible arrangement and you have learned that The Dewey Decimal Classification System did just that. All history books are together in the 900s; science is in another section, in the 500s; religion, art, music, and literature are other categories, each with its own number. The Dewey number 800 is the classification for literature. Since this is a very broad, all-encompassing classification, you can understand the value of breaking that general number down into smaller subdivisions. Among the numbers where poetry is to be found are 808.81 and 821.08, where anthologies are shelved. You can also try these numbers:

811—American poetry (individual poets, e.g. Marianne Moore)
821—British poetry (individual poets, e.g. John Keats)
841—French poetry (individual poets, e.g. François Villon)

It may have struck you that the middle digit changes for the country while the "1" remains at the end and stands for "poetry." This is helpful to know but you do not have to memorize even so interesting a device, since all libraries use some guide to which the patron may refer in order to learn the location, the call number, of any book in the library.

Fiction usually has no number and is put on the shelves in alphabetical order by the author's last name.

CARD CATALOG

You may have been introduced to the card catalog before. There are guidebooks to refresh your memory about the details (Florence Cleary's *Discovering Books and Libraries* is one). Here let us just see how the card catalog helps us with information about poets and poetry.

Having located the tray of the catalog which contains the cards that are headed POETRY we find some of the following headings:

POETICS
POETRY
POETRY—COLLECTIONS
POETRY—DICTIONARIES
POETRY—HISTORY AND CRITICISM
POETS, AMERICAN
POETS, FRENCH

Under each of these subject headings the catalog cards are arranged. For example, under the heading POETRY—COLLECTIONS we find the following:

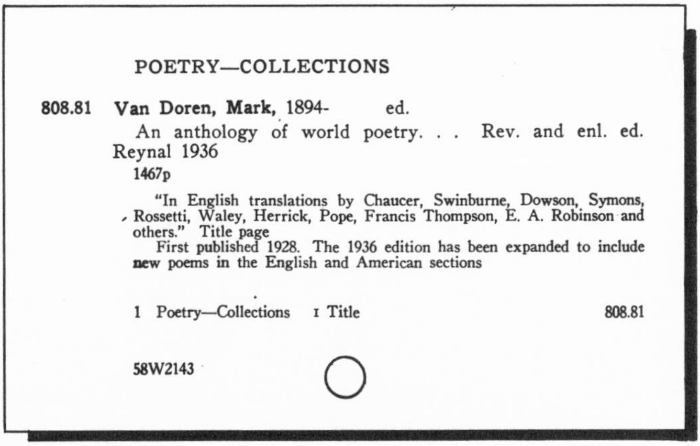
POETRY—COLLECTIONS

808.81 **Van Doren, Mark,** 1894- ed.
An anthology of world poetry. . . Rev. and enl. ed. Reynal 1936
1467p

"In English translations by Chaucer, Swinburne, Dowson, Symons, Rossetti, Waley, Herrick, Pope, Francis Thompson, E. A. Robinson and others." Title page
First published 1928. The 1936 edition has been expanded to include new poems in the English and American sections

1 Poetry—Collections I Title 808.81

58W2143

Figure 22. Sample subject catalog card

Figure 22 shows the catalog card for an anthology edited by Mark Van Doren. The book itself will be found where all the books marked 808.81 are shelved. Here we have to look for the letter "V" (for Van Doren) after we have come to the section that contains books numbered 808.81. This anthology of world poetry by Mark Van Doren will be between 808.81 U (an anthology by Louis Untermeyer) and 808.81 W (an anthology by Thomas Walsh).

The card catalog helps you to find materials if you know the subject, the author, or the title. For instance here is the author card (Figure 23) for the Van Doren anthology; in this case you could locate the book if you knew only that an editor named Van Doren had produced some collection of poetry you wanted.

808.81 **Van Doren, Mark,** 1894- ed.
An anthology of world poetry. . . Rev. and enl. ed. Reynal 1936
1467p
"In English translations by Chaucer, Swinburne, Dowson, Symons, Rossetti, Waley, Herrick, Pope, Francis Thompson, E. A. Robinson and others." Title page
First published 1928. The 1936 edition has been expanded to include new poems in the English and American sections

1 Poetry—Collections I Title 808.81

58W2143

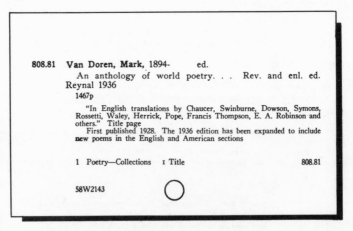

Figure 23. Sample author catalog card

Most of the libraries that you will be using in schools or in public library systems have a dictionary catalog—that is, all the cards whether they are for the subject or the author or the title of the material, are filed in one single alphabet. Some libraries divide the cards into two files, one for subjects only and the other for authors and titles. Some libraries may even have three separate alphabets. In any case, there will always be a guide card to explain how the catalog is arranged. Figure 24 shows such a card.

HOW TO USE THIS CATALOG

Non-fiction books are listed alphabetically under the author's name, title and subject. Find the book you want under any one of these classifications just as you would find a name in the telephone directory. "The", "An", and "A" are not considered.

For Example: **The book entitled "Outline of History", by H. G. Wells, will be listed under the title, "Outline of History", in the drawer containing O's; also under the author's surname, "Wells", in the drawer containing W's; and also under the subject, "History", in the drawer containing H's.**

The book's location on the shelves is indicated by the number in the corner of the card.

Books about persons are listed under surnames, which will be found on the top line of each card.

English fiction is shelved alphabetically according to the author's surnames. Neither books nor cards are numbered.

The Librarian will be glad to help you if you cannot find what you wish.

Figure 24. Sample library catalog guide card

In recent times with greater use of computer technology, some libraries have begun to use what are called book catalogs. Figure 25 shows a page from the book catalog of the New York Public Library, which uses three sets of book *catalogs*: one each for subjects, titles, and names. (Note that in the illustration the call number is in the lower right-hand side of each entry instead of the place to which you are probably accustomed, the upper left-hand corner of a catalog card.) The information in the book catalog is more condensed

poetry. Minneapolis [c1956] 225p. 70-97935 **Ccl** **[809.1-K]**

Leaping poetry . Boston [c1975] 93 p. ; 76-108704 **Ccl D Rr BLS** **[808.81-L]**

Levertov, Denise, 1923- The poet in the world. [New York, c1973] x, 275 p. 74-141914 **Ccl D Rr BLS** **[809.1-L]**

Mackail, John William, 1859-1945. Lectures on poetry. Freeport, N.Y. [1967] 334p. 70-295086 **Ccl** **[809.1-M]**

MacLeish, Archibald, 1892- Poetry and experience. Cambridge, Boston, 1961 [c1960] 204p. 70-416337 **Ccl BLS** **[809.1-M]**

MacNeice, Louis, 1907-1963. Modern poetry. Oxford [c1968] 205p. 70-189295 **Ccl** **[808.1-M]**

Maritain, Jacques, 1882-1973. Art and poetry. Port Washington, N.Y. [1968, c1943] 104p. 70-358585 **Ccl** **[700.1-M]**

Matthiessen, Francis Otto, 1902-1950. The achievement of T. S. Eliot. New York [c1958] 248p. 72-197347 **Ccl Fd My BLS** **[811-Eliot-M]**

Merwin, William S., 1927- (comp.) Selected translations, 1948-1968. New York [c1968] 176 p. 69-96536 **Ccl** **[808.81-M]**

Millett, Fred Benjamin, 1890- Reading poetry. New York [1967, c1968] 510p. 71-294389 **Ccl** **[808.107-M]**

Montes Brunet, Hugo. De Platón a Neruda. [Santiago, c1967] 126p. 74-126873 **Df** **[S-808.1-M]**

Múgica, Rafael. Inquisición de la poesía. [Madrid, c1972] 258 p. 76-104592 **Ccl** **[S-808.1-M]**

Nowottny, Winifred. The language poets use. [London, c1962] 225p. 71-306641 **Ccl** **[808.1-N]**

Paz, Octavio, 1914- The bow and the lyre (El arco y la lira). Austin [c1973] x, 281 p. 74-7352 **Ccl D** **[808.1-P]**

Pound, Ezra Loomis, 1885-1972. A. B. C. of reading. New York [1960, c1934] 206p. 70-533979 **Ccl BLS** **[809.1-P]**

Pratt, John Clark. The meaning of modern poetry. Garden City, N.Y. [c1962] 400p. 70-473488 **Ccl** **[808.1-P]**

Prescott, Frederick Clarke, 1871-1957. Poetry & myth. Port Washington, N.Y. [1967, c1927] 190p. 70-541279 **Ccl** **[808.1-P]**

Press, John. The chequer'd shade. London, New York [c1958] 229p. 70-543122 **Ccl** **[809.1-P]**

Press, John. The fire and the fountain. New York [1966] 255p. 71-148342 **Ccl** **[808.1-P]**

Read, Herbert Edward, Sir, 1893-1968. Poetry and anarchism. Freeport, N.Y. [1972] 126 p. 73-194557 **Ccl** **[824-Read]**

Reeves, James. Understanding poetry. New York [1968, c1965] 186p. 69-147129 **Ccl** **[808.1-R]**

Richards, Ivor Armstrong, 1893- Coleridge on imagination. Bloomington [c1960] 236 p. 69-120159 **Ccl** **[821-Coleridge-R]**

Rosenheim, Edward W. What happens in literature. Chicago [c1960] 162p. 73-119965 **Ccl D Fd Sg** **[807-R]**

Rosenthal, Macha Louis. Exploring poetry. New York [c1973] xxvii, 531 p. 73-145112 **Ccl D Ex BLS** **[821.008-R]**

Rukeyser, Muriel, 1913- The life of poetry. New York, 1968. 232 p. 69-112099 **Ccl** **[808.1-R]**

Savage, Derek S. The personal principle. Port Washington, N.Y. [1969] 196p. 70-151323 **Ccl** **[821.009-S]**

Schiller, Johann Christoph Friedrich von, 1759-1805. Naive, and sentimental poetry, and On the sublime. New York [1967,c1966] 220p. 69-101666 **Ccl** **[808.1-S]**

Scholes, Robert E. Elements of poetry. New York [c1969] 86p. 70-514082 **Ccl** **[808.1-S]**

Sewell, Elizabeth, 1919- The human metaphor. [Notre Dame, Ind., c1964] 212p. 70-261150 **Ccl** **[808.1-S]**

Sewell, Elizabeth, 1919- The Orphic voice. New York [1971, c1960] 463p. 74-70228 **Ccl** **[809.1-S]**

Sewell, Elizabeth, 1919- The structure of poetry. London [1951] 196p. 70-166110 **Ccl** **[808.1-S]**

Shairp, John Campbell, 1819-1885. Aspects of poetry. Freeport, N.Y. [1972] 401 p. 73-72763 **Ccl** **[808.1-S]**

Shapiro, Karl Jay, 1913- Beyond criticism. [Lincoln, c1953] 73p. 75-42699 **Ccl** **[808.1-S]**

Shapiro, Karl Jay, 1913- A primer for poets. Lincoln [c1953] 73p. 71-43299 **Ccl** **[808.1-S]**

Shelley, Percy Bysshe, 1792-1822. A defence of poetry. Indianapolis [c1965] xxxiii, 80p. 71-76806 **Ccl** **[808.1-S]**

Singh, Ghan Shyam. Leopardi and the theory of poetry. [Lexington, c1964] 365p. 71-267825 **Ccl** **[801.951-S]**

Sisson, Charles Hubert, 1914- In the Trojan ditch. Chester Springs, Pa. [c1975] 228p. 76-97444 **Ccl** **[821-Sisson]**

Solve, Melvin Theodor. Shelley: his theory of poetry. New York, 1964. 207p. 70-511593 **Ccl** **[821-Shelley-S]**

Sprigg, Christopher St. John, 1907-1937. Illusion and reality. New York [c1937] 342p. 75-77058 **Ccl** **[808.1-S]**

Squire, John Collings, Sir, 1884-1958. Essays on poetry. Freeport, N.Y. [1967] 228p. 72-228724 **Ccl** **[821.009-S]**

Squire, John Collings, Sir, 1884-1958. Flowers of speech. Freeport, N.Y. [1967] 151p. 71-429780 **Ccl** **[808.042-S]**

Stauffer, Donald Alfred, 1902-1952. The nature of poetry. New York [1962, c1946] 291p. 71-84156 **Ccl BLS** **[808.1-S]**

Tillyard, Eustace Mandeville Wetenhall, 1889-1962. Poetry direct and oblique. London [1945] 115p. 71-14806 **Ccl** **[808.1-T]**

Untermeyer, Louis, 1885- The pursuit of poetry. New York [c1969] 318p. 70-67615 **Ccl BLS** **[808.1-U]**

Valéry, Paul, 1871-1945. The art of poetry. New York [c1958] 345p. 71-62782 **Ccl** **[809.1-V]**

Warren, Alba Houghton. English poetic theory, 1825-1865. New York, 1966 [c1950] 243p. 71-106926 **Ccl** **[801.951-W]**

Whittemore, Reed, 1919- From zero to the absolute. New York [c1967] 210 p. 69-50744 **Ccl** **[809.1-W]**

Wimsatt, William Kurtz, 1907-1975. The verbal icon. [Lexington, c1954] 299p. 74-123372 **Ccl** **[808.1-W]**

Yeats, William Butler, 1865-1939. Letters on poetry from W. B. Yeats to Dorothy Wellesley. London, New York [c1964] 202p. 69-47076 **Ccl** **[B-Yeats-Y]**

POETRY - EARLY WORKS TO 1800.

Aristotle. Aristotle on the art of fiction. London [1968] 93p. 70-71119 **Ccl** **[882.009-A]**

Aristotle. Aristotle on the art of poetry. Ithaca, N.Y. [1967, c1913] 100p. 71-429095 **Ccl** **[801-A]**

Aristotle. Aristotle: Poetics. Ann Arbor [c1967] 124p. 71-153658 **Ccl BLS** **[882.009-A]**

Aristotle. Aristotle's Art of poetry. Oxford [1940] xxxii, 82p. 71-315739 **Ccl** **[882.009-A]**

Aristotle. Aristotle's Poetics. London, New York [1963] 208p. 70-70547 **Ccl** **[882.009-A]**

Aristotle. On poetry and style. Indianapolis [c1958] xxxii, 110p. 69-172730 **Ccl** **[801-A]**

Aristotle. Poética. Buenos Aires [c1947] 149p. 74-21718 **Df** **[S-882.009-A]**

Aristotle. Poetics. New York [c1961] 118p. 69-134588 **Ccl Fd** **[882.009-A]**

Aristotle. The poetics of Aristotle. Chapel Hill [c1942] 70p. 71-146514 **Ccl BLS** **[882.009-A]**

Aristotle. Politics and Poetics. New York [1957, c1952] 265p. 74-163186 **Cc4** **[320.01-A]**

Aristotle. Rhetoric. New York [c1954] 289p. 70-139733 **Ccl My BLS** **[808-A]**

Boccaccio, Giovanni, 1313-1375. Boccaccio on poetry. New York [c1956] L,213p. 70-363651 **Ccl** **[808.1-B]**

Daniel, Samuel, 1562-1619. Poems and a defence of ryme. Chicago [1965, c1930] 215p. 71-128528 **Ccl** **[821-Daniel]**

Durham, Willard Higley, 1883- (ed.) Critical essays of the eighteenth century. New York, 1961 [c1915] 445p. 70-164736 **Ccl** **[824.008-D]**

Horace. The art of poetry. Albany [c1974] xi, 83 p. 74-236509 **Ccl** **[871-Horace]**

Puttenham, Richard, 1520?-1601? (supposed author.) The arte of English poesie. Cambridge [Eng.] 1963. cx, 358p. 71-391195 **Ccl** **[808.1-P]**

Sidney, Philip, Sir, 1554-1586. An apology for poetry. [London, c1965] 244 p. 69-107428 **Ccl** **[808.1-S]**

Smith, George Gregory, 1865-1932. (ed.) Elizabethan critical essays. [London, 1904] 2v. 70-143972 **Ccl** **[820.9003-S]**

Tasso, Torquato, 1544-1595. Discourses on the heroic poem. Oxford [c1973] xxxiv, 232p. 74-50389 **Ccl** **[808.13-T]**

POETRY - ADDRESSES, ESSAYS, LECTURES.

Allen, Don Cameron, 1904- (ed.) The moment of poetry. Baltimore [c1962] 135p. 71-132503 **Ccl** **[808.1-A]**

Bogan, Louise, 1897-1970. Selected criticism. New York [c1955] 404p. 74-457456 **Ccl** **[809-B]**

Bowra, Cecil Maurice, Sir, 1898-1971. Inspiration and poetry. Freeport, N.Y. [1970, c1955] vii, 265 p. 72-201893 **Ccl** **[809.1-B]**

Burford, William. (comp.) The poet's vocation. [Austin [c1967] 71p. 70-558767 **Ccl** **[808.86-B]**

Ciardi, John, 1916- Dialogue with an audience. Philadelphia [c1963] 316 p. 69-78639 **Ccl** **[808.1-C]**

Cunningham, James Vincent. Tradition and poetic structure. Denver [c1960] 273p. 70-159622 **Ccl** **[821.009-C]**

Day-Lewis, Cecil, 1904-1972. The poetic image. London [1947] 157 p. 69-47406 **Ccl** **[808.1-D]**

Drew, Elizabeth A., 1887-1965. Discovering modern poetry. New York [c1961] 426p. 73-54715 **Ccl Ex BLS** **[821.9-D]**

Drinkwater, John, 1882-1937. The muse in council. Freeport, N.Y. [1970] 303p. 71-430858 **Ccl** **[821.009-D]**

Erskine, John, 1879-1951. The kinds of poetry. Port Washington, N.Y. [1966, c1920] 185p. 70-543805 **Ccl** **[809.1-E]**

Forster, Leonard Wilson, 1913- The poet's tongues. [London, New York, c1970] 101p. 73-127481 **Ccl** **[809.1-F]**

Graves, Robert, 1895- Oxford addresses on poetry. Garden City, N.Y. [c1962] 141p. 75-208134 **Ccl** **[809.1-G]**

Hearn, Lafcadio, 1850-1904. Books and habits. Freeport, N.Y. [1968] 328p. 71-565221 **Ccl** **[809-H]**

Highet, Gilbert, 1906- The powers of poetry. New York [c1960] 356 p. 69-112594 **Ccl** **[821.009-H]**

Kunitz, Stanley Jasspon, 1905- A kind of order, a kind of folly Boston [c1975] xii, 320 p. ;

To locate a book listed in this catalog, make note of the location symbol, for example Cc4, and the classmark, for example [917.3-D]. Consult a librarian if you need help.

Figure 25. From New York Public Library book catalog

than that on the card but the essential facts (author, title, date of publication, and location of the book in the library) are there.

While we are discussing possible variations among libraries, it might be useful to know that, although most libraries that you use are arranged by the Dewey decimal classification, there are other systems. One of the most important is that developed by the Library of Congress (LC), one of our national libraries. This is an arrangement most often used by large research libraries and college and university collections. In the LC classification the letters of the alphabet are used as the basis for subject divisions. The letter P is the general area for literature. David Morse's *Grandfather Rock* would be marked PN 6101.M462 in a library using this classification system. If you are interested in learning more about this system you can find information in *The New Library Key* by Margaret G. Cook.

Booklists are also a helpful source of titles, although your library may not own all the books found in them. Examples of booklists that recommend materials are *Books For You* issued by the National Council of Teachers of English (the poetry section is on pages 197–306) and *Books and the Teen-age Reader* by G. Robert Carlsen in which chapter 10 is devoted to a discussion of poetry and contains a bibliography of titles.

Indexes to Poetry

We have talked about the variety of books of poetry available and where they can be found on a library's shelves. Quite often, however, it is not a volume of poems but one specific poem for which we are searching. Narrowing the search is important, and we will see how that can be accomplished if we follow a few fairly simple procedures.

When you learned the parts of a book in your earlier school days, you became familiar with terms like title page, preface, table of contents, glossary—and index. The table of contents is a list of the chapters and other parts of a book in the order in which they occur. The index, on the other hand, is an alphabetical arrangement of all the names, events, titles, people, and topics that are covered in a book.

What kind of index would be helpful in an anthology of poetry—or even in a book of poems written by one author? One way to answer this question is to ask another: How do you usually remember a poem? If you are like most people, you will usually remember the title of a work before the name of the author. And often it will be the first line that comes to mind while the title and author elude you. On the other hand, there are times when we can recall the author of a poem without clearly remembering the title or the first line. Sometimes we want a poem to celebrate some occasion like St. Valentine's Day or Thanksgiving. Thus, books of poetry, frequently include an index of titles and first lines and anthologies also often have an index of authors. More extensive poetry reference titles may give additional help by including a subject index. In some books there are separate indexes for first lines, titles, and authors; others combine all three elements into a single index.

REMINDER: The introduction to a book usually explains how to use the book. Reading introductions is as important as reading the instructions on a tape recorder, record-player, toaster, or any other appliance you buy. They tell how the tool works.

In order to find the volume in which a certain poem is contained we might have to look through hundreds of anthologies. *Granger's Index to Poetry* does much of the labor for us. It provides a title and first-line index, an author index, and a subject index to about 12,000 poems included in 514 collections.

If you remembered only that famous first line "I shot an arrow into the air" you could look under that and learn that the title is "The Arrow and the Song" and that the author is Henry Wadsworth Longfellow. The collections in which the poem might be found are listed in abbreviated form, whether you look under the first line or under the title of the poem.

Another example of the usefulness of the *Granger* index is to supply you with possibilities for specific programs. For instance, if you were preparing a program on the subject of peace in the world, you could start by looking in the subject index in *Granger*'s under the heading PEACE (Figure 26). You would find some 78 poems listed by title with the author's name following. Having selected several poems that sound promising, you would then look in the title and first-line index in order to identify the anthologies in which they appear. Let us choose "Peace Was My Earliest Love" by Edna St. Vincent Millay. When we locate it in the title and first-line index (Figure 27), we find the abbreviation *NYTB*. All the abbreviations used in the index stand for the titles of the anthologies in which the poems themselves can be found. At the front of *Granger*'s is the entire list of abbreviations in alphabetical order and looking up *NYTB* we find that it stands for the name of the book we need: the *New York Times Book of Verse*, Thomas Lask, ed. (c1970) Macmillan Company. While the copyright date and publisher are given, it is

2157 **SUBJECT INDEX** **Peacocks**

Patriotic Songs, Swedish
Swedish National Hymn. Strandberg.
Patriotic Songs, Welsh
Men of Harlech. *Unknown.*
Patriotism
Ad Patriam. Scollard.
Barbara Frietchie. Whittier.
Border March. *Fr.* The Monastery. Scott.
Breathes There the Man with Soul So Dead. *Fr.* The Lay of the Last Minstrel. Scott.
Bruce to His Men at Bannockburn. Burns.
Call of the Bugles, The. Hovoy.
Celebrations. Clarke.
Children's Song, The. Kipling.
Dear Harp of My Country. Moore.
Dulce et Decorum Est. Owen.
Fatherland, The. J. R. Lowell.
Flag Goes By, The. Bennett.
I am an American. Lieberman.
I Hear America Singing. Whitman.
In Westminster Abbey. Betjeman.
Kid Has Gone to the Colors, The. Herschell.
My Native Land. *Fr.* The Lay of the Last Minstrel. Scott.
Nationality. Gilmore.
Oh, Breathe Not His Name! Moore.
Our Country's Call. Bryant.
Patriot, The. R. Browning.
Patriotism. "Coolidge."
Petition, A. Vernède.
Pro Patria Mori. Moore.
Sail on, O Ship of State! *Fr.* The Building of the Ship. Longfellow.
Scots Wha Hae. Burns.
Soldier, The. *Fr.* 1914. Brooke.
There Is a Land. Montgomery.
To Those Who Reproved the Author for Too Sanguine Patriotism. Woodberry.
Yesterday. Anderson.
Young Hero, The. Tyrtaeus.
Patriotic Anthology, The (PaA). Introduced by Carl Van Doren.
Patriotic Poems America Loves (PAL). Jean Anne Vincent, comp.
Poems of American Patriotism (PAP). Brander Matthews, ed.
Poetry of Freedom, The (PoFr.). William Rose Benet *and* Norman Cousins, eds.
Sourcebook of Poetry (SoP). Al Bryant, comp.
Patrons.
Miserly Patron, A. *Unknown.*
Patroness. Barrax.
Paul, Saint
Paul. Marlatt.
Paul. Oxenham.
Saint Paul, *sels.* Myers.
To St. Peter and St. Paul. Constable.
Pavlova, Anna
Elegy on the Death of Mme Anna Pavlova, *sel.* Meyerstein.
Pawlet, Lady Jane, Marchioness of Winton
Elegie on the Lady Jane Pawlet, Marchion. of Winton, An. Jonson.
Pawnshops
Pawnbroker, The. Kumin.
Pawnshop Window. Grenville.
Peace
And They Shall Beat Their Swords into Plowshares. Micah, Bible, *O.T.*
As Brothers Live Together. *Fr.* The Song of Hiawatha. Longfellow.
Bells of Peace, The. Fisher.
Bucolic. Merwin.
Bugle Song of Peace. Clark.
Child of Peace, The. Lagerlöf.
Christ of the Andes, The. Markham.
Christian Soldier, The. Studdert-Kennedy.
Dear Lord and Father of Mankind. *Fr.* The Brewing of Soma. Whittier.
Disarmament. Whittier.
Even during War. *Fr.* Letter to the Front. Rukeyser.
Evening Star, The. Carmichael.
Flag of Peace, The. Gilman.
Gospel of Peace, The. Roche.
He Shall Speak Peace. Clark.
He Shall Speak Peace unto the Nations. Walters.
He Walks at Peace. *Fr.* Tao Teh King. *Unknown.*
History of Peace, A. Graves.
Hope's Forecast. Fuller.
Hush, All Ye Sounds of War. Draper.
Hymnal: "Bringer of sun, arrower of evening, star-begetter and moon-riser." Vinal.
In Distrust of Merits. Moore.
In the End of Days. Isaiah, Bible, *O.T.*
In the Way of Peace. Watt.
Let Us Have Peace. Turner.
Man unto His Fellow Man. *Fr.* On a Note of Triumph. Corwin.
Message of Peace, The. Howe.
Message of Peace, A. O'Reilly.
More than Flowers We Have Brought. Turner.
New Mars, The. Coates.
New Victory, The. Widdemer.
O Brother Man. Whittier.
Ode to Peace. *Unknown.*
Peace. Bhartrihari.
Peace. *Fr.* 1914. Brooke.
Peace. Cary.
Peace. Clare.
Peace. De la Mare.
Peace. Edman.
Peace. Greenberg.
Peace. Herbert.
Peace. Hopkins.
Peace. Markham.
Peace. Oxenham.
Peace. Pulsifer.
Peace. Sangster.
Peace. Scollard.
Peace. Vaughan.
Peace. Warren.
Peace. Whitney.
Peace and Rest. Davies.
Peace, like a Lamb. Clark.
Peace Must Come as a Troubadour. Drennan.
Peace on Earth. Bacchylides.
Peace on Earth. Cole.
Peace on Earth. S. Longfellow.
Peace on Earth. Sears.
Peace Triumphant. Rice.
Peace Universal. Thorne.
Peace Was My Earliest Love. Millay.
Per Pacem ad Lucem. Procter.
Prayer to Peace. *Fr.* Cresophontes. Euripides.
Prepare. Bynner.
Prince of Peace, The. Fosdick.
Reconciliation. Wheelock.
Reign of Peace, The. Starck.
Reign of Peace, The. Thornton.
Rose of Peace, The. Yeats.
Scythians, The. Blok.
Shalom Aleichem. *Unknown.*
To Men Unborn. Hamilton.
When the Cannon Booms No More. Carruth.
When the Great Grey Ships Come In. Carryl.
When War Shall Be No More. *Fr.* The Arsenal at Springfield. Longfellow.
Where the Rainbow Ends. R. Lowell.
Why. Freeman.
Winds of God, The. Scollard.
You cannot traffick in peace. *Fr.* The Uncelestial City. Wolfe.
See also **Veterans' Day.**
Peach Trees
Peach, The. Brown.
Peach, The. Lamb.
Peach Tree, The. E. Sitwell.
Peach Tree in the Garden of an Empty House. Press.
Peach Tree with Fruit. Colum.
Peacock, Margaret Love
Margaret Love Peacock for Her Tombstone, 1826. Peacock.
Peacock, Thomas Love
You are now/ In London, that great sea. *Fr.* Letter to Maria Gisborne. Shelley.
Peacocks
Peacock and Nightingale. Finch.

Figure 26. From *Granger's Index to Poetry*, subject index

Peace **TITLE AND FIRST LINE INDEX** **1058**

Peace (continued)
Woman Courting Him. John Cleveland. AnAnS-2
Peace by Night. Sister Mary Madeleva. GoBC
Peace Call, The. Edgar Lloyd Hampton. PEDC
Peace, childish Cupid, peace: thy fingered eye. Epigram. Francis Quarles. *Fr.* Emblems. EP
Peace, come away; the song of woe. In Memoriam A. H. H., LVII. Tennyson. EPN; OAEP; TOP; ViPo; VP
Peace, deep and rich. Prayer to Peace. Euripides. *Fr.* Cresophontes. PoPl
Peace Delegate. Douglas Livingstone. PeSA
Peace does not mean the end of all our striving. Peace and Joy [*or* The Christian Soldier]. G. A. Studdert-Kennedy. *Fr.* The Suffering God. MaRV; OQP; TRV
Peace-Giver, The. Swinburne. *See* Christmas Antiphon, A.
Peace Hymn for England and America. George Huntington. PaA
Peace Hymn of the Republic. Henry van Dyke. SoP; TRV
Peace in her chamber, wheresoe'er. First Love Remembered. Dante Gabriel Rossetti. PoVP
Peace in the sober house of Jonas dwelt. Jonas Kindred's Household. George Crabbe. *Fr.* The Frank Courtship. OBNC
Peace in the Welsh Hills. Vernon Watkins. ChMP; GTBS-P
Peace in the World. John Galsworthy. MaRV; PoLF
Peace in thy hands. The Ghost. Walter de la Mare. OAEP (2d ed.); POTE
Peace is declared, and I return. The Return. Kipling. MoBrPo; NeMA
Peace is not an elusive thing. Peace. Barbara Drake Johnson. SoP
"Peace Is the Tranquillity of Order." Robert Wilberforce. GoBC; JKCP (1955 ed.)
Peace lies profound on these forgotten acres. Meditation by Mascoma Lake. Donald C. Babcock. NePoAm-2
Peace, like a Lamb. Leonard Clark. WePo
Peace Message, The. Burton Egbert Stevenson. PAH
Peace Must Come As a Troubadour. Marie Drennan. OQP
Peace mutt'ring thoughts, and do not grudge to keep. Content. George Herbert. MaMe
Peace now and ever on this gravestone be. At My Father's Grave. Matthias Claudius. WoL
Peace of a Good Mind, The. Sir Thomas More. *Fr.* The Twelve Weapons of Spiritual Battle. EnRePo
Peace of Christ, The. St. John, Bible, *N.T.*. *See* My Peace I Give unto You.
Peace of Christ, The. John Antes La Trobe. BePJ
Peace of great doors be for you, The. For You. Carl Sandburg. MAP; MoAmPo; MoRP; WaKn
Peace of Heaven, The. Henry Vaughan. *See* Peace.
Peace of joys, The. Three Blessings. *Unknown.* BoPe
Peace of the Roses, The. Thomas Philipps. ACP
Peace of Wild Things, The. Wendell Berry. NYTB
Peace on Earth. Anatolius, *tr. fr. Greek.* BePJ
Peace on Earth. Bacchylides, *tr. fr. Greek by* John Addington Symonds. AWP; JAWP; WBP
Peace on Earth. Helen Wieand Cole. ChIP; OQP
Peace on Earth. Sanuel Longfellow. PGD
Peace on Earth. Edmund H. Sears. *See* It Came upon the Midnight Clear.
Peace on Earth. William Carlos Williams. LiTA; LOW; MAP; NP; PFY; ViBoPo
Peace on New England, on the shingled white houses, on golden. Jehu. Louis MacNeice. LiTG; LiTM (rev. ed.); MoAB; WaP
Peace on the earth,/ Joyfully sang the angels long ago. Through the Ages. Margaret Hope. PGD
Peace! peace! A mighty Power, which is as darkness. Shelley. *Fr.* Prometheus Unbound. OAEP
Peace, peace be unto all the world. War and Peace. Alexander Petofi. PoFr
Peace, peace! he is not dead, he doth not sleep. He Is Not Dead [*or* Against Oblivion *or* An Elegy on the Death of John Keats.] Shelley. *Fr.* Adonais. FaBoEn; LO; MaRV; OBNC; TreFS
Peace, peace! I know 'twas brave. Content. Henry Vaughan. SCEP-1
Peace, peace, my friend; these subjects fly. George Crabbe. *Fr.* Sir Eustace Grey. PoEL-4
Peace, peace, my hony, do not cry. Christs Reply. Edward Taylor. *Fr.* God's Determinations. MAmP; MWA-1; PoEL-3
Peace, peace on earth! the heart of man forever. Peace on Earth. Samuel Longfellow. PGD
Peace, peace, peace, make no noise. A Ditty. John Day. *Fr.* Humour Out of Breath. EIL
Peace, Perfect Peace. Edward H. Bickersteth. BePJ; BLRP; FaChP; SoP; WGRP
Peace-Pipe, The. Longfellow. *Fr.* The Song of Hiawatha. AnNE
Peace pratler, do not lowre [*or* lour]. Conscience. George Herbert. AnAnS-1; EP; MaMe; MeP
Peace, Shepherd, peace! What boots it singing on? Genius Loci. Margaret L. Woods. HBV; OBEV; OBVV
Peace, the one-time radiant goddess. The Child of Peace. Selma Lagerlof. PoPl
Peace! The perfect word is sounding, like a universal hymn. In the Dawn. Odell Shepard. WGRP
Peace, the wild valley streaked with torrents. The Straw. Robert Graves. MoVE
Peace, there is peace in this awaking. Waking. Patrick MacDonogh. NeIP
Peace through Prayer. Longfellow. *See* Oft Have I Seen.
Peace to all such! but were there one whose fires. Atticus [*or* Characters from the Satires: Atticus *or* Portrait of Atticus]. Pope. *Fr.* Epistle to Dr. Arbuthnot. AWP; InPo; JAWP; MaPo; OBEC; PoFS; PoSa; SeCePo; ShBV-4; UnPo (1st ed.); ViBoPo; WBP; WHA
Peace to the quiet dead. The Elegy of the Kremlin Bells. Marya Zaturenska. *Fr.* Elegies over John Reed. NP
Peace to the Slumberers! Thomas Moore. HBV; OnYI
Peace to the Statue. *Unknown, tr. fr. Greek by* Lord Neaves. OnPM
Peace to these little broken leaves. Leaves. W. H. Davies. MoBrPo
Peace to-night, heroic spirit! Requiem for a Young Soldier. Florence Earle Coates. OHIP
Peace Triumphant. Cale Young Rice. PEDC
Peace Universal. Anna H. Thorne. PEDC; PoRL
"Peace upon earth!" was said. We sing it. Christmas: 1924. Thomas Hardy. PV
Peace, war, religion. This Tokyo. Gary Snyder. NeAP
Peace Was My Earliest Love. Edna St. Vincent Millay. NYTB
Peace, wayward barne! O cease thy moan! Song. Richard Brome. *Fr.* The Northern Lass. SeCL
Peace! What Do Tears Avail? "Barry Cornwall." VA
Peace you were always there. Prayer. James Kirkup. BoPe
Peaceable Kingdom, The. Isaiah, XI: 6-9, Bible, *O.T.* FaPON (XI: 6); LiTW
Peaceable Kingdom, The. Marge Piercy. TwCP; WOW
Peaceable Race, The. T. A. Daly. HBV
Peaceful, archangelic sun, A. The Ruined Farm. William Plomer. BoSA
Peaceful bite of hamburger and your mind is blown into space, A. New York. Tony Towle. ANYP
Peaceful Death. Walt Whitman. OQP
Peaceful life;—just toil and rest, A. Lincoln. James Whitcomb Riley. DD; LiPo; OHIP
Peaceful Night, The. Milton. *Fr.* On the Morning of Christ's Nativity. ChrBoLe
("But peaceful was the night.") FaBoCh; LoGBV
Peaceful Shepherd, The. Robert Frost. *Fr.* A Sky Pair. MAP; MoAB; MoAmPo; MoRP
Peaceful spot is Piper's Flat, A. The folk that live around. How McDougal Topped the Score. Thomas E. Spencer. PoAu-1
Peaceful Western Wind, The. Thomas Campion. EnRePo; LoBV
Peacefulness. Henry W. Frost. SoP
Peacemaker, The. W. H. Davies. BoPe
Peacemaker, The. Joyce Kilmer. CAW; MaRV; PoFr
Peach, The. Abbie Farwell Brown. GFA
Peach, The. Charles *and* Mary Lamb. OTPC (1923 ed.)
Peachblossoms flutter like pink butterflies, The. Prose Poem: Indifference. Judith Gautier. OnPM
Peach Tree, The. Edith Sitwell. NP
Peach Tree in the Garden of an Empty House. John Press. NYTB
Peach Tree with Fruit. Padraic Colum. BoNaP
Peaches, The. Joel Oppenheimer. CoPo

Figure 27. From *Granger's Index to Poetry*, title and first-line index

the title of this anthology that is of most importance to us.

Armed with the information in *Granger's* we head for the library 's card catalog (or book catalog), look up *New York Times Book of Verse*, note the call number, and go to the shelf where the book is located. Once you have the book, what is your next step? You look in the index for the title of the poem (in this case) or for the author, Millay, in order to find out on which page "Peace Was My Earliest Love" appears.

If it is only the first line of a poem that is known, *Granger's Index* can again be used to learn the title of the poem and the anthology which contains it. In Figure 27 the first line "Peace is declared, and I return" is from a poem by Rudyard Kipling entitled "The Return," which appears in two anthologies, MoBrPo and NeMa. Referring to the list of abbreviations in the front of *Granger*'s we find that the first collection is *Modern British Poetry*, edited by Louis Untermeyer, and the second—NeMa—is *New Modern American and British Poetry*, by the same editor.

Another useful tool is Brewton's *Index to Poetry for Children and Young People* which, with its supplements, is a guide to over 200 collections of poems. This is very useful for finding poetry, for example, to read aloud to younger brothers and sisters, or perhaps to young people with whom you are babysitting. Figure 28 shows a typical page in the Brewton volumes. Note that first-line entires are distinguished from title entries by quotation marks and that title entries contain the abbreviation for the collection in which you can find the whole poem. Note also that when there are several poems with the same title, Brewton gives you the first line of each so that you can tell which is the one you are searching for.

Flowers—*Continued*
"**March** winds and April showers." Mother Goose.—BrSg
Spring.—BrMg
Maytime magic. M. Watts.—BrSg
"**The moon** over the mountains." Issa.—IsF
Names. D. Aldis.—BrSg—HoB
"**The night** opens the flower in secret." R. Tagore.—LeMf
"**Of Brussels** it was not." E. Dickinson.—DiPe
"**Of what** use are twigs." Buson.—BeCs
Planting flowers on the eastern embankment. Po Chü-i.—CoBn
The round. P. Booth.—CoBn
"**The short** night." Issa.—LeOw
Slow flowers, fast weeds. From King Richard III. W. Shakespeare.—ShS
Some flowers o' the spring. From The winter's tale. W. Shakespeare.—GrCt
"**A spark** in the sun." H. Behn.—BeCs—BrSg
A spike of green. B. Baker.—BrSg
"**Spring** is almost gone." Buson.—BeCs
Starry night II. E. Merriam.—MeI
Stay-at-home. A. Fisher.—FiC
"**Stillness.**" Chora.—LeI
Summer days. A. Fisher.—FiC
Summer shower. S. Robinson.—ThA
A tale. E. Thomas.—GrCt
Thief. Unknown.—CoBb
This spot. Unknown.—BrSm
Three don'ts. I. O. Eastwick.—BrSg
To blossoms. R. Herrick.—CoBn—SmM
Tom Tinker's ground. Mother Goose.—ReOn
Under the window. K. Greenaway.—GrT
"**Violets**, daffodils." E. J. Coatsworth.—ArT-3
"**We** human beings." Issa.—IsF
"**White** coral bells upon a slender stalk." Unknown.—LaPd
The wild flower's song. W. Blake.—BlP
Window-boxes. E. Farjeon.—BrSg
Winter flower store. D. Aldis.—BrSg
"**With** feeble steps." Issa.—LeOw
"**Within** one petal of this flower." Unknown.—BaS
The wood of flowers. J. Stephens.—LaPd—StS
Flowers. Harry Behn.—BrSg
Flowers at night. Aileen Fisher.—BrSg—FiI
Flowers by the sea. William Carlos Williams.—BoGj—HoL
Flowers: For Heliodora. Meleager of Gadara, tr. by Dudley Fitts.—GrS
"**Flowers** for sale." Unknown.—WyC
Flowers in the valley. Unknown.—BlO—GrS
"The **flowers** left thick at nightfall in the wood." See In memoriam, Easter, 1915
"**Flowers** look like balls of wool." Peter White.—LeM
Flowers of darkness. Frank Marshall Davis.—AdIa—BoA
"The **flowers** of this wide world all bloom and fade." See A bird song in the ravine
"The **flowers** to the tree's root." Sūtoku.—BaS
"**Fluffy**, yellow, and trim." See The ducklings
Flutes
"O moon, why must you." Koyo.—BeCs
"There was a young lady of Bute." E. Lear
Nonsense verses.—HuS-3
"There was an old man with a flute." E. Lear.—BrLl
"**Fluttering** helplessly." Thea Boughton.—LeM
Fly ("A fly buzzes up the pane") Elizabeth Jane Coatsworth.—CoDh
The **fly** ("Little fly") William Blake.—BlO—BlP
The **fly** ("Lord, shall I always go in black") Carmen Bernos de Gasztold, tr. fr. the French by Rumer Godden.—GaC
The **fly** and the flea. See "A flea and a fly in a flue"
Fly away. Elizabeth Jane Coatsworth.—CoSb
"**Fly** away, fly away over the sea." See The swallow
"A **fly** buzzes up the pane." See Fly
Fly-fishing. See Rural sports
"**Fly**, white butterflies, out to sea." See Envoi
Flying. Kaye Starbird.—LaPd
Flying a ribbon. Kathleen Fraser.—FrS
"The **flying** butterfly." Issa, tr. fr. the Japanese by R. H. Blyth.—IsF
Flying crooked. Robert Graves.—HoL—ReO
The **flying** fish. John Gray.—GrCt
The **flying** pig. See "Dickery, dickery, dare"
Flying saucers
Go fly a saucer. D. McCord.—LiT
The **flying** sea. Roger Mortimer.—LeM
Foal. Mary Britton Miller.—ArT-3—CoB—LaPd
Foam flowers. Yasuhide, tr. by Shotaro Kimura and Charlotte M. A. Peake.—LeMw
Fog
Fog ("The fog comes") C. Sandburg.—ArT-3—HoB—HuS-3—LaP—ThA
Fog ("Fog is a puff of smoke") S. Ingbritson.—LeM
The fog ("I saw the fog grow thick") W. H. Davies.—ArT-3—LaC
Fog ("Over the oily swell it heaved, it rolled") C. Garstin.—CoSs
Fog ("Waking, I knew the sea had come again") E. J. Coatsworth.—CoDh
Fog, the magician. M. Cane.—ThA
The sounding fog. S. N. Pulsifer.—LaPd
"We rowed into fog." Shiki.—BeCs
"The yellow fog that rubs its back upon the window-panes." From The love song of J. Alfred Prufrock. T. S. Eliot.—ArT-3
Yellow fog.—HaL
Fog ("The fog comes") Carl Sandburg.—ArT-3—HoB—HuS-3—LaP—ThA
Fog ("Fog is a puff of smoke") Scott Ingbritson.—LeM
The **fog** ("I saw the fog grow thick") William Henry Davies.—ArT-3—LaC
Fog ("Over the oily swell it heaved, it rolled") Crosbie Garstin.—CoSs
Fog ("Waking, I knew the sea had come again") Elizabeth Jane Coatsworth.—CoDh
"The **fog** comes." See Fog

Figure 28. From Brewton's *Index to Poetry for Children and Young People*

Still another helpful reference title is the *Subject Index to Poetry for Children and Young People 1957–1975* compiled by Smith and Andrews. It has analyzed 263 anthologies and offers a very wide variety of subjects from ABBEYS to ZOOS. Many of the topics are subdivided into numerous sub-topics. Special attention has been given to locating poems that are scientific or geographical in content, and subjects of ethnic and current interest are also included. Here is one example from this index:

> LOVE, FIRST: see also HUMOR—LOVE, FIRST
> Dream Love. C. Rossetti.
> De-CH: 350

The capitalized heading is the subject and you note that additional subject headings may be suggested. Under the subjects are listed the poems on that topic, arranged alphabetically by title. The poem we have selected here is entitled "Dream Love" by the poet Rossetti. At the front of the index we look, in alphabetical order, for the abbreviation De-CH and find that it stands for the book by De la Mare, Walter entitled *Come Hither*. The front of the index lists all the anthologies giving not only author and title but publisher, date of publication, and the suggested age levels of interest for the poetry included in the collection.

The Sound of Poetry

Poems are meant to be heard—whether they are simply read aloud or performed more elaborately. Poetry readings are presented at coffee bars or outside in parks as well as in auditoriums. In a book entitled *Sounds and Silences*, Robert Boynton and Maynard Mack have gathered together poems for performing. They say, "Like singing in the shower, performing a poem requires only a self audience. . . ." Not too many years ago, it was not unusual for family gatherings to include some recitations. Certainly, some poems take on added meaning when read aloud to a small group of family, friends, or fellow-students.

It is now possible to listen to poetry recordings in libraries. The records or tapes may be recorded by the poets themselves or the poems may be read by some famous actors or actresses. An example of the former is the record *Poetry and Voice of May Swenson*, of the latter, *Three Hundred Years of Great American Poetry*, read by Vincent Price, Julie Harris, Eddie Albert, Helen Gahagan Douglas, and Ed Begley. Still another example is the set of 6 cassettes entitled *Twentieth Century Poets* (Volume 1) which records William Butler Yeats, Stephen Spender, Langston Hughes, Richard Wilbur, W. H. Auden, and James Dickey reciting their own work. Sometimes recordings tell something *about* the poems as well as give the actual words. Often a booklet accompanies the recording and contains some background information about the poet.

Listen to a recording in which the poet reads her or his own work and then to another in which a professional performer does the reading. Is there a difference between the two versions? Which do you prefer? Why?

How do you find out which recordings your school media center or public library has? Exactly as you do with any other materials—in most libraries.

The card catalog may contain cards for records and tapes as well as for books. If this is the case in your library, you should, most likely, look for the recording under title or subject. The examples in Figures 29 and 30 illustrate a title card and a subject card.

Depending on the policy of the library, you may be able to go directly to the shelf where recordings are kept and find the one you need or you may have to request it at the desk. In some libraries there may be a separate catalog for non-print resources or possibly, in small collections, a typed list of such holdings, somewhat like a book catalog.

```
  KIT  Symbolism in poetry.  Coleman Film
808.1    enterprises.  RMI Film Productions, 1971.
  S
           filmstrip  and disc
```

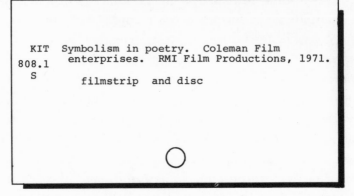

Figure 29. Sample audiovisual title catalog card

```
          POETICS
  KIT  The poetic experience. Guidance
808.1     Associates, 1969.
  P
          2 filmstrips with cassettes or discs

        Discussion of poetry from nursery
       rhymes to modern poetry with some
       quotations from poems.
```

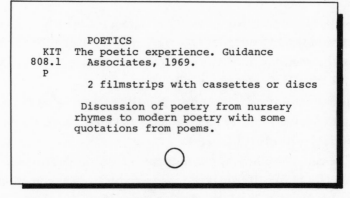

Figure 30. Sample audiovisual subject catalog card

If, after consulting your library's catalog, you do not find the poet whose works you would like to hear, it is possible that no recording exists. However, before making this assumption, you should consult the *Schwann Record and Tape Guide*. There are two publications: *Schwann—1*, revised monthly, lists LPs, cartridges, and cassettes featuring classical music, rock, blues, country and western, jazz, etc.; *Schwann—2*, appearing semi-annually, is the source for poetry recordings, which are listed under the heading "Poetry, Prose, Speech."

Many librarians welcome suggestions for additions to their recordings collection and you might recommend a favorite title that is not in the library.

Adding Another Dimension

There are some materials in your media center that combine sight and sound. For instance, in one kit, *The Poetic Experience*, consisting of two filmstrips and two cassettes, we can learn about the elements of poetry by hearing some examples of the work of a few poets, and actually seeing on film representations of figures of speech such as "simile" and "metaphor," which are characteristic of poetic writing. *The Poetic Experience* uses excerpts from the poetry of Countee Cullen, Stephen Crane, William Carlos Williams, and Lawrence Ferlinghetti, among others, together with pictures of landscapes, people, and other things to help us understand what poetry is. As is often the case with audiovisual resources, a handbook that accompanies the kit gives some suggestions about what to look for and what to think about, as you listen and look. You can stop the viewer and tape cassette player any time to think more deeply about what you have seen and heard. New ideas may come to you about a poem that you have read or heard or about a poem you may wish to write.

Poetry has been called the art of painting with words. *Haiku—A Photographic Interpretation* is a combination of filmstrip and narrative in which pictures of natural beauty supply a fitting accompaniment to this unique, Japanese form of poetry.

Another form of pictorial material is the slide. *The Poetry of Rock* is a slide/cassette kit that uses photographs, reproductions of famous paintings, and other visuals to amplify the meanings expressed in the lyrics of many well-known songs. Among the songs are "Bridge Over Troubled Waters" (Paul Simon); "You Light Up My Life" (Carole King); "You're So Vain" (Carly Simon); and "Suzanne" (Leonard Cohen). Earlier in this chapter we read about the relationship between rock and more traditional poetry. This audiovisual kit is a good way to explore this relationship further.

Critical Evaluations

We like to form our own opinions about the movies we see, the records we buy, or the clothes we wear but it is also common for most people to want to know what the "experts" think. For that reason we read reviews of movies, concerts, shows, rock groups, or books. In the case of books it is often useful to know the opinion of a poet's work, for example, held by someone who has made a deep and detailed study of that writer.

Literary criticism can be puzzling since it often happens that critics will disagree. One reviewer will praise the poems of a poet; another will pinpoint the negative aspects of the work. You can find such examples in the excerpts of reviews that appear in the issues of *Book Review Digest*, which selects statements from more than 70 journals and periodicals. For example, there are two reviews of *Houseboat Days* by John Ashbery, one of the outstanding American poets of modern times, in the *Book Review Digest* for 1977. One review, which appeared in *Christian Science Monitor*, is less complimentary than one that appeared in *Newsweek*. Since *Book Review Digest* tells you the date of the issue and the length of the original review, you may decide whether you would like to read the entire review and come to some conclusion for yourself. The original review will also identify the reviewer and sometimes that will help you to determine how objective the review is.

Some books of criticism cover many writers while others concentrate on one. In the card catalog the books that are general in coverage are filed under the broad heading POETRY followed by the subdivision HISTORY AND CRITICISM. Here are two examples from a card catalog:

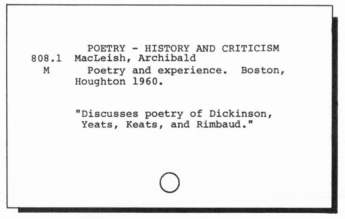

```
          POETRY - HISTORY AND CRITICISM
808.1  MacLeish, Archibald
  M       Poetry and experience.  Boston,
       Houghton 1960.

       "Discusses poetry of Dickinson,
        Yeats, Keats, and Rimbaud."
```

Figure 31. Sample subject catalog card

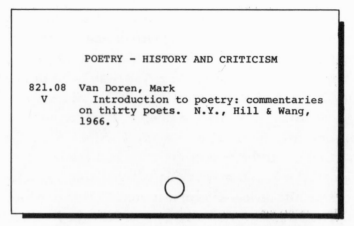

POETRY - HISTORY AND CRITICISM

821.08 Van Doren, Mark
V Introduction to poetry: commentaries
on thirty poets. N.Y., Hill & Wang,
1966.

Figure 32. Sample subject catalog card

If you are looking for a critical analysis of Sylvia Plath's poetry, will either of these two books help you?

> REMINDER: It is important to read the catalog card carefully in order to save yourself the disappointment of searching for a book that turns out to be useless to you.

The book by MacLeish is obviously not what you need, since the annotation says it deals only with four poets, none of whom is Plath. Van Doren's book might be helpful but it is hard to tell from the card. What is your next step?

You will go to the section where the 821.08 books are shelved, look for the "V" for Van Doren, and, with luck, you will find *Introduction to Poetry*. Next you check the index of the book and look for "Plath."

Of course, if it *is* one specific writer who interests you, the shortest road is to look in the catalog under that name. Let us see what happens if we look for Sylvia Plath.

Finding the tray in which "PL . . ." would be filed, we find the following cards:

811 Plath, Sylvia
P Ariel. Harper 1966

Poems by Plath

B Plath, Sylvia
PLATH Letters home. Harper 1970

Autobiography by Plath

PLATH, SYLVIA
811 Newman, Charles Hamilton, comp.
N The art of Sylvia Plath; a symposium. Bloomington, Indiana University
Press, 1970

Selected criticism

Plath as subject

Figure 33. Sample catalog cards

What kinds of books do these three cards represent? The first is a collection of poems by Plath (call number 811 is for American poetry); the second book is also by Plath and has been classified by the library as biography (the call number "B" stands for both biography and—in this case—autobiography).

In the third card, unlike the first two, we note that the name on the top line is typed entirely in capital letters. This indicates that Plath is the *subject* of the book.

Who is the author of the book about Plath? What is the title? Where will you find it? What does "symposium" mean? Charles Hamilton Newman is the compiler (abbreviated here as "comp.") of a book that contains the critical views of a number of different people. The book is entitled *The Art of Sylvia Plath*. The dictionary, to which one goes for the explanation of a new word, tells us that "symposium" may mean a discussion, a conference, or a collection of writings. This book is just what you want and so you go to the shelf labeled 811 and look for the "N" authors within that section until you find Newman's book.

There are also series that specialize in critical analysis of writers, including poets. One series, Twentieth Century Views, is devoted to such poets as Dylan Thomas and Emily Dickinson. Other series are the United States Authors series and the Modern Literature Monographs. The recently begun Modern Writer Series (Barnes and Noble) has already issued a volume on Sylvia Plath.

Some very good, brief literary analysis of American writers comes in the University of Minnesota Pamphlets on American Writers. For British writers a similar series called Writers and Their Work is available. Libraries have differing policies about the storage of pamphlets. Some keep this form of material in pamphlet boxes and put them on the book shelves where they would belong in the Dewey classification. Other libraries put pamphlets in folders in a file cabinet, often called the vertical file or information file. Sensibly, these files are arranged only by subjects. What subject would you look under for pamphlet material on Sylvia Plath? Under the name is the most direct way but that might produce nothing. What other possibilities are there? AMERICAN LITERATURE is one possibility; POETRY is another. The point to keep in mind, always, is that any search does require your thinking and imagination.

If you do find a folder on your poet in the vertical file, there is a possibility that you will also find newspaper or magazine clippings and even picture material there since the vertical file is used for all types of printed material that cannot be classified as a book or a magazine.

Biography of the Writer

Psychologists have told us a great deal about the influences that affect a person's growth. We have come to understand that many factors in childhood—family life, schooling, friends, the community—have a bearing on how people think and act. For that reason it adds much to our understanding of an author's work if we know something of her or his background. You may wish a great deal of information or just a sketch.

Biographies and autobiographies—both marked B, plus the name of the person whose life it is—are usually shelved in one section of the library labeled BIOGRAPHY. In some libraries, however, a biography is placed in the same section as the subject for which the person has been known. For example, a biography of Reggie Jackson would be found in the 700s, the Dewey number for sports, under this system of classification; the life of Albert Einstein would be with the 500s and the other books on science. This arrangement is an exception, however, and your best bet is to go to the biography section for a biography of your poet. Remember that in biographies the books are arranged in alphabetical order by the name of the subject, not by the author as in other sections.

Figure 34. Arrangement of biography on library shelf

> REMINDER: The names of authors do not determine how books are arranged in the biography section, except in the case of autobiographies, when the author and the subject of the book are the same.

Note in Figure 34 that Dickinson precedes Thomas, which in turn precedes Whitman, all of those being the subjects of biographies. Notice also that while the spines of books are not consistent in the placement of the author and title the call number is always at the bottom and is the solid clue to locating the book. It is also important to keep in mind that many times the title of a biography or autobiography gives no clue as to *whole* life is being described. The last book, entitled *Listen America*, is a biography of Walt Whitman and the call number reads,

B
WHITMAN

Frequently what we want is a brief outline of the author's life. A library has several special biographical dictionaries that range from those that include brief biographies of thousands of people from all periods of time to those that concentrate on one special kind of coverage.

Webster's Biographical Dictionary covers about 40,000 names of people famous in all kinds of activity and in all periods of history. Entries vary from two lines to a long paragraph.

Examples of biographical dictionaries that are directed to a specific area are *Who's Who of American Women*; *Who's Who in Show Business*; *Who's Who in the Theatre*; *Who Was Who in American Sports*.

Since our specific interest in this chapter is poets, the best source for our biographical sketch will be in one of the seven volumes in the Wilson Author Series. An index to the series helps us to turn immediately to the right volume. For example, if we wish a biographical sketch (rather than a full biography) about Sylvia Plath we look in the *Index to the Wilson Authors Series* (Figure 35) and find the following entry: "Plath, Sylvia—W."

In the front of the index is this list of titles in the Author Series: It tells us that the letter "W" stands for the volume entitled *World Authors: 1950–1970*. Finding this volume—probably in the reference section of the library—we turn to

Petroni, Guglielmo—W
Petrov, Eugene—T, T-1
Petrović, Petar II Njegoš—E
Petry, Ann—T, T-1
Pettie, George—B
Petty, Sir William—B
Pétursson, Hallgrímur—E
Pevsner, Sir Nikolaus (Bernhard Leon)—W
Peyrefitte, (Pierre) Roger—W
Pfeiffer, Emily Jane—B-1
Phaer or Phayer, Thomas—B
Phelps, Elizabeth Stuart. *See* Ward, Elizabeth Stuart (Phelps)—A
Phelps, Elizabeth (Stuart)—A
Phelps, William Lyon—T, T-1
"Philenia." *See* Morton, Sarah Wentworth (Apthorp)—A
Philippe, Charles Louis—E
Philippe Mouskés. *See* Mouskés, Philippe—E
Philips, Ambrose—B
Philips, John—B
Philips, Katherine—B
Phillips, David Graham—T, T-1
Phillips, Edward—B
Phillips, Henry Wallace—T
Phillips, John—B
Phillips, Samuel—B-1
Phillips, Stephen—T
Phillips, Watts—B-1
Phillips, Wendell—A
Phillips, William Addison—A
Phillpotts, Eden—T, T-1
"Philodicaios." *See* Young, Thomas—A
"Philomusus." *See* Locker, Jacob—E
"Phoenix, John." *See* Derby, George Horatio—A
Piatt, John James—A
Piatt, Sarah Morgan (Bryan)—A
Piccolomini, Enea Silvio (or Aeneas Silvius), Pope Pius II—E
Pichette, Henry—W
Picken, Andrew—B-1
Picken, Ebenezer—B-1
Pickering, John—A
Pickett, Albert James—A
Pickthall, Marjorie Lowry Christie—T, T-1
Pickthall, Marmaduke—T, T-1
Pico della Mirandola, Giovanni, Count—E
Picton, Thomas—A
Pidgin, Charles Felton—T
Pierce, Benjamin—A
Pierce, Gilbert Ashville—A
Pierpont, John—A
Pike, Albert—A
Pike, James Shepherd—A
Pike, Mary Hayden (Green)—A
Pilkington, Mrs. Mary—B-1
Pilnyak, Boris—T, T-1
Pincherle, Alberto. *See* "Moravia, A."—T-1
Pinckney, Josephine—T-1
"Pindar, Peter." *See* Wolcot, John—B
Pinero, Sir Arthur Wing—B-1
Pinget, Robert—W
Pinkney, Edward Coote—A
Pinski, David—T, T-1
Pinter, Harold—W
Pinto, Fernão Mendes—E
Piovene, Guido, Count—W
Piozzi, Mrs. Hester Lynch Thrale—B
Pirandello, Luigi—T, T-1
Pisan, Christine de—E
Pisarev, Dmitry Ivanovich—E
Pisemsky, Alexey Feofilaktovich—E
"Pitcairn, Frank." *See* Cockburn, (Francis) Claud—W
Pitkin, Timothy—A
Pitkin, Walter Boughton—T, T-1
Pitter, Ruth—T, T-1
Pius II, Pope. *See* Piccolomini, Enea Silvio—E
Pjetursson, Hallgrímur. *See* Pétursson, Hallgrímur—E
Place, Francis—B-1
"Plaidy, Jean." *See* Hibbert, Eleanor Burford—W
Planché, James Robinson—B-1
Platen-Hallermünde, August Graf von—E
Plath, Sylvia—W
Plievier, Theodor—T-1
Plomer, William Charles Franklyn—T, T-1
Plumb, J(ohn) H(arold)—W
Plummer, Jonathan—A
Plunkett, Edward John Morton Drax. *See* Dunsany—T, T-1
Plunkett, Joseph Mary—T
Pocock, Isaac—B-1
Podhoretz, Norman—W
Podmore, Frank—T
Poe, Edgar Allan—A
Poggioli, Renato—W
Pohl, Frederik—W
Poirier, Louis. *See* "Gracq, J."—T-1
Polanyi, Michael—W
Polenz, Wilhelm von—E
Poli, Umberto. *See* "Saba," Umberto—W
Poliziano (or Politian), Angelo—E
Pollard, Albert Frederick—T, T-1
Pollard, Edward Alfred—A
Pollen, John Hungerford—B-1
Pollock, Channing—T, T-1
Pollock, Sir Frederick, 3d Bart.—T, T-1
Pollock, Walter Herries—T
Pollok, Robert—B-1
Polnay, Peter de. *See* De Polnay, P.—T-1
Polo, Marco—E
Pomeroy, "Brick." *See* Pomeroy, Marcus Mills—A
Pomeroy, Marcus Mills—A
Pomfret, John—B
Ponge, Francis—W
Pontano, Giovanni Gioviano—E
Pontoppidan, Henrik—T, T-1
Pool, Maria Louise—A
Poole, Ernest—T, T-1
Poole, John—B-1
Poole, Reginald Stuart—B-1
Poole, William Frederick—A
Poore, Benjamin Perley—A
Poorten. *See* Schwartz—T, T-1
Pope, Alexander—B
Pope, Dudley (Bernard Egerton)—W
Pope-Hennessey, Dame Una (Birch)—T-1
Pope-Hennessy, James—W
Popper, Karl Raimund—T-1
"Porcupine, Peter." *See* Cobbett, William—B-1
"Porlock, Martin." *See* MacDonald, P.—T, T-1
Porson, Richard—B
Porter, Anna Maria—B-1
Porter, Mrs. Eleanor (Hodgman)—T, T-1
Porter, Mrs. Gene (Stratton)—T, T-1
Porter, Harold Everett—T
Porter, Henry—B

52 INDEX TO THE WILSON AUTHORS SERIES

Figure 35. From *Index to the Wilson Authors Series*

"Plath" in its alphabetical order and find a 1600-word account of the poet's short life, her special attachment to her father, her marriage to the British poet, Ted Hughes, the influence of Robert Lowell on her writing, and a discussion of two of her works, *The Bell Jar* and *Ariel*. The sketch, which includes a photograph of Plath, ends with a list of her principal works.

Another reference title that gives biographical information about writers is the series *Contemporary Authors: A Bio-Bibliographical Guide to Current Writers in Fiction, General Nonfiction, Poetry, Journalism, Drama, Motion Pictures, Television, and Other Fields*. The entries vary in length but this reference work is particularly useful for the large number of writers from all parts of the world, on whom it provides information. Each entry is broken up into sections called Personal; Career; Writings; Works in Progress; Sidelights; Sources. *Contemporary Authors* is published twice a year (4 volumes bound as 1). The second volume of the year provides a cumulative index to all previous volumes.

Current Biography

Some poets are of more recent prominence. A very important library reference tool that gives biographical information on people in the public eye is the magazine called *Current Biography*. It is published monthly except December. It is also available as an annual volume.

Athough we are going to check *Current Biography* for a sketch of a modern American poet, Adrienne Rich, you will also find it most useful for biographical information about people in a wide variety of occupations: government, science, business, sports, entertainment, as well as literature. It is the

Previn, André (George) May 72
Previn, Dory Sep 75
Prey, Hermann Feb 75
Pribichevich, Stoyan obit Jul 76
Pride, Charley Apr 75
Priest, Ivy (Maude) Baker obit Aug 75
Priestley, J(ohn) B(oynton) May 76
Prince, Harold Apr 71
Prinze, Freddie Jun 75 obit Mar 77
Prío Socarrás, Carlos obit Jun 77
Pritchett, V(ictor) S(awdon) Jan 74
Proell, Annemarie Sep 76
Prouty, Winston L(ewis) obit Oct 71
Pryor, Richard Feb 76
Puckett, B(enjamin) Earl obit Apr 76
Puente, Tito Nov 77
Puzo, Mario Mar 75

Qaddafi, Muammar el- Sep 73
Quayle, Anthony Dec 71
Queler, Eve Jul 72

Rabe, David Jul 73
Rabin, Yitzhak Sep 74
Radcliffe, Cyril John, 1st Viscount Radcliffe obit May 77
Radford, Arthur W(illiam) obit Oct 73
Radhakrishnan, Sir Sarvepalli obit Jun 75
Radziwill, Lee (Bouvier) Apr 77
Rahman, Sheik Mujibur Jan 73 obit Oct 75
Rajagopalachari, Chakravarti obit Feb 73
Rakosi, Matyas obit Mar 71
Raman, Sir (Chandrasekhara) Venkata obit Jan 71
Ramspeck, Robert (C. Word) obit Dec 72
Rance, Sir Hubert Elvin obit Mar 74
Ranganathan, S(hiyali) R(amamrita) obit Dec 72
Rank, Joseph Arthur Rank, 1st Baron obit May 72
Ransom, John Crowe obit Sep 74
Rathbone, Monroe J(ackson) obit Sep 76
Rather, Dan May 75
Ravdin, I(sidor) S(chwaner) obit Oct 72
Ray, Dixy Lee Jun 73
Ray, Man obit Jan 77
Ray, Robert D. Jan 77
Reading, Stella (Charnaud Isaacs), Marchioness of obit Jul 71
Reardon, John (Robert) Nov 74
Reber, Samuel obit Feb 72
Reddy, Helen Apr 75
Redford, Robert Apr 71
Reed, Sir Carol obit Jun 76
Reed, Rex Jan 72
Reed, Willis Jan 73
Reese, Della Sep 71
Rehnquist, William H(ubbs) Apr 72
Reich, Charles A(lan) Jun 72
Reid, Charlotte T(hompson) Jan 75
Reith, John Charles Walsham, 1st Baron obit Jul 71
Rennert, Günther Jun 76
Revel, Jean-François Feb 75
Reynolds, Burt Oct 72
Rhodes, James A(llen) Apr 76
Rhodes, John J(acob 2d) Sep 76
Rhys, Jean Dec 72
Riad, Mahmoud Nov 71
Rich, Adrienne (Cecile) Feb 76
Rich, Buddy Jun 73
Rich, Daniel Catton obit Feb 77
Richards, Dickinson W(oodruff) obit Apr 73
Richards, I(vor) A(rmstrong) Dec 72
Richardson, Elliot L(ee) Mar 71
Richler, Mordecai May 75
Richter, Burton Sep 77
Richter, Charles Francis May 75
Rickenbacker, Edward Vernon obit Oct 73
Riefenstahl, Leni May 75
Riefler, Winfield W(illiam) obit Jun 74
Rieve, Emil obit Mar 75
Rigg, Diana Oct 74
Righter, Carroll Oct 72
Riklis, Meshulam Dec 71
Riles, Wilson (Camanza) Dec 71
Rinfret, Pierre A(ndré) Jul 72
Ritter, Thelma obit Feb 74 (died Feb 69)
Rivera, Geraldo May 75
Rivers, L(ucius) Mendel obit Feb 71
Rizzo, Frank L(azarro) Mar 73
Roa (y García), Raúl Nov 73
Robbe-Grillet, Alain Dec 74
Roberts, C. Wesley obit Jun 75
Robertson, A. Willis obit Dec 71
Robertson, Sir Brian (Hubert) obit Jun 74
Robeson, Paul Mar 76 obit Mar 76
Robey, Ralph W(est) obit Sep 72
Robinson, Brooks Sep 73
Robinson, Edward G. obit Mar 73
Robinson, Frank Jun 71
Robinson, Jackie obit Dec 72
Robsjohn-Gibbings, T(erence) H(arold) obit Feb 77
Roche, Josephine (Aspinwall) obit Sep 76
Rockefeller, Winthrop obit Apr 73
Rogers, Fred M(cFeely) Jul 71
Rohmer, Eric Apr 77
Rojas Pinilla, Gustavo obit Mar 75
Rollins, Sonny Apr 76
Romero Barceló, Carlos Oct 77
Romnes, H(aakon) I(ngolf) obit Jan 74
Rooney, John J(oseph) obit Jan 76
Rooth, Ivar obit Apr 72
Roper, Elmo (Burns, Jr.) obit Jun 71
Rose, Alex obit Feb 77
Rose, Leonard Jan 77
Rose, Pete Aug 75
Rosen, Samuel Feb 74
Rosenman, Samuel I(rving) obit Sep 73
Ross, Diana Mar 73
Rossellini, Roberto obit Aug 77
Rosset, Barnet (Lee, Jr.) Apr 72
Rothschild, Guy (Edouard Alphonse Paul), Baron de Mar 73
Roudebush, Richard L(owell) Jun 76
Rovere, Richard H(alworth) Apr 77
Rowlands, Gena Nov 75
Royall, Kenneth C(laiborne) obit Sep 71
Rubin, Reuven obit Jan 75
Ruckelshaus, William D(oyle) Jul 71
Rudd, Paul Sep 77
Rudolph, Paul (Marvin) Feb 72
Ruiz Cortines, Adolfo obit Jan 74
Rush, (David) Kenneth May 75
Russell, Bill See Russell, W. F. Jul 75
Russell, Ken Oct 75
Russell, Richard B(revard, Jr.) obit Mar 71
Russell, Rosalind obit Feb 77

498 CURRENT BIOGRAPHY 1977

Figure 36. From index of *Current Biography Yearbook 1977*

place where you can find a sketch of Nadia Comaneci, gymnast, as well as of Andrew Young, statesman.

In our search for Rich, Adrienne, do we have to look through all those bound volumes and all the paper issues for the current year? Not at all. The indexes to *Current Biography* make it possible for you to find out quickly if the name you are searching for is anywhere in all of those books. You need to look in only three indexes to locate a biographical sketch: the most recent monthly (paper) issue covers all the preceding issues for the current year; the most recent bound volume includes all the names from 1971 through that year (Figure 36); the Cumulated Index 1940–1970 contains the names in all the other volumes since the series began.

Since we may not be sure when, or if, Ms. Rich was written up, we start with the monthly index and find nothing. The next step is to look in the index of the bound volume for 1977, where we find that she is included in the 1976 edition. Step three is not necessary then in this instance, since we found what we wanted in alphabetical order in the 1976 volume. As is usual in *Current Biography*, a picture of Adrienne Rich accompanies her sketch, as does a list of references from which information in the sketch was drawn and which you can consult if you wish.

Readers' Guide to Periodical Literature

We know that often the information contained in books needs updating because some change has occurred since the date of publication. Pamphlets may be more current than books but magazines which libraries call periodical literature, are more useful since they do come out periodically—some every week, some every two weeks, many every month, and still another group issued quarterly.

There are actually thousands of magazines published, but most libraries make a selection among those because of budget limitations and they choose those that are more useful as well as more popular. Even when the number of magazines available in a library is reduced to about 200, it still makes for quite a problem when the library user needs a piece of information from one of them. Just as the card catalog assists you in the location of a book or audiovisual resource, so the index to magazines, the *Readers' Guide to Periodical Literature*, helps you to locate an article quickly.

Since magazines come out often this index keeps up-to-date by publishing an issue twice a month except in February, July, and August, when one issue a month is published. The entries are interfiled and a bound volume appears annually. The *Readers' Guide* indexes about 180 magazines mostly by subject and author with title entries for stories. Smaller libraries (often junior high or middle school libraries) sometimes subscribe to *Abridged Readers' Guide*, which indexes over 50 magazines.

Poets often have single poems published in magazines before a collection is ready to be printed in book form. Sometimes an article on a poet by a well-known literary critic will appear in a magazine. For these reasons, *Readers' Guide* should not be overlooked when you are doing research either for an assignment or for some personal interest.

Although Sylvia Plath's death occurred some time ago there is still strong interest in her writing. If we wish to see what new articles have appeared about her, we start with the most recent issue of *Readers' Guide* and work back. The 1977 issues show nothing. At last, we come to the issue dated August 1976 and find the following entry:

PLATH, Sylvia
Poet as cult goddess. S. Maloff. por Commonweal 103:371-4 Je 4 '76 *

The pattern for the entry is always the same:

"Poet as cult goddess"—title of the article

S. Maloff—author of the article (sometimes there is no author indicated)

por—abbreviation for "portrait"

Commonweal—name of the magazine

103: —volume number, needed when using large libraries which bind back issues of magazines

371-4—page numbers, indicating the length of article

Je 4 '76 —date of magazine issue: month, *day*, and year

Continuing to work back we come to many other articles in the bound volume for March 1975–February 1976. Under "Plath" we find an entry which leads us to an excerpt from her book *Letters Home*. Then under a subhead "about" we find the following:

Ariel's flight: the death of Sylvia Plath. N. J. C. Andreasen. il Sat Eve Post 247: 58-9+ Mr '75 *
Letters home, by S. Plath. Review
Ms il pors 4:45-9 D '75. H. Rosenstein *
Newsweek il pors 86:83 D 22 '75. M. Jefferson *
Time il pors 106:101-2 N 24 '75. M. Duffy *

You may wish to read all three reviews in order to compare them or you may want only the most detailed. Which one is the longest review? We look at the numbers *after the colon* which stand for the page or pages of the articles. *Ms* magazine has 45–9; *Newsweek* "83"; *Time* "101–2." *Ms* magazine has devoted the most space to the review. All of the above entries include the abbreviations "il" and "pors" indicating that you can find pictures of Sylvia Plath in all three articles.

> REMINDER: It is important to look *first* at the date of the *Readers' Guide* that you are consulting. If you are checking on something or someone important in 1976—perhaps the election campaign of Jimmy Carter—you start with the issue for that time. If you want the *latest* information on a topic, such as the most recent poetry awards, you must look in the most recent *Readers' Guide* and work your way back until you find an entry relating to your subject.

UPDATING MAGAZINE INFORMATION

We live in an age of instant and constant information. The daily newspaper adds considerably to the flow of up-to-date information. For example, the New York *Times* of Sunday, May 22, 1977 carried an article entitled "Can (or Should) Rock Music Appeal to Adult Sensibilities?" This article might contain worthwhile information to add to that in David Morse's *Grandfather Rock*. The way to locate the article is through the New York *Times Index*. (This reference tool is described fully in Chapter 5, page 81.) The *Times Index* will indicate newspaper coverage on poetry readings, prizes, and other happenings.

In our era we must not overlook the program listings for radio and television since excellent presentations related to this topic, poetry, are available in those media.

YOU AS THE POET

At the beginning of this chapter we pointed out that many young people do write poetry whether it is read by anyone other than the poet or not. Kenneth Koch, a poet and teacher, has written two books telling how he started people, both young and old, writing poetry: *Wishes, Lies and Dreams* and *I Never Told Anybody*. Mr. Koch's advice may be useful to anyone interested in poetry. The card catalog in your library will direct you to those two books on the shelves. What will you look under in the catalog? Either the "K" tray for the author or the two drawers where the title cards would be filed; "W" for the first, "I" for the second. The call number of each will give you its exact location in the 800 section.

The vertical file or information file of the library may also carry brochures from the following organizations which are related to the art and craft of writing poetry: Poets and Writers (201 W. 54 Street, New York, NY 10019); National Endowment for the Arts—Literature Programs (Mail Stop 607 Washington, D.C. 20506); Poetry in the Schools (a program supported by your state's Council on the Arts).

Additional help for the beginning poet can be found in such magazines as *Poetry*, a monthly publication that contains both poetry and critical evaluations, and *The Writer*, which, in its monthly issues, not only discusses the techniques of writing in all literary forms, but also gives information on how to get your poetry published. Advice on publishing can also be found in *The Whole Word Catalogue 2*, a collection of ideas about writing drama, film, and video productions as well as poetry.

It is wise to remember that getting anything published is never easy, and having poetry published is more difficult still. However, your school publications are excellent outlets and the yearbooks and literary magazines often look for the writings of beginning poets. Local newspapers are another possibility for the publication of a single poem. Eventually—who can tell?—an award may be in your future. Meanwhile, there is the pleasure of being a writer for yourself.

SUGGESTED MATERIALS

Abridged Readers' Guide. New York: Wilson.
Adoff, Arnold, ed. *The Poetry of Black America: Anthology of the 20th Century*. New York: Harper, 1973.
Ashbery, John. *Houseboat Days*. New York: Viking Press, 1977.
Book Review Digest. New York: Wilson.
Boynton, Robert W. and Maynard Mack. *Sounds and Silences*. Rochelle Park, NJ: Hayden, 1975.
Brewton, John E. and others. *Index to Poetry for Children and Young People, 1965–1969*. New York: Wilson, 1972. *Supplement, 1970–1975*, 1978.
Browning, Elizabeth Barrett. *Sonnets from the Portuguese*. Many editions.
Carlsen, G. Robert. *Books and the Teen-Age Reader*. New York: Harper, 1972.
Christian Science Monitor. Boston, MA: Christian Science Publishing Society.
Cleary, Florence Damon. *Discovering Books and Libraries*. 2nd ed. New York: Wilson.
Cole, William, ed. *Fireside Book of Humorous Poetry*. New York: Simon and Schuster, 1959.
Contemporary Authors: a Bio-Bibliographical Guide to Current Authors and Their Works. Detroit, MI: Gale.
Cook, Margaret G. *The New Library Key*. 3rd ed. New York: Wilson, 1975.
Current Biography. New York: Wilson. *Cumulated Index, 1940–1970*.
Eberhart, Richard and Seldon Rodman, eds. *War and the Poet*. Greenwich, CT: Devin-Adair, 1945.

Ellmann, Richard, ed. *New Oxford Book of American Verse*. New York: Oxford University Press, 1976.

Granger's Index to Poetry. 6th ed. James Smith, ed. New York: Columbia University Press, 1973.

Haiku—A Photographic Interpretation. 2 filmstrips and records. Laguna Beach, CA: Lyceum Productions, 1971.

Hughes, Langston. *New Negro Poets: U.S.A.* Bloomington, IN: Indiana University Press, 1970.

Klemer, D. J., ed. *Modern Love Poems*. New York: Doubleday, 1961.

Koch, Kenneth. *I Never Told Anybody; Teaching Poetry Writing in a Nursing Home*. New York: Random, 1977.

———. *Wishes, Lies and Dreams; a New Way of Teaching Children to Write Poetry*. New York: Chelsea, 1970.

Lask, Thomas, ed. *New York Times Book of Verse*. New York: Macmillan, 1970.

Livingston, Myra Cohn, ed. *O Frabjous Day! Poetry for Holidays and Special Occasions*. New York: Atheneum, 1977.

Morrison, Lillian. *The Sidewalk Racer; and Other Poems of Sports and Motion* New York: Lothrop, 1977.

Morse, David. *Grandfather Rock; the New Poetry and the Old*. New York: Delacorte, 1972.

National Council of Teachers of English. *Books for You*. Urbana, IL: NCTE, 1976.

Newsweek (periodical). New York: Newsweek, Inc.

Peck, Richard, ed. *Pictures that Storm Inside My Head*. New York: Avon, 1976.

Plath, Sylvia, *Ariel*. New York: Harper, 1966.

———. *The Bell Jar*. New York: Harper, 1971.

The Poetic Experience. 2 filmstrips and cassettes. New York: Guidance Associates, 1969.

Poetry (periodical). Chicago, IL: Modern Poetry Association.

Poetry and Voice of May Swenson. Cassette or record. New York: Caedmon, 1976.

The Poetry of Rock: A Reflection of Human Values. 2 carousels of slides and cassettes or records. White Plains, NY: Center for Humanities.

Readers' Guide to Periodical Literature. New York: Wilson.

Reit, Ann, comp. *Alone Amid All This Noise*. New York: Four Winds Press, 1976.

Smith, Dorothy B. Frizzell and Eva L. Andrews, comps. *Subject Index to Poetry for Children and Young People 1957–1975*. Chicago, IL: American Library Association, 1977.

Smith, Stevie. *Collected Poems*. New York: Oxford University Press, 1976.

Teachers and Writers Collaborative. *The Whole Word Catalogue 2*. Bill Zavatsky and Ron Padgett, eds. New York: McGraw-Hill, 1977.

Three Hundred Years of Great American Poetry. Recording. New York, NY: Caedmon.

Twentieth Century Poets (Vol 1). 6 cassettes. New Rochelle, NY: Spoken Arts.

Webster's Biographical Dictionary. Springfield, MA: Merriam, 1971.

Who's Who in the Theatre: A Biographical Record of the Contemporary Stage. Ian Herbert and others, eds. Detroit, MI: 1977.

Who's Who of American Women. Chicago, IL: Marquis.

World Authors 1950–1970: A Companion Volume to Twentieth Century Authors. John Wakeman, ed. New York: Wilson.

The Writer (periodical). Boston, MA.

Chapter 7

VALUES TO LIVE BY

In both our private and public lives we are constantly having to make decisions or form opinions about what action we should take on certain questions. In the personal area we must consider whether it is "right" or "wrong" for us to consume alcoholic drinks, experiment with drugs, engage in premarital sexual relationships. As citizens of the United States we try to reach "moral" conclusions about racial relationships, attitudes toward non-democratic countries, the use of nuclear devices for peace or war, our collective responsibility toward the millions of people who go to bed hungry every night.

One book recently published, *Social Ethics* by Thomas A. Mappes and Jane S. Zembaty, lists the issues that the authors consider the most crucial. Their topics include abortion, euthanasia (inducing a merciful death), the death penalty, sexual equality, discrimination, sexual integrity, pornography and censorship, violence, economic justice, and environmental and population control. For each of these very important issues, there are statements by experts in law, sociology, philosophy, psychology, and politics.

Thoughtful men and women have always tried to formulate a philosophy for living a "good life." Part of the problem has been in trying to define the term. Simply stated, it means a life that has been led according to values that are deemed important. Some important values are freedom, honesty, loyalty, kindness, self-discipline, brotherhood, conscientiousness, friendship, patriotism, sportsmanship, respect for the law. Not all people, however, will agree on the importance of every one of these values, and as societies change, bringing alterations in customs and interpersonal relationships, so do values and moral education. Even when several people agree on the importance of a value, for example patriotism, they may not agree on its definition. Which statement expresses the more moral patriotic attitude: "My country right or wrong" or "I love my country but am honor-bound to speak out when I think it is not acting according to our democratic principles"?

As long ago as the fourth century B.C. the Greek philosopher Socrates said, "The life which is unexamined is not worth living." This examination becomes more revealing, more rewarding when we know what some wise people, philosophers, have considered to be the basis of the good life.

In current vocabulary we hear a good deal about "life-style" but life-style is a matter of choice, of personal preference, and therefore it is simply an expression of your own notion of what life is all about for you. How do you try to recognize what your "style" is? One helpful way to begin is by reading something in that field.

If you have undertaken some research for a social studies or literature assignment, you often may have found that you could make a good start with an encyclopedia article. Since the topic we are considering here—the good life—is rather abstract, we have to be more precise about what we are attempting to understand. Is it behavior? Morals? Interpersonal relationships? We can test out any of the words that come to mind. Experimenting with a variety of them will lead you, by way of the *see* or *see also* references to the subject selected as covering this area of human behavior. That term, generally, is *ethics* which, in turn, is often considered within the framework of philosophy or moral philosophy.

All of the encyclopedias that you have used in other subjects will tell you something about ethics or moral philosophy. Of course they will differ in the amount of information, the difficulty of the ideas presented, the degree of scholarship in the article, and the number of related topics that are included in the article. The *New Columbia Encyclopedia*, a one-volume encyclopedia, defines the term and mentions a few important names that you can investigate further. Larger encyclopedias like *Compton's, World Book, Americana, Collier's, International,* and *Britannica* give more information, with *Compton*'s and *World Book* giving the simplest explanations and *Britannica* the most detailed. Your choice will depend on how comfortable you are with the style, the amount of detail, the level of vocabulary of one encyclopedia over the others.

The new *Britannica*, known as "Britannica 3," has an unusual arrangement. The one-volume Propaedia gives an outline of all knowledge. The ten-volume Micropaedia contains brief information on thousands of subjects and also acts as an index to the third part of the set, the nineteen–volume

Macropaedia, which contains very long and detailed articles. You can remember that "micro" is from the Greek word for small and "macro" the word for large: therefore, a small amount of information compared with a large amount.

There are some encyclopedias that deal only with a specific subject area. For the subject of this chapter, the *Encyclopedia of Philosophy* will give you a thorough discussion of the history and problems of ethics as well as references to numerous related articles like "Duty"; "Choosing, Deciding and Doing"; "Ends and Means," and others.

Another reference work that may be useful to the student who is seriously drawn to this topic is the *Dictionary of the History of Ideas: Studies of Selected Pivotal Ideas.* In four volumes (plus an index volume) fundamental ideas in the sciences, mathematics, logic, law, literature, religion, and philosophy are covered. The sample page from the index volume (Figure 37) will illustrate how broad the contents are.

Encyclopedia articles frequently conclude with lists of suggested readings or bibliographies. If we are deeply interested in a subject, an encyclopedia article may sharpen our appetite for books, films, filmstrips, and kits on the subject of values in general or quite specific issues like responsibility, individual privacy, or the right to dissent.

The book mentioned earlier in this chapter, *Social Ethics*, deals with specific moral issues, while a book like *Values in Transition* by Gail Inlow is more general in its treatment. The author defines traditional cultural values and then discusses values that exist in many areas such as economics, politics, science and technology, philosophy, the black community. *Values in Transition* might serve as an introduction (although not an easy one) to your exploration, for example,

Aristotle, I 463a; II 149b–150b, 236b–237a; III 354a, 440a, 554b; IV 4b, 6b, 49b, 175b, 320a, 321a, 451b, 452a
asceticism, IV 320b
atomism, IV 319a
Basilides of Alexandria, II 329a–329b
behaviorism, IV 72b, 73a
Bellarmine, III 441b
Bentham, III 444a–444b
Bernstein, Eduard, III 162b–163a, 164b
Bible, III 440b, 441a, 445b
biology, III 646b
birth, IV 322a
Bruno, II 347b, 348b
Buddhism, I 252a–252b, 253b–254a; III 446a
Burnet, III 258a
Calvin, III 441b
capitalism, IV 70a
catharsis, I 267b–268a
Cato, IV 321b
causation, IV 320a
Chain of Being, I 328b–329a
chance, II 226b, 227a, 227b, 233a
Chapman, III 294b
charity, II 212b, 215a
China, III 430a, 430b
Christianity, I 407b; III 440b, 441a, 441b, 445b, 446a; IV 176a–176b, 177a, 322a
Chrysippus, IV 321b, 322a
Cicero, III 16b; IV 319b, 321b, 322a
city-state, IV 320a
classification of the sciences, I 463a, 464b, 465a
Cleanthes, IV 321b
Clement of Alexandria, III 441a; IV 322a
color, IV 71b
comedy, III 440a
commerce, I 253b–254a; III 443b
communism, IV 70a, 291b
Comte, III 644a
conscience, IV 70a, 71a
Counter-Enlightenment, II 101a
courage, IV 320b
crime, IV 70a
criticism, IV 321b
cruelty, IV 72a
Cudworth, III 441a–441b
culture, III 442b, 443b, 444a, 447a; IV 70a, 71a, 71b, 73a, 73b, 320a–320b
cynicism, I 627b, 629a, 629b–630a, 633a, 633b; IV 320b
death, IV 70b, 71b
deism, I 651a
Democritus, IV 319a
desire, IV 72a
destiny, III 442a; IV 319a
Dewey, III 446b, 447a; IV 186a
Diogenes of Sinope, IV 320b
diplomacy, III 443b
disarmament, III 444b
divination, IV 320a
Doukhobors, III 441a
drama, III 440a
dueling, IV 70a
duty, IV 71a
economics, III 442a, 444a, 445b, 446b
education, II 77a–77b, 78b; III 440a
egoistic interpretation of, III 231a, 231b, 233a
Einstein, III 445b, 446b–447a
emancipation, III 444b
Emerson, III 430a, 430b
emotion, IV 72a
emotive theory, III 234b–235a
empathy, II 85b
empiricism, III 443b
Engels, III 159b
Enlightenment, II 90a, 96b; III 446a
Epictetus, IV 319a, 321b, 322a
Epicureanism, IV 8a, 319a
Epicurus, IV 321b
equality, II 142a
equity, II 148a–154a
eschatology, II 159a
Euripides, III 440a
evil, II 162b, 163a, 163b, 165a, 167a–167b; IV 70b, 71a, 72b, 319a, 320a, 321a
evolution, III 646b, 647a; IV 71a, 180a, 181a
evolutionism, II 181a
existentialism, II 192a; III 158a, 158b, 159b, 160a
faith, II 212b, 215a
fascism, III 674a
fate, II 226b, 227a, 227b, 233a
Faust (legend), III 251a
fear, IV 71b
Ficino, III 506a
Fichte, IV 209b
fortune, II 226b, 227a, 227b, 233a
Fox, III 441a
France, III 444b
free will, II 236b–237a; IV 320b
freedom of speech, II 259a
Freud, III 445b, 446b, 447a; IV 96b
Galen, IV 321b
game theory, II 273a
Gandhi, III 441b–442a; IV 73a
Genghis Khan, IV 73a
Gnosticism, II 328a–328b, 331a
God, II 334b, 347b, 348b; III 440b; 441a, 441b, 445b; IV 70b, 72a, 319a–320b
good, IV 70b, 71b, 72b, 173b–186b, 319b, 320a, 320b, 321a, 321b
Gothic, II 372a–372b
Great Britain, III 538a
Greece (ancient), III 353a, 440a, 440b, 585a; IV 319a, 320a–320b
Grotius, III 441b–442a
happiness, II 374b–375a, 375b, 378a, 379a, 379b, 380a, 380b, 381b, 383a; IV 70b, 319b, 320b, 321a, 321b
harmony, II 390b
health, IV 321a, 321b
Hector (myth), III 440a
Hegel, II 408b; III 445a; IV 180a, 290b
Heraclitus, IV 320b
hierarchy, II 444a
Hillel, III 440b
history, III 440a, 440b, 443b, 444a, 445a; IV 320a–320b
Hitler, IV 73a
Hobbes, III 441b, 442b, 443a, 443b, 445b, 446a; IV 72a, 72b, 177a–177b
Hobhouse, IV 71a
holy, II 512a, 513a, 513b
Homer, III 440b
homosexuality, IV 70a, 70b
hope, II 212b, 215a
human nature, III 442b, 443b, 446a, 577a, 644a; IV 72a, 72b
human sacrifice, IV 71a
humanism, III 446a; IV 129b
humanitarianism, III 441a
Hume, III 231b, 232a, 233a, 233b, 235a, 444a; IV 70a–70b, 71b, 72a, 72b
Hutcheson, III 231a–232a; IV 70b, 71b–72b
idea, II 544b, 548b, 603a–603b
ideal, II 549a, 550b, 551a
idealism, III 443a, 443b, 444a, 445b
ideology, II 554a
imperialism, III 445a
impressionism, II 576a
India, III 446a
individualism, II 603a–603b; IV 49b
industry, III 445a, 445b, 446a
infanticide, IV 70a
injury, IV 71a
internationalism, III 442a, 444b, 446a
intolerance, III 446b
Jainism, III 446a
James, William, III 447a
joy, IV 321a
Judaism, III 440b, 487b, 488a; IV 176a
judgment, IV 71b, 72a, 73a; IV 321a
justice, III 443a, 444b; IV 320b
Kames, III 234b
Kant, II 551a; III 233b, 442a–442b, 443a–444a, 444b, 445a, 445b, 555b–556a, 639b; IV 179a–179b, 181a, 322a
kindness, IV 72a
knowledge, IV 71a, 321a
Kropotkin, III 445a
language, IV 72b, 319b, 321b
law, III 1a, 2a, 6a, 440b, 441b, 442a, 443a–444b, 445b, 447a; IV 72b
Lecky, IV 70b, 71b
Leibniz, III 442a, 443b
Leonardo da Vinci, IV 442a–442b
Lévy-Bruhl, IV 70b–71a
Lieber, III 444a
Lincoln, III 444a
logic, III 568b; IV 319a, 319b–320a, 320b, 322a
logos, III 440b; IV 319a, 320a, 320b, 321a
love, III 440b, 441a, 445b, 447a
Lovejoy, III 552b
Luther, III 441b
lying, IV 71a, 72b
Machiavelli, III 116a–125a, 441b
Mandeville, III 231a
Marcus Aurelius, III 440b; IV 321b, 322a
Maritain, III 441a, 445b
Marxism, III 148a, 151b, 158a, 158b, 159b, 160a,

Figure 37. From *Dictionary of the History of Ideas*, index

of the scientist's moral responsibility for the results of his research and its applications.

If some of these suggestions seem far beyond your level of interest, remember that there is a wide range of interests and abilities among people. What is so satisfying about using a library is that there is something for everyone regardless of the amount or kind of information wanted. There are resources that do not demand quite as much of the library user as long encyclopedia articles. Under the broad heading of ETHICS or ETHICS, SOCIAL, or MORAL RESPONSIBILITY, or MORAL SENSE, the catalogs might direct you to *What Is It Really Like Out There?* by Thomas Moorman, a book that discusses, among various topics, a search for truth, brainwashing, and personal growth. Under the heading ADOLESCENCE or ADOLESCENT PSYCHOLOGY, you may find *Who Are You?* by Elizabeth McGough, which discusses values, dating, and relationships with parents and others—in short a guide to self-understanding.

The Center for Humanities, which produces slide and record or cassette kits, has prepared some programs on the topic we are considering in this chapter. *Deciding Right from Wrong: The Dilemma of Morality Today* presents the problem by way of real examples such as the case of Kitty Genovese whose street murder went unheeded by neighbors who were aware from within their homes that something terrible was going on outside their windows. Other illustrations included in this kit are Sergeant Alvin York (hero of World War I); Senator Edmund G. Ross, who cast the deciding vote in the case of Andrew Johnson's impeachment trial; Theodore Roosevelt and the Panama Canal; and President Truman and the use of the atomic bomb.

Another title from the same producer is ***Values in Conflict in History***, which describes the case of Alfred Dreyfus, a famous incident in modern French history; the Sepoy rebellion in India; Galileo and the Copernican theory; and the impact of industrialization on nineteenth-century England.

There are several other titles in this series and their value lies not only in the interesting way the material is presented—with slides that include reproductions of famous paintings or illustrations from films—but also in the many books that are used as examples and that could be the basis of your own further study. Each of the kits has an accompanying booklet so that you can identify the slide and the titles of the examples used.

Another filmstrip and tape program is entitled *Understanding Values*. The six filmstrips and tapes in the set cover: Stealing; Cheating and Chiseling; Lies, Half-Truths and Untold Truths; Others' Values/Your Values; Who Cares/Staying Involved; Right, Wrong, or Maybe.

Typical incidents are portrayed that necessitate making decisions—moral decisions arising from the values *you* esteem. There are breaks indicated in the strips where discussion can take place if you are viewing this with a group of friends or classmates.

I Had No Choice But to Obey is a filmstrip and tape kit that illustrates dilemmas faced in war, sports, school situations involving authority's objectives, and moral consequences.

Recreational Books with a Message

There are many novels, biographies, plays, operas, and poems that add to our perspective on ethical behavior, personal responsibility, and moral sense. Let us consider some of them.

Robert Bolt's *A Man for All Seasons* is a play based on the life of Sir Thomas More. Its theme is the conflict between More and Henry VIII and the message with which we are left is that More is willing to face death rather than compromise his religious principles. Other plays in which characters insist on following their principles in spite of personal danger are Jean Anouilh's *Antigone* (based on the play by Sophocles) and Henrik Ibsen's *An Enemy of the People.*

Harper Lee's *To Kill A Mockingbird* is, on the surface, a story of small town life in Alabama in the 1930s, but its deeper theme is the brave position of Atticus Finch, a white lawyer, who takes up the legal defense of a black man falsely accused of rape. An unusual legal trial is also the plot of Jessamyn West's *Massacre at Fall Creek*, in which equal justice for Indians and white men is sought.

Some books help us to understand the values of other ethnic groups. In Margaret Craven's *I Heard the Owl Call My Name*, Mark Brian, a young priest whose death is imminent, begins to achieve an understanding and appreciation of the non-Christian rituals and customs of the Indians of British Columbia who are his congregation. Another Indian group is the subject of Hal Borland's *When the Legends Die* in which young Thomas Black Bull faces a destructive conflict between the values of his Ute ancestors and those of the white men among whom he must live. Alfred Kazin's *A Walker in the City* is a sensitive, autobiographical account of how it was to live among Jewish immigrants in Brownsville, a community in East Brooklyn. Also revealing the customs and moral values of some Jewish families is the novel by Chaim Potok,

The Chosen, which describes the society of the Hasidic and Orthodox Jews.

Some cities are a mixture of many cultures. *Two Blocks Apart* by Charlotte Mayerson describes the lives and aspirations of Juan Gonzalez and Peter Quinn, seventeen years old and neighbors, but living in very different economic conditions.

The manner in which we face death reveals something about our values. David Hendin has written an overview of the subject in *Death as a Fact of Life*, but true accounts of the courage shown by people who have actually faced death are more powerful. In *Eric* by Doris Lund we learn of the incredible bravery of a seventeen-year-old youth who fills his life as completely as possible despite the fact that he knows he is dying from leukemia. This book brings to mind that classic, *Death Be Not Proud* by John Gunther.

You can probably recall many books you have read or films you have seen in which the characters are more important and of more interest than the events of the plot. There are lists that help you to find resources by their themes and the following two can be consulted by you in your libraries.

Reading Ladders for Human Relations, edited by Virginia Reid, is arranged under headings like "Creating a Positive Self-Image," "Living With Others," "Appreciating Different Cultures," and "Coping With Change." Each section contains books for a wide range of reading levels, with a simple code to indicate the level of a title. There are old favorites and recent titles, and each is described.

Another helpful guide is one prepared by the National Council of Teachers of English and it is a very full and up-to-date list. *Books for You: A Booklist for Senior High*

Students divides its suggestions into categories like "Mystery," "Adventure," "Science Fiction," but for the topic of this chapter the headings that are likely to direct you to pertinent titles would be, for example, "Problems of Modern Humanity," "Problems and Young People," "Ethnic Experiences," "Utopias and Communes." There is a sentence or two describing the contents of each book.

Special Lists

Libraries prepare their own special guides and some of them are very valuable. Don't overlook them. Enoch Pratt in Baltimore, Boston Public Library, and Los Angeles Public Library are well-known for their attention to the interests of young people. Your library's vertical file may have such lists.

Probably one of the best-known lists is published annually by the New York Public Library and is called *Books for the Teen Age*. It is arranged under broad topics like "Humor," "True Adventure," and "Overcoming Odds," but for our subject the heading PHILOSOPHY refers us to "Adventures in Ideas" under which we find such titles as Robert Pirsig's *Zen and the Art of Motorcycle Maintenance*, Charlie Simon's *Martin Buber*, Daniel Cohen's *The New Believers* as well as older titles like Ralph Waldo Emerson's *Essays* and Henry David Thoreau's *Walden*.

Films are a thought-provoking resource and, while it is unusual for a library to run a film for just one viewer, there may be programs of films that include something you wish to see. Check the publicity announcements put out by your public library. Also, you might suggest to your classroom teacher that a certain film be borrowed from the school library collection for group showing.

Some film recommendations in connection with the topic of ethical behavior and moral responsibility are:

Is It Always Right to be Right? Narrated by Orson Welles. Stresses the need for interdependence.

Neighbors. The story of two men who fight over a flower that grows at the boundary of their two properties.

Toys. Shows children looking into a store-window at a display of toys which come to life and become engaged in a war.

Miguel—Up From Puerto Rico. Describes the difficult adjustment necessary for those who come up from a small tropical island to live in a big city.

Many special films like these are produced each year and compete for awards at film festivals. The best ones have been listed in a useful guide called *Superfilms: An International Guide to Award-Winning Educational Films* by Salvatore Parlato. They are arranged in an alphabetical list by title, but a topical index at the front of the book helps you to locate a film by subject. The description of each film includes the running time and whether it is in color or black and white.

Resources from Community Agencies

Organizations like the Young Men's Christian Association, Young Women's Christian Association, and the Young Men's and Young Women's Hebrew Association, usually offer group discussions on such topics as moral education. Often a list of suggested readings is available to supplement these discussions. One excellent example is the annual booklist published by the National Conference of Christians and Jews, *Books for Brotherhood*.

School and public libraries often post announcements of

discussion groups or other outside activities and usually acquire the publications and booklists that are useful to their patrons. Make it a practice not only to check the bulletin boards for such meetings but also to see what new materials have been added to the vertical file.

Televison and Values

In your reading, thinking, and discussions on the subject of the good life for you and your family, the most visible influence since your birth may have been that most pervasive form of mass communication, the television set. Programs have appeared that deal with ethical behavior among doctors, political leaders, businessmen—and young people. Your advance program guides will let you know when such programs will be shown. You are often able to benefit from some of these programs by sending for printed transcripts, which some of the channels offer for a minimum fee and which allow you to consider some of the arguments presented in your own time and at your own pace of understanding.

We cannot leave the subject of television without pointing out that it is itself a means of shaping values. As part of a broad understanding of how we come to adopt certain values the following books on the television medium may be instructive: *The Plug-In Drug* by Marie Winn; *Television: The Critical View*, edited by Horace Newcomb; and *The Good Guys, The Bad Guys and the First Amendment* by Fred W. Friendly.

Magazines

As is true with other topics covered in this book, the topic of ethics is discussed in magazine articles. Perhaps not as absolutely current as television but allowing you to consider the content with more sustained attention, magazine articles add to the list of your resources on a research hunt. The *Readers' Guide to Periodical Literature* can be used to locate articles that may have appeared in over 180 magazines. It is published twice a month (once in February, July, and August), and cumulated during the year. An annual volume with a single alphabet is published, making it easier to check through the list of subjects and authors. If we look under ETHICS as on the sample page (Figure 38)—just as we did in the encyclopedias, card catalog, vertical file—we find articles listed or references to headings where those articles *are* listed. In our illustration we note that the topic we want has been subdivided into quite specific areas. We can then check all of these suggestions, if we are doing research in depth, or concentrate on one aspect of ethics. Let us follow up on BUSINESS ETHICS (Figure 39). We see that six articles have been listed (as well as two additional subject headings for further consideration).

Can we translate the information in the fourth entry? First comes the title of the article (in this case a speech or address made on January 29, 1977). Next comes the author's name, followed by the magazine in which the article appears (sometimes abbreviated and explained in the list of abbreviations in front of each issue). Then comes the volume number *before* the colon (used in libraries that bind the old issues of magazines into annual volumes). The numbers immediately *after* the colon, 292-4, are page numbers and indicate the article is three pages long. The final notation, Mr 1'77, is the date of the magazine's issue.

Test yourself on the other articles. Can you understand the parts of the entries? In what periodical does the article

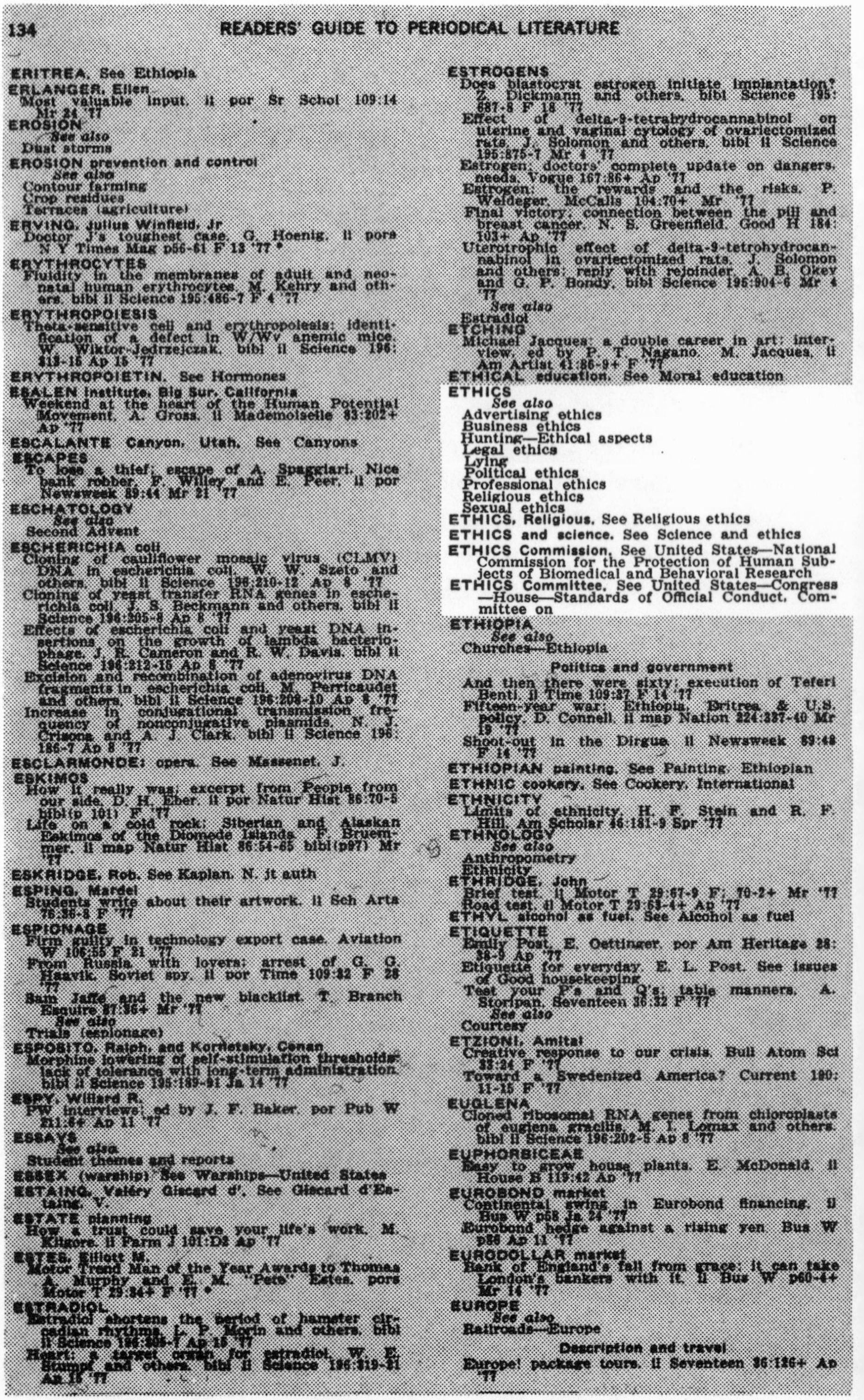

134 READERS' GUIDE TO PERIODICAL LITERATURE

ERITREA. See Ethiopia
ERLANGER, Ellen
Most valuable input. il por Sr Schol 109:14 Mr 24 '77
EROSION
See also
Dust storms
EROSION prevention and control
See also
Contour farming
Crop residues
Terraces (agriculture)
ERVING, Julius Winfield, Jr
Doctor J's toughest case. G. Hoenig. il pors N Y Times Mag p56-61 F 13 '77 *
ERYTHROCYTES
Fluidity in the membranes of adult and neonatal human erythrocytes. M. Kehry and others. bibl il Science 195:486-7 F 4 '77
ERYTHROPOIESIS
Theta-sensitive cell and erythropoiesis: identification of a defect in W/Wv anemic mice. W. Wiktor-Jedrzejczak. bibl il Science 196:313-15 Ap 15 '77
ERYTHROPOIETIN. See Hormones
ESALEN Institute, Big Sur, California
Weekend at the heart of the Human Potential Movement. A. Gross. il Mademoiselle 83:202+ Ap '77
ESCALANTE Canyon, Utah. See Canyons
ESCAPES
To lose a thief; escape of A. Spaggiari, Nice bank robber. F. Willey and E. Peer. il por Newsweek 89:44 Mr 21 '77
ESCHATOLOGY
See also
Second Advent
ESCHERICHIA coli
Cloning of cauliflower mosaic virus (CLMV) DNA in escherichia coli. W. W. Szeto and others. bibl il Science 196:210-12 Ap 8 '77
Cloning of yeast transfer RNA genes in escherichia coli. J. S. Beckmann and others. bibl il Science 196:205-8 Ap 8 '77
Effects of escherichia coli and yeast DNA insertions on the growth of lambda bacteriophage. J. R. Cameron and R. W. Davis. bibl il Science 196:212-15 Ap 8 '77
Excision and recombination of adenovirus DNA fragments in escherichia coli. M. Perricaudet and others. bibl il Science 196:208-10 Ap 8 '77
Increase in conjugational transmission frequency of nonconjugative plasmids. N. J. Crisona and A. J. Clark. bibl il Science 196:186-7 Ap 8 '77
ESCLARMONDE: opera. See Massenet, J.
ESKIMOS
How it really was; excerpt from People from our side. D. H. Eber. il por Natur Hist 86:70-5 bibl(p 101) F '77
Life on a cold rock; Siberian and Alaskan Eskimos of the Diomede Islands. F. Bruemmer. il map Natur Hist 86:54-65 bibl(p97) Mr '77
ESKRIDGE, Rob. See Kaplan, N. jt auth
ESPING, Mardel
Students write about their artwork. il Sch Arts 76:36-8 F '77
ESPIONAGE
Firm guilty in technology export case. Aviation W 106:55 F 21 '77
From Russia with lovers; arrest of G. G. Haavik, Soviet spy. il por Time 109:32 F 28 '77
Sam Jaffe and the new blacklist. T. Branch Esquire 87:36+ Mr '77
See also
Trials (espionage)
ESPOSITO, Ralph, and Kornetsky, Conan
Morphine lowering of self-stimulation thresholds: lack of tolerance with long-term administration. bibl il Science 195:189-91 Ja 14 '77
ESPY, Willard R.
PW interviews; ed by J. F. Baker. por Pub W 211:6+ Ap 11 '77
ESSAYS
See also
Student themes and reports
ESSEX (warship) See Warships—United States
ESTAING, Valéry Giscard d'. See Giscard d'Estaing, V.
ESTATE planning
How a trust could save your life's work. M. Kilgore. il Farm J 101:D2 Ap '77
ESTES, Elliott M.
Motor Trend Man of the Year Awards to Thomas A. Murphy and E. M. "Pete" Estes. pors Motor T 29:34+ F '77 *
ESTRADIOL
Estradiol shortens the period of hamster circadian rhythms. L. P. Morin and others. bibl il Science 196:305-7 Ap 15 '77
Heart: a target organ for estradiol. W. E. Stumpf and others. bibl il Science 196:319-21 Ap 15 '77
ESTROGENS
Does blastocyst estrogen initiate implantation? Z. Dickmann and others. bibl Science 195:687-8 F 18 '77
Effect of delta-9-tetrahydrocannabinol on uterine and vaginal cytology of ovariectomized rats. J. Solomon and others. bibl il Science 195:875-7 Mr 4 '77
Estrogen: doctors' complete update on dangers, needs. Vogue 167:86+ Ap '77
Estrogen: the rewards and the risks. P. Weideger. McCalls 104:70+ Mr '77
Final victory; connection between the pill and breast cancer. N. S. Greenfield. Good H 184:103+ Ap '77
Uterotrophic effect of delta-9-tetrohydrocannabinol in ovariectomized rats. J. Solomon and others; reply with rejoinder. A. B. Okey and G. P. Bondy. bibl Science 195:904-6 Mr 4 '77
See also
Estradiol
ETCHING
Michael Jacques: a double career in art; interview, ed by P. T. Nagano. M. Jacques. il Am Artist 41:86-9+ F '77
ETHICAL education. See Moral education
ETHICS
See also
Advertising ethics
Business ethics
Hunting—Ethical aspects
Legal ethics
Lying
Political ethics
Professional ethics
Religious ethics
Sexual ethics
ETHICS, Religious. See Religious ethics
ETHICS and science. See Science and ethics
ETHICS Commission. See United States—National Commission for the Protection of Human Subjects of Biomedical and Behavioral Research
ETHICS Committee. See United States—Congress—House—Standards of Official Conduct, Committee on
ETHIOPIA
See also
Churches—Ethiopia
Politics and government
And then there were sixty; execution of Teferi Benti. il Time 109:37 F 14 '77
Fifteen-year war: Ethiopia, Eritrea & U.S. policy. D. Connell. il map Nation 224:337-40 Mr 19 '77
Shoot-out in the Dirgue. il Newsweek 89:48 F 14 '77
ETHIOPIAN painting. See Painting, Ethiopian
ETHNIC cookery. See Cookery, International
ETHNICITY
Limits of ethnicity. H. F. Stein and R. F. Hill. Am Scholar 46:181-9 Spr '77
ETHNOLOGY
See also
Anthropometry
Ethnicity
ETHRIDGE, John
Brief test. il Motor T 29:67-9 F; 70-2+ Mr '77
Road test. il Motor T 29:63-4+ Ap '77
ETHYL alcohol as fuel. See Alcohol as fuel
ETIQUETTE
Emily Post. E. Oettinger. por Am Heritage 28:38-9 Ap '77
Etiquette for everyday. E. L. Post. See issues of Good housekeeping
Test your P's and Q's; table manners. A. Storipan. Seventeen 36:32 F '77
See also
Courtesy
ETZIONI, Amitai
Creative response to our crisis. Bull Atom Sci 33:24 F '77
Toward a Swedenized America? Current 190:11-15 F '77
EUGLENA
Cloned ribosomal RNA genes from chloroplasts of euglena gracilis. M. I. Lomax and others. bibl il Science 196:202-5 Ap 8 '77
EUPHORBICEAE
Easy to grow house plants. E. McDonald. il House B 119:42 Ap '77
EUROBOND market
Continental swing in Eurobond financing. il Bus W p58 Ja 24 '77
Eurobond hedge against a rising yen. Bus W p86 Ap 11 '77
EURODOLLAR market
Bank of England's fall from grace; it can take London's bankers with it. il Bus W p60-4+ Mr 14 '77
EUROPE
See also
Railroads—Europe
Description and travel
Europe! package tours. il Seventeen 36:126+ Ap '77

Figure 38. From *Readers' Guide to Periodical Literature*

62 READERS' GUIDE TO PERIODICAL LITERATURE

BUSINESS and religion
Dissidents gear up for annual meetings. J. Perham. il Duns R 109:74-5+ Ap '77

BUSINESS and society. See Business—Social aspects

BUSINESS and the environmental movement. See Industry and the environmental movement

BUSINESS budget. See Budget. Business

BUSINESS conditions
Big surge ahead in business: interview. C. L. Schultze. il pors U.S. News 82:23-4 F 28 '77
Business is edgy about the upturn. il Bus W p42-3 Ap 18 '77
Business outlook; ed by W. B. Franklin. See issues of Business week
Business roundup. See issues of Fortune
Carter business boom shaping up? with interview with B. Lance. U.S. News 82:15-18 F 7 '77
Economic diary. See issues of Business week
Economy resumes its upward thrust: what business leaders see ahead. il Nations Bus 65:32-4+ Ap '77
Surge ahead for business—. il U.S. News 82:20-1 Ap 4 '77
See also
Business failures
Business forecasting
Economic conditions
Inflation (finance)
Production
United States—Economic conditions

BUSINESS consolidations and mergers. See Corporations—Acquisitions and mergers

BUSINESS consultants
Big business in credibility: economic consulting. il Bus W p84+ Mr 7 '77
Should CPAs be management consultants? staff study of the Senate Subcommittee on Reports, Accounting and Management. il Bus W p70+ Ap 18 '77

BUSINESS crimes. See Commercial crimes

BUINESS districts
Business prospects in the inner city. R. N. Farmer. Intellect 105:263-4 F '77
Pedestrian malls not cure for downtown ills; excerpt from address, September 1976. J. P. Butler, Jr. Am City & County 92:60 Ja '77

BUSINESS education
See also
Business schools and colleges

BUSINESS English. See English language—Business English

BUSINESS enterprises
Big bankroll for new business; venture capital. T. J. Murray. il Duns R 109:52-4+ F '77

BUSINESS ethics
Big rip-off in purchasing. R. Levy. il Duns R 109:76-7+ Mr '77
Dissidents gear up for annual meetings. J. Perham. il Duns R 109:74-5+ Ap '77
Emersons: dubious payments American-style. A. Hershman. il por Duns R 109:73-5 Mr '77
Ethics: another kind of oil shortage; individual responsibility; address, January 29, 1977. G. J. Gore. Vital Speeches 43:292-4 Mr 1 '77
Is the ethics of business changing? readers' survey. S. N. Brenner and E. A. Molander; discussion. il Harvard Bus R 55:47+ Mr '77
Pressure to compromise personal ethics; results of studies at Pitney-Bowes and Uniroyal. il Bus W p 107 Ja 31 '77
See also
Accounting ethics
Advertising ethics

BUSINESS executives. See Executives

BUSINESS failures
Alchemist: I. Jones, professional liquidator. E. Dyson. por Forbes 119:34 Ja 15 '77
It's expensive to go broke; legal costs surrounding W. T. Grant bankruptcy case. H. Seneker. Forbes 119:21-2 F 1 '77
Sanitas: struggling out of bankruptcy. Bus W p27-8 Ap 4 '77
$3-billion cram-down? L. Minard. il Forbes 119:74+ Ap 15 '77

BUSINESS forecasting
Business: a look ahead. G. Heiman. See issues of Nation's business
Even better times coming: as top business economists see it. il U.S. News 82:69-70 Ap 18 '77
Managing for an uncertain future: Union Carbide in 1996; address, November 19, 1976. W. S. Sneath. Vital Speeches 43:196-9 Ja 15 '77
Outlook for 1977: favorable. il Nations Bus 65:54-6+ Ja '77

BUSINESS in the Arts Awards
Where art and business meet. il Forbes 119:6 F 1 '77

BUSINESS Leadership, Hall of Fame for. See Halls of fame

BUSINESS liquidation. See Liquidation

BUSINESS literature
See also
Business—Bibliography

BUSINESS management
Executive trends. J. Costello. Nations Bus 65:4+ Ap '77
Film director's approach to managing creativity; A. Penn's Night moves. E. Morley and A. Silver. il por Harvard Bus R 55:59-70 Mr '77
Leading businesswoman's perspective on management. interview. J. Spain. il pors Nations Bus 65:70-2+ Mr '77
Learning a lesson from David; February 17, 1977. R. W. Bunke. Vital Speeches 43:376-9 Ap 1 '77
Lessons of leadership. See issues of Nation's business
Meeting the greater competition of tomorrow. J. W. Hanley. pors Nations Bus 65:37-40 Mr '77
See also
Bank management
Budget. Business
Communication in management
Computers—Business use
Construction industry—Management
Diversification in industry
Executives
Factory management
Personnel management
Service industries—management

Japan

Profit in breaking Japanese traditions: management techniques of U.S. subsidiaries. il Bus W p51-2 F 14 '77

BUSINESS organization. See Business management

BUSINESS planning
Anticipate your long-term foreign exchange risks. H. Hagemann. il Harvard Bus R 55:81-8 Mr '77
Shirt-sleeve approach to long-range plans. R. E. Linneman and J. D. Kennell. bibl f il Harvard Bus R 55:141-50 Mr '77

BUSINESS report writing. See Report writing

BUSINESS Roundtable (organization) See Lobbying

BUSINESS schools and colleges
Is business school for you. S. Horwitz. Seventeen 36:36 Ap '77
Mystery of the business graduate who can't write; teaching specialized writing courses. il Nations Bus 65:60-2 F '77
Tourney of young tycoons; MBA tournament involving business problem solving. P. Witteman. il Time 109:63 Ja 31 '77

Graduates

In hotter pursuit of MBAs. il Bus W p98 F 7 '77
My son, the MBA. il Forbes 119:41-4 Mr 1 '77

BUSINESS statistics
Figures of the week. See issues of Business week

BUSINESS travel
How to make that trip abroad more exciting. F. J. Gross. Harvard Bus R 55:14 Mr '77

BUSINESS trips. See Business travel.

BUSINESSMEN
Businessmen in the news. See issues of Fortune
Faces behind the figures. See issues of Forbes
Money men. See issues of Forbes
See also
Entrepreneurs

BUSINESSWOMEN. See Business and professional women

BUSTANOBY, Andre
How to cope with discouragement. Chr Today 21:28+ Ja 7 '77
Why pastors drop out. Chr Today 21:14-16 Ja 7 '77

BUTLER, Jerome P. Jr
Pedestrian malls not cure for downtown ills; excerpt from address, September 1976. Am City & County 92:60 Ja '77

BUTLER, Robert Neil
Dr Robert N. Butler issues urgent call for more doctors trained in geriatrics. por Ret Liv 16:14-15 D '76 *

BUTLER, Ron
True confessions. C. J. Baker. il pors Hot Rod 30:32-3+ Mr '77 *

BUTTER
Butter lamb for the Easter Sunday breakfast table. il Sunset 158:200 Ap '77

BUTTERFIELD, Jan
Re-placing women artists in history. il Art N 76:40-4 Mr '77

BUTTERFLIES
Its fate is up in the air; protecting the habitat of the El Segundo blue butterfly. R. H. Boyle. il Sports Illus 46:54+ F 28 '77

BUTTONS

Collectors and collecting

Button collecting:
Emerald Isle. D. F. Brown. Hobbies 82:139 Mr '77
Heads. D. F. Brown. il Hobbies 81:156-7 F '77
Transfer buttons or decals. D. F. Brown. il Hobbies 82:138-9 Ap '77

Figure 39. From *Readers' Guide to Periodical Literature*

appear that is entitled "Is the ethics of business changing?" What does the abbreviation "Bus W" mean? Who wrote the first article listed under the heading BUSINESS ETHICS?

> REMINDER: In using the *Readers' Guide* note the date of the issue to see what period of time is covered. If you are looking for the most current information, begin with the most recent *Readers' Guide* and work back. If you are checking on something that happened at an earlier date, look for the index for that year.

SUMMARY

Your consideration of values, your search for a good life, will be strengthened by your reading, by your viewing of films, and by your listening to the words of past and present thinkers. It will also be influenced by discussions within your family, in your school, and among your friends. The adult leaders whom you admire are also a factor.

In your own lives you will face hard, practical questions, the answers to which will be based on your definitions of "right" and "wrong." Mercy killings, for instance, involve legal and medical problems. Who should receive food stamps and whether there should be restrictions on how those can be used is a question of moral judgment that involves sociological and perhaps even agricultural considerations.

"The life which is unexamined is not worth living," said Socrates, and the wisest people point out that this examination is a life-long need. How sound a basis for good living is "Everybody's doing it."?

The popularity of books on human behavior and dilemmas of what is right, or on the struggle between good and evil, indicates how central to your life is your reading, seeing, discussing—and thinking before you decide. Remember, too, that some decisions must face reconsideration in the face of new information.

SUGGESTED MATERIALS

Anouilh, Jean. *Antigone*, in *Anouilh: Five Plays* (Vol. I). New York: Hill and Wang, 1958.
———. *Antigone* (French). New York: Larousse, 1974.
Bolt, Robert. *A Man for All Seasons*. New York: Random, 1962.
Books for Brotherhood. New York: National Conference of Christians and Jews.
Books for the Teen Age. New York: New York Public Library, Office of Young Adult Services.
Borland, Hal. *When The Legends Die*. Philadelphia, PA: Lippincott, 1963.
Cohen, Daniel. The New Believers: Young Religion in America. New York: Evans, 1975.
Collier's Encyclopedia. New York: Collier.
Compton's Pictured Encyclopedia. Chicago IL: Compton.
Craven, Margaret. *I Heard the Owl Call My Name*. New York: Doubleday, 1973.
Deciding Right from Wrong; the Dilemma of Morality. Slides and cassettes or records. White Plains, NY: Center for Humanities.
Dictionary of the History of Ideas: Studies of Selected Pivotal Ideas. Philip Wiener, ed. 4 vols. and index. New York: Scribner, 1973.
Emerson, Ralph Waldo. *Essays*. New York: Dutton.
Encyclopaedia Britannica. Chicago IL: Encyclopaedia Britannica.
Encyclopedia Americana. Chicago IL: Encyclopedia Americana.
Encyclopedia of Philosophy. Paul Edwards, ed. New York: Macmillan-Free Press, 1967.
Friendly, Fred W. *The Good Guys, the Bad Guys and the First Amendment*. New York: Random, 1976.
Gunther, John. *Death Be Not Proud*. New York: Harper, 1971.

Hendin, David. *Death as a Fact of Life.* New York: Norton, 1973.

I Had No Choice But to Obey. Filmstrips and cassettes. Denoyer-Geppert Audiovisuals.

Ibsen, Henrik. *An Enemy of the People*, in *Four Major Plays* (Vol. 2). New York: New American Library, 1970.

Inlow, Gail M. *Values in Transition: A Handbook.* New York: Wiley, 1972.

International Encyclopedia of the Social Sciences. David L. Sills, ed. New York: Macmillan.

Is It Always Right to Be Right? Film 8 min. color. Malibu, CA: Stephen Bosustow Productions, 1971.

Kazin, Alfred. *A Walker in the City.* New York: Harcourt, Brace, Jovanovich, 1969.

Lee, Harper, *To Kill a Mockingbird.* New York: Lippincott, 1960.

Lund, Doris. *Eric.* Philadelphia, PA: Lippincott, 1974.

McGough, Elizabeth. *Who Are You? A Teen-Ager's Guide to Self-Understanding.* New York: Morrow, 1976.

Mappes, Thomas A. and Jane S. Zembaty. *Social Ethics: Morality and Social Policy.* New York: McGraw-Hill, 1977.

Mayerson, Charlotte. *Two Blocks Apart: Juan Gonzalez and Peter Quinn.* New York: Holt, Rinehart and Winston, 1965.

Miguel—Up From Puerto Rico. Film 15 min color. New York: Learning Corporation of America, 1970.

Moorman, Thomas. *What Is It Really Like Out There? Objective Knowing.* New York: Atheneum, 1977.

National Council of Teachers of English. *Books For You: A Booklist for Senior High School Students.* Urbana, IL: NCTE, 1976.

Neighbors. Film 8 min color. Chicago: International Film Bureau, 1952.

New Columbia Encyclopedia. New York: Columbia University Press, 1975.

Newcomb, Horace, ed. *Television: The Critical View.* New York: Oxford University Press, 1976.

Parlato, Salvatore J., Jr. *Superfilms: An International Guide to Award-Winning Educational Films.* Metuchen, NJ: Scarecrow Press, 1976.

Pirsig, Robert M. *Zen and the Art of Motorcycle Maintenance: An Inquiry into Values.* New York: Morrow, 1974.

Potok, Chaim. *The Chosen*. New York: Simon and Schuster, 1967.
Readers' Guide to Periodical Literature. New York: Wilson.
Reid, Virginia M., ed. *Reading Ladders for Human Relations*. 5th ed. Washington, D.C.: American Council on Education, 1972.
Sears List of Subject Headings. 11th ed. New York: Wilson.
Simon, Charlie M. *Martin Buber: Wisdom in Our Times*. New York: Dutton, 1969.
Sophocles. *Antigone* (recording). New York: Caedmon. LC R67-2925; cassettes CDL 5320.
Thoreau, Henry David. *Walden*. New York: Doubleday. Also Harper, Macmillan, and Houghton Mifflin.
Toys. Film 8 min color. New York: McGraw-Hill, 1966.
Understanding Values. 6 filmstrips and cassettes. Jamaica, NY: Eye Gate Media.
Values in Conflict in History. Slides and cassettes or records. White Plains, NY: Center for Humanities.
West, Jessamyn. *Massacre at Fall Creek*. New York: Harcourt Brace Jovanovich, 1975.
Winn, Marie. *The Plug-in Drug*. New York: Grossman, 1977.
World Book Encyclopedia. Chicago, IL: Field Enterprises Education Corp.

Chapter 8

GETTING IT TOGETHER

The preceding chapters have given suggestions for searching out information in several different subject areas. These can serve as models for many other topics. For example, if you were doing research on disarmament, the chapter "Living in One World" could serve as a guide. If you wanted information on the safety of mopeds, the suggestions in the chapter entitled "Being a Well-Informed Citizen" might help you.

What you have in this book is a *pattern for procedure.* The titles of the resources may change constantly as new films, recordings, pamphlets, books, and encyclopedias are added to your library's holdings. Like a flowing river, the resources of the libraries you use—school or public—are forever renewed. Not only is it possible that the contents will change but also the format in which information comes may be in a shape that is new to you. Regardless of what the future may bring in terms of these new formats, libraries will always try to find ways to index, analyze, display, and retrieve that information. It is also true that, whatever the shape of the information carrier, there will always remain the need for you to learn by using the resources, by applying thought and imagination to your research, and by remembering that the more you are exposed to libraries and their collections, the more comfortable and capable you will be with them.

In like manner, of course, the references you have used (encyclopedias, card catalog, *Readers' Guide*) help you by offering *see also* or *see* suggestions. For example,

JOBS *see also* EMPLOYMENT AGENCIES, OCCUPATIONS;
MORAL VALUES *see* ETHICS, CHARACTER EDUCATION, MORAL PHILOSOPHY;
GAMES *see also* AMUSEMENTS, SPORTS, ENTERTAINMENT, RECREATION, names of games like CHESS, TENNIS, SOCCER.

Another kind of directional signal is in the bibliographies at the end of articles, books, or filmstrips. These lists of resources can direct you to other materials that you may wish to consult.

How to Organize Information

First, you must decide exactly what it is you want to find out. For example, nuclear power is a very broad subject, but it can be narrowed down to more manageable topics like the peaceful uses of nuclear energy. Having decided on the goal of your search, jot down the various aspects that might be part of that topic. Some possibilities are the background of nuclear energy (history, discovery) and some of the famous scientists connected with its development (Enrico Fermi, Albert Einstein). Nuclear weaponry will, of course, be eliminated since we have decided on peaceful applications. Other sub-topics that might occur to you are the use of nuclear energy in space science, in medical science, and as an alternative to other forms of energy (fuel oil, coal, etc.). Since there is controversy about nuclear energy as a fuel, you may wish to read articles supporting both sides of the argument.

When you have listed all your preliminary thoughts—each on a card or in a loose-leaf notebook—arrange them so that those that go together logically will be researched at the same time.

The materials you use will be determined by what kind of information you need for the answers:

For background:
Encyclopedias, general and special. (Consult the index of this book for details about these sources and the others listed here.)

Books and audiovisual materials. (Consult the card or book catalog under headings like NUCLEAR ENERGY or ATOMIC ENERGY, NUCLEAR PHYSICS, NUCLEAR REACTORS.)

For statistics
Almanacs, yearbooks, statistical abstracts.

For biographical information
Encyclopedias, biographical dictionaries like *Who's Who, Current Biography*, special science biographical dictionaries.

For pro and con discussion
Editorial Research Reports and vertical file materials. Magazine articles found through the *Readers' Guide* and, if more depth is needed, other indexes that analyze special magazines. New York *Times Index.*

Up-to-the-minute information
Daily newspaper and special coverage on television.

NOTETAKING

As you use any or all of these resources you will be taking notes. Copying word for word from anything does not insure your understanding it, and you cannot use the material that way without giving credit to the author. (Plagiarism is the "stealing" of another's words to present them as your own.) With photocopying machines in libraries you may be saved the time of sitting in the library while you read, but you must still do the reading, thinking, and selecting when you get home.

Underline (if the copy is your own) or write down the most important ideas. You can invent a shorthand of your own to save time. These notes should be kept with the cards or loose-leaf pages on which you did your original planning. That enables you to re-arrange them as you think through how much of what you have read and noted you want to keep for the final report.

The End Product

Make an outline and then a draft of your report so that you can expand or eliminate material before you type out the finished report. Sometimes you will want to give a direct quote. Supply a note about the source of that. It is called a footnote and is often at the foot of the page. If it is not there, it is put at the end of the chapter or at the back of the book, after all the chapters. It is marked so that we know there is going to be a citation. Here is an example:

In a paragraph about the use of nuclear reactors, you may want to quote what another person has said: "The future of radioactive wastes is, clearly, a political and emotional issue—part of the massive battle over atomic energy that is raging today in Europe and will rage in America before long."[1]

At the bottom of the page will appear this note:

[1]William Hines, "Anti-Nuclear Ferment in Europe," *The Progressive*, September 1977, p. 21.

At the end of your report you will want to show all the resources that you consulted. This is called a bibliography, even though it will contain not only books, pamphlets, magazine articles, and newspaper clippings but possibly also films, recordings, and kits. In this list the same information that you gave in your footnote must also be given but with the author's name in inverted order. Here is a sample bibliography on our topic "Nuclear Energy: Advantages and Disadvantages."

1. American Assembly, Columbia University. *The Nuclear Power Controversy.* Englewood Cliffs, N.J.: Prentice-Hall, 1976.

2. Feiveson, H. A. and T. B. Tyler. "Security Implications of Alternative Fission Futures." *Bulletin of the Atomic Scientists*, vol. 32, pp. 14-18+ (December, 1976).

3. Hines, William. "Anti-Nuclear Ferment in Europe." *The Progressive*, vol. 41, pp. 19-21 (September, 1977).

4. Lapp, Ralph E. *The Nuclear Controversy*. Greenwich, Conn.: Fact Systems, 1974.

5. Novick, Sheldon. *The Careless Atom.* Boston: Houghton Mifflin, 1969.

6. "Nuclear Fuels," *McGraw-Hill Yearbook of Science and Technology*, 1971, pp. 291-293.

7. International Atomic Energy Agency. *Nuclear Power and the Environment.* Vienna: 1973.

8. *Nuclear Radiation.* 6 filmstrips with 3 cassettes. New York: Eye Gate Media.

9. "Nuclear Reactors," *Collier's Encyclopedia*, 1977 ed., vol. 17, pp. 714–719.

10. "Nuclear Reactors," *Van Nostrand's Scientific Encyclopedia,* pp. 1630-1661.

11. "Reactors, Nuclear," *McGraw-Hill Encyclopedia of Science and Technology,* 1977 ed., vol. 11, pp. 375-386.

12. Salmon, Alan. *The Nuclear Reactor.* New York: John Wiley & Sons, 1964.

13. Seaborg, Glenn T. and William R. Corliss. *Man and the Atom.* New York: Dutton, 1971.

14. Woodbury, David O. *Atoms for Peace.* New York: Dodd, Mead, 1965, pp. 50–59, "What Is a Reactor?"

Note that there is a variety of sources: books, articles in encyclopedias or magazines, audiovisual material. Items 1, 5, 12, 13, and 14 are books and were found through the card catalog search under the subject headings NUCLEAR REACTORS; ATOMIC ENERGY; ENERGY. Item 8, a kit composed of filmstrips and cassettes, was also found in the catalog. Entries 2 and 3 were located by subject in the *Readers' Guide to Periodical Literature*. Items 6, 9, 10, 11 came from searching the one-volume and multi-volume sets of general and science encyclopedias. Numbers 4 and 7 were discovered in the vertical file under ATOMIC ENERGY.

Other sources you might have used would include *Facts on File, Editorial Research Reports* and the New York *Times Index*.

Guides to Writing Reports

In addition to the brief information given here on "getting it together," you can review the steps involved in gathering and organizing information by looking at an excellent slide-tape program entitled *The Research Paper Made Easy*, a three-part audiovisual program that covers planning the report, doing the research, and writing the paper. Also helpful for more detailed information are two paperbacks (which perhaps should be part of your personal library): Hubbell's *Writing Term Papers and Reports* and Turabian's *Manual for Writers of Term Papers, Theses and Dissertations.*

Other Kinds of Reports

You may not necessarily report on your research in written form, as a paper to be handed in. It is possible that, if you have freedom to choose how to share your information, you may decide to make it an oral report. In that case, your outline will be a guide to your "speech" and you may use index cards as a reminder of how to progress from one point to the next.

Oral reports are often enlivened by the use of illustrations: pictures, diagrams, transparencies, slides, films, etc. Some people have made reports using their own slides plus a cassette tape, or by showing an original film with a running narrative that can also be put on tape. These require at least as much planning as a written report, plus some very careful rehearsal to make sure all the elements fit together.

Producing your own audiovisual materials may be fairly simple or very complicated. Only if you are well-versed in writing a script should you attempt to produce a movie. Slides, however, and filmstrips have been made even by very young children. What you should know is exactly what materials you will need to photograph or sketch and how to use them. Your school or public library may have a course in audiovisual production or you may be able to follow the steps in a book such as *Planning and Producing Audiovisual Materials* by Jerrold Kemp.

EQUIPMENT

Both for presenting your own audiovisual reports and for using those materials that the library has purchased, you should become acquainted with a few machines that you are likely to see and that are available to you in your library media centers.

Newspapers and magazines may be available to you on microfilm. A *microfilm reader* is needed for that and looks like the illustration in Figure 40. The librarian will show you

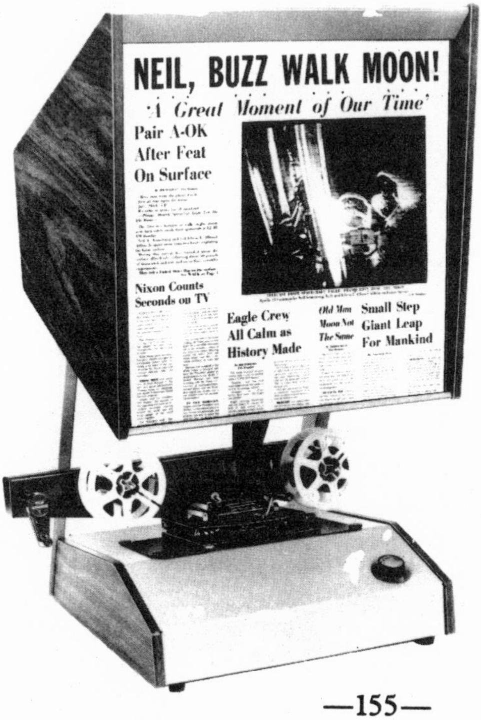

Figure 40.
Microfilm Reader

how to put the film into the machine and you will find that the second time you will be able to do it yourself. Some readers come with copying facilities that enable you to make a copy of the page you are reading for further study at home.

Slides require a projector (Figure 41) and a screen. If you are showing your report to a class you will need a large screen. If you are viewing materials by yourself, a small screen may be permanently mounted on the wall of a conference room or a carrel (a small study space usually large enough for an individual student or library patron).

Figure 41. Carousel Slide Projector

Another type of projector is used with filmstrips (Figure 42). There are also machines that take *filmstrip, or slides, plus cassette tapes* (Figures 43 and 44) because more and more resources are being produced as sound filmstrips or kits.

It is fairly easy to use some of the 16mm *movie projectors* (Figure 45) because they are self-threading but a few minutes of practice will make you just as comfortable with the other type too. *Super 8* movies are popular for making home movies and those require their own projector.

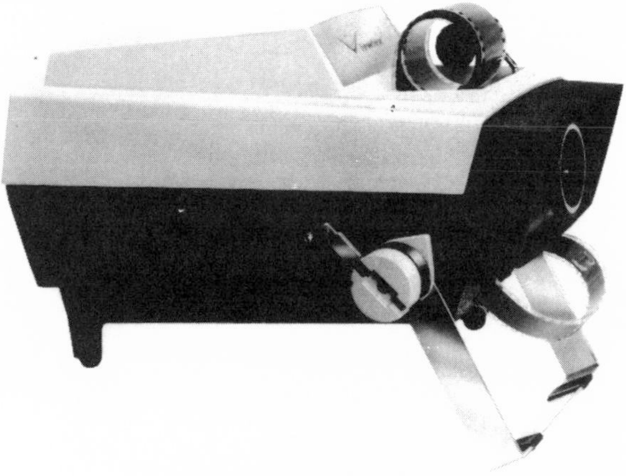

Figure 42. Filmstrip Projector

Figure 43. Filmstrip/Cassette Tape Viewer

Figure 44.
Slide/Cassette
Tape Projector

Figure 45.
16 MM Film Projector

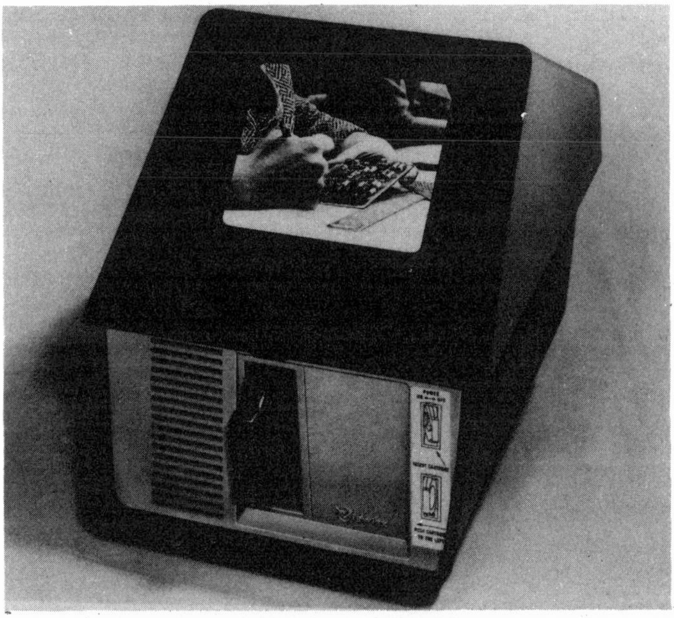

Figure 46. 8 MM Loop Cartridge Viewer

In some subject areas there are very short films that run on a continous loop that never needs to be rewound. These 8 millimeter cartridge films usually describe one specific activity and generally take about 3 to 4 minutes. For example there are short films used in an *8mm projector* (Figure 46), on bisecting an angle, on the amoeba, or techniques in power volleyball, on gymnastics.

Transparencies are projected by an *overhead projector* (Figure 47) and are easily made with special grease pencils or other markers. This kind of visual allows you to speak directly to your audience as you show your material in a lighted room, unlike motion pictures, slides, and some filmstrips that require darkened rooms.

Figure 47. Overhead Projector

Opaque projectors (Figure 48) are useful for showing pictures in their original state, that is as they look in a book, magazine or art print. These also need darkened rooms.

Some public libraries have acquired *video cartridges* (Figure 49) and a special player is needed to view those.

None of these machines is very complicated and you can easily learn how to handle them efficiently. They do require considerate handling just as your own tape recorder, record player, microphone, and camera do. You know that, even with home appliances, it may take time for a maintenance person

Figure 48. Opaque Projector

Figure 49. Video Cassette Recorder

to do the repair job. In that interval you are left without the convenience of the equipment, so handle with care.

Remember that the most important equipment that you need for your information-search is your mind—and your eyes. Libraries try to keep in mind the fact that many people have trouble with their eyes and for them they have acquired books in large print and even talking books so that you can hear a book if you are not able to read it.

As for one's mind, too often it is allowed to be unexercised. If you have ever had to stay in bed for an extended period of time you know how weak your legs become from disuse. That also happens to a mind when it is not used regularly.

Odds and Ends

Libraries are like elastic. You can start out in as small a way as you wish—then stretch your library use to almost any lengths.

The chapters in this book have given you many suggestions and titles. Depending on your personal objectives you may use one or several of the sources mentioned. You may decide you need only a slide/tape introduction to a specific topic or you may go even beyond the most advanced materials described here.

It has not been the aim of this guide to list every possible resource that your local libraries can offer. That would be neither possible nor practical. The suggestions you have found here will lead you to subject headings in indexes, catalogs, information files, and to sections of the library itself where you will discover for yourself additional, newer materials.

The following special resources are useful when you are

tracking down the availability of certain titles. *Books in Print* is an annual list with entries by author and by title; its companion volume is *Subject Guide to Books in Print*. The growth of the paperback industry and the great popularity of the smaller format (because we can all own a personal library at those prices) has brought into being *Paperbound Books in Print*, which is issued as an annual list with entries by title, author, and subject. It is updated twice a year with supplements in May and September.

Other Useful Library Resources

Sometimes you need to know how certain books or films have been reviewed by critics. *Readers' Guide to Periodical Literature* helps you to find those reviews and lists book reviews in a special section at the back of each issue. Also helpful is *Book Review Digest*, which covers reviews in more than 70 journals and gives excerpts from the reviews. It also includes a title and subject index in each issue.

No attempt has been made to cover the whole world of knowledge in this short book, but if you use the approaches that have been described as typical, you can help yourself to information in almost any field. You will discover for yourself that each area has its own special reference titles. Thus, in music there are special works like *Concise Oxford Dictionary of Music* and Logan's *Illustrated Encyclopedia of Rock*; in mathematics, James's *Mathematics Dictionary* and Stonaker's *Famous Mathematicians*.

There are guides to flowers, minerals, automobiles, mopeds, kites—and every other interest under the sun. The library catalog, card format or book format, will give you a clue to the location of titles—and then the whole library world is open to your browsing, tasting, testing, and consideration of what book or pamphlet, or filmstrip, or record will serve your needs.

Often in speeches or essays the addition of a pertinent quote from a well-known person adds importance to the statement. Quotations can be found in such references as Bartlett's *Familiar Quotations*, which gives over 20,000 quotations arranged in chronological order by the authors of those quotations, or Stevenson's *Home Book of Quotations*, which contains about 50,000 entries and is arranged by subject. Both of these reference books have an index of key words so that if you are trying to find the source of a quotation you can locate it in the index under any of the important words in the quote. For example, if you have read somewhere "My library was dukedom large enough" and wanted to know where it originated you could check the index under "library" or "dukedom." Either entry would refer you to the page containing the quotation.

Other quotation collections exist. Some are specifically for one author, such as *A Treasury of Lincoln Quotations. Great Treasury of Western Thought* includes very long passages from important writings and arranges them under 20 broad headings, including "War and Peace," "Medicine and Health," "Ethics," "Family," "Love."

In writing your reports you may need help in checking on a word or question of grammar. Dictionaries are well-known to you but books of synonyms may not be. *Roget's Thesaurus of English Words and Phrases* and *Funk and Wagnalls Standard Handbook of Synonyms, Antonyms and Prepositions* can help you add variety to the way you express yourself. A book like John E. Warriner's *English Grammar and Composition* will answer questions of punctuation as well as of correct usage.

The Library—A Necessity Not A Luxury

Your school and public libraries will be your usual sources of information. It is worth noting, however, that many a community has dozens of libraries not as readily visible as those two. In addition to the libraries that colleges and universities maintain, museums, medical societies, publishers, banks, business corporations—all these often have their own collections of materials intended, of course, for their own patrons. Occasionally, some students may be given special permission to use these resources when their research is so advanced that the school and public library collections cannot satisfy their needs.

There is no aspect of life that cannot benefit from your having the library habit. It may be to further your education, improve your employment opportunities, take care of your home, enliven your leisure time, find out about your ability to write a poem, bring up a healthy family—and, in general, to understand and cope with the world in which we live.

SUGGESTED MATERIALS

Adler, Mortimer and Charles Van Doren, eds. *Great Treasury of Western Thought*. New York: Bowker, 1977.

Bartlett, John. *Familiar Quotations: A Collection of Passages, Phrases and Proverbs Traced to Their Sources in Ancient and Modern Literature*. 14th rev. and enl. ed. Boston, MA: Little, Brown, 1968.

Book Review Digest. New York: Wilson.

Books in Print: An Author-Title-Series Index to the Publishers' Trade List Annual. New York: Bowker.

Editorial Research Reports: Washington, D.C.: Congressional Quarterly.

Facts on File: A Weekly Digest of World Events with Cumulative Index. New York: Facts on File.

Fernald, James C. *Funk & Wagnalls Standard Handbook of Synonyms, Antonyms & Prepositions*. New York: Funk, 1947.

Hubbell, George Shelton. *Writing Term Papers and Reports*. New York: Barnes and Noble, 1969.

James, Robert C. and Edwin F. Beckenbach. *Mathematics Dictionary*. 4th ed. New York: Van Nostrand Reinhold, 1976.

Kemp, Jerrold. *Planning and Producing Audiovisual Materials*. 3rd ed. New York: Crowell, 1975.

Logan, Nick and Bob Woffinden. *The Illustrated Encyclopedia of Rock*. New York: Crown, 1977.

Paperbound Books in Print. New York: Bowker

Public Affairs Information Service Bulletin. New York: PAIS, Inc.

Readers' Guide to Periodical Literature. New York: Wilson.

The Research Paper Made Easy: From Assignment to Completion. 3 carousels of slides and cassettes or discs. White Plains, NY: Center for Humanities.

Roget's Thesaurus of English Words and Phrases. Dutch, Robert A., ed. New York: St. Martin's Press, 1965.

Scholes, Percy H. *Concise Oxford Dictionary of Music*. 2nd ed. J. O. Ward, ed. New York: Oxford University Press, 1964.

Stevenson, Burton, ed. *The Home Book of Quotations: Classical and Modern.* 10th rev. ed. New York: Dodd, Mead, 1967.

Stonaker, Frances B. *Famous Mathematicians.* Philadelphia, PA: Lippincott, 1966.

Subject Guide to Books in Print. New York: Bowker.

A Treasury of Lincoln Quotations. New York: Doubleday, 1965.

Turabian, Kate L. *A Manual for Writers of Term Papers, Theses, and Dissertations.* 4th ed. Chicago, IL: University of Chicago Press, 1973.

Warriner, John E. and others. *English Grammar and Composition.* Heritage ed. New York: Harcourt Brace Jovanovich, 1977.

TEST QUESTIONS

1. Leon Uris wrote a best-seller entitled *Trinity* in 1976. Where can you find excerpts of some of the reviews of that book?

2. There was a remarkable rescue of hostages from a hijacked plane at Entebbe. Where do you look to find out where Entebbe is?

3. What is the most logical biographical reference to use for a sketch of Rod McKuen?

4. How can you find out how many biographies of President Carter your library has?

5. What is the name of an encyclopedia which specializes in scientific subjects?

6. You are planning to buy new stereo equipment. How can you get some help on deciding which to purchase?

7. You know that the Rt. Hon. Margaret Thatcher is an important political figure in England. Where can you find brief biographical information about her?

8. "The boy stood on the burning deck" has been used as a first line for some parodies but it is the first line of a serious poem. How can you find the name of the original poem, who wrote it, and where to see the entire poem?

9. You have heard someone mention a book entitled *What Every Kid Should Know*. You would like to know who

wrote it and you do not find it, under its title, in your library. How can you find out the author and whether the book is in print?

10. A friend read a book about cloning and recommended it to you. You do not know whether it is fiction or fact. The title is *Joshua Son of None*. How can you tell from the catalog which it is?

11. Which biographical dictionary will give you a sketch of Robert Lowell, American poet, and a picture?

12. What is a book catalog?

13. What index will help you if you are looking for articles on stocks and bonds in magazines that are not listed in the *Readers' Guide to Periodical Literature*?

14. You noted the word "compiler" on a catalog card? Where will you find the meaning of the word?

15. Where can you find information about the Nobel Prize winners for the current year?

16. Where can you find a list of Pulitzer Prize awards for 1968?

17. You know that government agencies have issued some pamphlets on the energy crisis. Where would you look for those in your library?

18. The Concorde plane has been much in the news and it is likely that discussions took place on an international level. You want to know the name of our ambassador to France and France's Ambassador to the United States. What is the best place to look for that kind of information?

19. What library resource is SIRS?

What reference title will help you locate reviews for A. Eagan's *Why Am I So Miserable if These Are the Best Years of My Life?*

21. How can you get articles that have been written about the Strategic Arms Limitation Talks?

22. You would like to join a club that is interested in folk dancing. What help can your library give you?

23. You want an overall discussion on the changing American family with some information about likely trends. What resource publishes booklets on such issues regularly?

24. What is the vertical file? What kinds of materials do you expect to find there?

POSTSCRIPT TO THE TEACHER

The rationale for this book has been to promote the idea that libraries are an important practical resource for solving some of the basic problems faced by youth (and by all people). Persuaded that education is not totally school-based, the author has used as themes those topics that appear to have particular pertinence for young people today. It is no surprise, however, that these themes upon closer examination appear to be those that have always figured prominently in growth and maturation.

The chapters include specific suggestions for using various materials to solve a problem, answer a need, or expand a budding interest, as well as to supply information. The patterns of research—steps to take in doing a search—can be extrapolated for application to other topics.

The contribution of the teacher toward the formation of a life-long library habit is incalculable. The prestige and authority of the classroom teacher are strong levers. It is to be hoped that students will become independent and committed patrons of libraries early in their school days. The interest shown by teachers, the importance attached by teachers to the use of a wide range of resources outside of the textbook, are the sine qua non for the most effective use of library media centers and their resources.

Also desirable is the encouragement by teachers of the use of imaginative and novel ways of presenting reports. In many schools—for example, Stuyvesant High School and the United Nations International School in New York—slide/tape projects have been prepared by the students on these topics: superstition, Russian emigrés in New York City, mystery of death, operation of a lever, nuclear power, Cantonese opéra, witchcraft, the school football team, UFOs, song birds of America.

Slides and filmstrips can be photographed or done by hand. Tapes to accompany the pictorial material require reading, thinking, planning, writing, as well as speaking, clearly.

The added resources of audiovisual materials in library media centers have special appeal to a generation born entirely within the television era. The fascination of those stimuli has increased the need for teachers and media specialists to guide young people in evaluating the messages carried by those media—just as they do with printed messages.

This approach does not disparage the medium of the book. In fact, it enhances those qualities that make the book perdurable: its portability, comparative low cost, ready accessibility without equipment, and availability for repeated use. We know, however, that music and poetry should be heard, that paintings must be seen and that certain activities are best understood through "active" conveyors of information.

All of these library materials combine to present a multifaceted opportunity to make learning a pleasurable and rewarding pursuit. The only catastrophe would be to allow this resource to die from inattention.

INDEX

AAAS Science Book List, 31
AAAS Science Books and Films, 31
Abbreviations in informational sources, 10, 11, 33, 46, 81, 85, 101-2, 141
Abridged Readers' Guide, 122
Adler, M. and Van Doren, C., eds. *Great Treasury of Western Thought,* 164
Adoff, A., ed. *Poetry of Black America,* 92
Ali, M. *The Greatest,* 51
Almanacs, 13, 17, 34, 71, 150
Alone Amid All This Noise, 92
Alphabetical order, 3
American Civil Liberties Union. *The Rights of Students,* 16
American Heritage Dictionary of the English Language, 68
American Universities and Colleges, 55
Anouilh, J. *Antigone,* 136
Answers and Questions: The Palestine Issue (pamphlet), 76
Antigone, 136
Antonyms, handbook of, 164
Applied Science and Technology Index, 31, 33
Arab World (Reference Shelf), 76
Area Handbook Series, 71
Ariel, 92, 119
Art of Sylvia Plath, 114
Arthur Ashe, Portrait in Motion, 51
Ashbery, J. *Houseboat Days,* 111
Ashe, A. *Arthur Ashe, Portrait in Motion,* 51
Atlantic Monthly (periodical), 83
Atlases, 68-69
Audiovisual materials, production of, 154-5
Audiovisual resources, 5, 18-19, 74, 107, 109, 150, 171; equipment, 5, 155-60; kits, 110, 134-5; in vocational areas, 52
Autobiography (M. Fonteyn), 51

Background information sources, 26-7, 150
Barnewall, G. G. *Your Future as a Job Applicant,* 49
Barron's Educational Series, 59
Barron's Guide to Two-Year Colleges, 57
Barron's Handbook of American College Financial Aid, 59
Barron's Handbook of Junior and Community College Financial Aid, 59
Barron's How to Prepare for the American College Testing Program, 62
Barron's Profiles of American Colleges, 56
Bartlett, J. *Familiar Quotations,* 164
Beery, Mary. *Young Teens and Money,* 10
Bell Jar, 92, 119
Bibliographies, 30, 149; of audiovisual resources, 52
Bibliography (sample), 152-3
Biographical dictionaries, 27-8, 72, 117, 150
Biography, information sources, 27-8, 49, 72, 117, 150; arrangement, 115-17
Bird, C. *Case Against College,* 41
Blakiston's Gould Medical Dictionary, 28
Blaze, W. and others. *Guide to Alternative Colleges and Universities,* 58
Bolt, R. *Man for All Seasons,* 136
Bombed, Buzzed, Smashed, or . . . Sober, 29
Book catalogs, 8, 18, 97
Book Review Digest, 111, 163
Booklists, 99, 137, 139
Books and the Teen-age Reader, 99
Books for Brotherhood (booklist), 139
Books for the Teen Age (booklist), 138
Books for You, 99, 137-8
Books in Print, 163
Borland, H. *When the Legends Die,* 136
Boynton, R. and Mack, M. *Sounds and Silences,* 106
Bradley, B. *Life on the Run,* 51
Brewton, J. E. and others. *Index to Poetry for Children and Young People, 1965–1969,* 104
"Britannica 3" *(Encyclopaedia Britannica),* 131
Browning, E. B. *Sonnets from the Portuguese,* 92
Browsing, 3, 49, 50, 56, 94, 163
Bulletin of the Atomic Scientists, 31
Busch, P. S. *What About VD?,* 29
Business Periodicals Index, 12, 48
Buyer Beware (filmstrip and cassette), 10

Call numbers, 3, 18, 30, 94, 96, 114, 116-117, 125
See also Dewey decimal classification
Capek, K. *R.U.R.,* 30
Card catalogs, 3, 8, 15, 18, 48, 95, 107, 150
Career Directions series, 52
Careers, Inc., 45
Careers, information sources, 40-53

Index

Carlsen, G. R. *Books and the Teen-age Reader,* 99
Case Against College, 41
Cass, J. and Birnbaum, M. *Comparative Guide to American Colleges,* 54
Catalog cards, 8-10, 48; author cards, 8, 96; call number, 29-30; parts of, 3; subject cards, 48, 107, 111-12; title cards, 8, 108
Catalogs, library. *See* Book catalogs; Card catalogs; College catalogs; Dictionary catalogs.
Cattell's American Men and Women of Science, 28
Center for Humanities, 134
Changing Times (periodical), 15
Choosing the Kind of Job You Want (filmstrips and cassettes), 52
Chosen, The, 136
Christian Science Monitor (newspaper), 111
Chronical Guidance Publications, 45
Citizenship, information sources, 15-17
Cleary, F. D. *Discovering Books and Libraries,* 95
Cohen, D. *The New Believers,* 138
Cole, W., ed. *Fireside Book of Humorous Poetry,* 93
Collections of reprinted articles, 35-6
College Blue Book, 56
College Boards Examination, 62
College catalogs, 57
College directories, 53-4
College, information sources, 53-62; costs, 59; testing, 62
Collier's Encyclopedia, 26, 70, 71, 131
Columbia-Lippincott Gazetteer of the World, 68
Community agencies as publishers of resource material, 139
Community Resources file, 42
Comparative Guide to American Colleges, 54
Complete Illustrated Book of Better Health, 29
Compton's Pictured Encyclopedia, 131
Concise Oxford Dictionary of Music, 163
Consumer Complaints (film), 10
Consumer Information Catalog, 12
Consumer information sources, 10-12
Consumer Reports (periodical), 10, 12
Consumers' Research Magazine, 10
Contemporary Authors, 119
Controversial material, evaluation of, 76-7, 81, 87-8
Cook, M. G. *The New Library Key,* 99
Coyne, J. and Hebert, T. *This Way Out,* 58
Craven, M. *I Heard the Owl Call My Name,* 136
Cross-references, 5, 15, 26-8; *see* and *see also,* 131, 149
Current Biography, 27, 51, 72, 85, 119, 150
Current Career and Occupational Literature 44
Current History (periodical), 31, 83
Current information sources, 14, 31, 79, 124, 150

Death as a Fact of Life, 137
Death Be Not Proud, 137
Death Penalty (Reference Shelf), 36
Deciding Right from Wrong (slides and cassettes), 134
Dewey decimal classification, 9, 18, 27, 56, 94, 99, 116
Dickinson, W. B., ed. *Editorial Research Reports,* 14
Dictionaries, 68
Dictionary catalogs, 96
Dictionary of the History of Ideas, 132
Directory of Medical Specialists, 28
Discovering Books and Libraries, 95
Discussion topics, information sources, 150
Dollars and Sense: The Teen-Age Consumer's Guide, 10

Eat, Drink and Be Wary (film), 29
Eberhart, R., ed. *War and the Poet,* 93
Editorial Research Reports, 14, 36, 77, 1 0
Edwards, P., ed. *Encyclopedia of Philosophy,* 132
Ellmann, R., ed. *New Oxford Book of American Verse,* 92
Emerson, R. W. *Essays,* 138
Encounters with Tomorrow: Science Fiction and Human Values (filmstrips and cassettes), 29
Encyclopaedia Britannica, 71, 131
Encyclopedia Americana, 13, 70, 71, 131
Encyclopedia of Careers and Vocational Guidance, 43
Encyclopedia of Philosophy, 132

Index

Encyclopedias, 13-14, 26-7, 70-71, 131, 150; of careers, 43-4; of philosophy, 132
Enemy of the People, 136
English Grammar and Composition, 164
Equipment, audiovisual, 155-60
Eric, 137
Essays (Emerson), 138
Essence of Accounting (filmstrips and cassettes), 52
Ethical Challenge: Four Biomedical Case Studies (slides and cassettes), 29
Ethics of Genetic Control (slides and cassettes), 29
Ethnic values, 136-7
Every Vote Counts, 15
Eyes on the Arab World (filmstrips and cassettes), 74

Facts on File, 36, 77
Familiar Quotations, 164
Family, information sources, 17-20
Famous Mathematicians, 163
Fernald, J. *Funk and Wagnalls Standard Handbook of Synonyms, Antonyms and Prepositions,* 164
Fiction, 94
Films, 138-9; guide to, 139
Filmstrip projector, 156-7
Financial Aids for Higher Education 76–77 Catalog, 61
Fireside Book of Humorous Poetry, 93
Fishbein, M., ed. *Modern Medical Adviser,* 28
Fletcher, J. F. *The Ethics of Genetic Control,* 29
Fonteyn, M. *Autobiography,* 51
Footnotes, 151
Foreign Affairs (periodical), 83
Formats of library material, 4, 30, 51, 148
Fractured Family, 20
Friendly, F. *The Good Guys, the Bad Guys and the First Amendment,* 140
Funk and Wagnalls Standard College Dictionary, 68
Funk and Wagnalls Standard Handbook of Synonyms, Antonyms and Prepositions, 164

Gazetteers, 67-8
General Science Index, 33
Genetic experimentation information sources, 29
Genetics: Man the Creator (film), 29
Geographical information sources, 67-9
Getting Ready for Marriage, 20
Good Guys, the Bad Guys and the First Amendment, 140
Goode's World Atlas, 69
Goodfield, J. *Playing God,* 29
Goodman, L. *Current Career and Occupational Literature,* 44
Government documents, 34, 44, 61
Government publications, 16-17
Grammar, 164
Grandfather Rock; the New Poetry and the Old, 93
Granger's Index to Poetry, 101
Great Treasury of Western Thought, 164
Greatest, The, 51
Gruber, E. C. and Bramson, M. *Scholastic Aptitude Test,* 62
Guide cards, in library catalogs, 97
Guide to Alternative Colleges and Universities, 58
Guide to Career Education, 44
Guide to External and Continuing Education, 58
Gunther, J. *Death Be Not Proud,* 137

Haiku–A Photographic Interpretation (filmstrips and cassettes), 110
Hammond Ambassador World Atlas, 69
Harper's (periodical), 83
Headings. *See* Subject headings
Health: A Quality of Life, 29
Health and medicine, information sources, 25-36
"Health—Getting It and Keeping It" (outline), 26
Hendin, D. *Death as a Fact of Life,* 137
Historical information sources, 70
Home Book of Quotations, 164
Houseboat Days, 111
How Can I Pay for College? (filmstrips and cassettes), 59
How to Buy a Used Car (film), 10
Hubbell, G. *Writing Term Papers and Reports,* 154
Hughes, L., ed. *New Negro Poets: U.S.A.,* 92
Human Resources file, 42
I Can Be Anything, 49
I Had No Choic But to Obey (filmstrip and tape), 135
I Heard the Owl Call My Name, 136

I Never Told Anybody, 125
Ibsen, H. *An Enemy of the People,* 136
Illustrated Encyclopedia of Rock, 163
Index to Poetry for Children and Young People, 1965–1969, 104
Index to the Wilson Authors Series, 117
Indexes: in books, 14, 31, 43, 100; of encyclopedias, 27; to periodicals, 11, 31, 33, 121-2, 144; to poetry, 101, 104
Information: organization of, 149; types of, 150
Information center, 2
Information file. *See* Vertical file.
Information Please Almanac, 17, 34, 71
Inlow, G. *Values in Transition,* 132
International Encyclopedia of the Social Sciences, 131
International Who's Who, 74
Is It Always Right to be Right? (film), 139
Israel Is Born (recording), 74

James, R. C. and Beckenbach, E. F. *Mathematics Dictionary,* 163
Jerusalem, Key to Peace, 76
Jobs: How People Create Their Own, 49
Jobs in Health Service (filmstrips and cassettes), 52

Kazin, A. *A Walker in the City,* 136
Keefe, J. *The Teenager and the Interview,* 49
Keeslar, O. *Financial Aids for Higher Education 76–27* Catalog, 61
Kemp, J. *Planning and Producing Audiovisual Materials,* 155
Kesselman, J. *Stopping Out,* 41
Klemer, D. J. *Modern Love Poems,* 92
Koch, K. *I Never Told Anybody; Teaching Poetry Writing in a Nursing Home,* 125; *Wishes, Lies and Dreams: A New Way of Teaching Children to Write Poetry,* 125

Langone, J. *Bombed, Buzzed, Smashed, or . . . Sober,* 29
Lask, T., ed. *New York Times Book of Verse,* 101
Lederer, M. *Guide to Career Education,* 44
Lee, H. *To Kill A Mockingbird,* 136
Legislative Manual of New York, 17
Leidy, W. P., comp. *Popular Guide to Government Publications,* 34
Lemback, R. *Teenage Jobs,* 49
Letters Home, 123
Librarians, role of, 6
Library lists, information sources, 138-40
Library: media center, 51; use of, 3-6, 42, 134, 149, 162, 165, 170
Library of Congress classification, 99
Library, physical layout, 3, 87
Life on the Run, 51
Lipkin, M. *Straight Talk About Your Health Care,* 29
Literary criticism, information sources, 110
Livingston, M. C., ed. *O Frabjous Day; Poetry for Holidays and Special Occasions,* 92
Logan, N. and Woffinden, B. *The Illustrated Encyclopedia of Rock,* 163
Lovejoy's Career and Vocational School Guide, 44
Lovejoy's College Guide, 56
Lund, D. *Eric,* 137

McDonough, M. and Hansen, A. J. *The College Boards Examination,* 62
Mace, D. R. *Getting Ready for Marriage,* 20
McGough, Elizabeth. *Dollars and Sense: The Teen-Age Consumer's Guide,* 10; *Who Are You?,* 134
McGraw-Hill Encyclopedia of Science and Technology, 27
Macropaedia (Encyclopaedia Brittannica), 132
Mademoiselle (periodical), 45
Magazines, 10, 31, 45, 79-83; indexes, 10-11, 31-33, 121-3, 140-41
Man for All Seasons, 136
Manpower (periodical), 45
Map files, 68
Mappes, T. and Zembaty, J. *Social Ethics,* 129
Martin Buber, 138
Massacre at Fall Creek, 136
Mate Selection: Making the Best Choice (filmstrips and cassettes), 20
Mathematics Dictionary, 163
Mayerson, C. *Two Blocks Apart,* 137
Media centers, libraries as, 2
Media specialist, 5
Medical Care in the United States (Reference Shelf), 36

Medicine and health, information sources, 28-9, 25-36
Merck Manual of Diagnosis and Therapy, 29
Microfilm reader (equipment), 155
Microforms, 2
Micropaedia (*Encyclopaedia Britannica*), 131
Middle East, information sources, 70
Middle East Journal (periodical), 86
Miguel–Up From Puerto Rico (film), 139
Mitchell, J. S. *I Can Be Anything,* 49
Modern British Poetry, 104
Modern Literature Monographs, 114
Modern Love Poems, 92
Modern Medical Adviser, 28
Modern Writer Series, 114
Monthly Catalog of Government Publications, 45
Monthly Checklist of State Publications, 17
Monthly Labor Review, 15
Moorman, T. *What Is It Really Like Out There?,* 134
Morrison, L. *The Sidewalk Racer,* 93
Morse, D. *Grandfather Rock,* 93
Movie projectors, 159
Municipal Yearbook, 15

National Commission on Resources for Youth. *New Roles for Youth in the School and Community,* 21
National Conference of Christians and Jews. *Books for Brotherhood,* 139
National Council of Teachers of English. *Books for You: A Booklist for Senior High Students,* 99, 137-8
Natural History (periodical), 31
Neighbors (film), 139
New Believers, 138
New Columbia Encyclopedia, 14, 131
New Israelis, 74
New Library Key, 99
New Middle East (periodical), 86
New Modern American and British Poetry, 104
New Negro Poets: U.S.A., 92
New Oxford Book of American Verse, 92
New Roles for Youth in the School and Community, 21
New York Public Library. *Books for the Teen Age* (booklist), 138
New York Public Library catalog, 97
New York Red Book, 17
New York *Times,* 81, 124; *Index,* 36, 81, 124, 150; *Magazine,* 83
New York Times Atlas of the World, 69
New York Times Book of Verse, 101
Newcomb, H. *Television: The Critical View,* 140
Newman, C. H., comp. *The Art of Sylvia Plath,* 114
Newman, J. *What Everyone Needs to Know About Law,* 16
Newspapers, 12, 79, 124, 150
Newsweek (periodical), 83, 111
Nicholsen, M. E. *People in Books,* 49
Norwick, K. P. *Your Legal Rights,* 16
Notetaking, 5, 11, 150-51
Now You Are a Voter (filmstrips and cassettes), 15
"Nuclear Energy: Advantages and Disadvantages" (bibliography), 152-3
Nutrition: Foods, Fads, Frauds, Facts (filmstrips and cassettes), 29
Nutrition, information sources, 29

O Frabjous Day, 92
Occupational Education, 53
Occupational Outlook Handbook, 44
Occupational Outlook Quarterly, 44
Occupations, information sources, 40-53
Ocean Environment (Reference Shelf), 36
O'Donnell, James. *Every Vote Counts: A Teen-Age Guide to the Electoral Process,* 15
Official College Entrance Examination Board Guide to Financial Aid for Students and Parents, 59
Official Congressional Directory for the Use of the U.S. Congress, 17
Opaque projectors, 160
Oral reports, 154
Osen, L. M. *Women in Mathematics,* 51
Outlines, preparation of, 25-6, 151
Overhead projectors, 15
Oxford Economic Atlas of the World, 70

Palestine Digest (pamphlet), 76
Pamphlets, 14, 17, 34, 44, 76, 114-15
Pamphlets on American Writers, 114
Paperbacks, 62, 162
Paperbound Books in Print, 163

Parlato, S. *Superfilms: An International Guide to Award-Winning Educational Films,* 139
Paycheck Puzzle (filmstrip), 7
Peck, R., ed. *Pictures That Storm Inside My Head,* 93
People in Books, 49
Periodicals. *See* Magazines.
Personal finance, information sources, 7-9, 8-10
Philosophy, information sources, 129-44
Pictures That Storm Inside My Head, 93
Pirsig, R. *Zen and the Art of Motorcycle Maintenance,* 138
Plagiarism, 151
Planning and Producing Audiovisual Materials, 155
Plath, Sylvia, 112, 122-4; *Ariel,* 92, 119; *The Bell Jar,* 92; *Letters Home,* 123
Playing God: Genetic Engineering and the Manipulation of Life, 29
Plug-In Drug, 140
Poetic Experience (filmstrips and cassettes), 109
Poetry: indexes, 99-101, 106; information sources, 92-6; recordings, 107
Poetry (periodical), 125
Poetry and Voice of May Swenson (recording), 107
Poetry of Black America, 92
Poetry of Rock: A Reflection of Human Values (slides and cassettes), 110
Political Economy, 21
Popular Guide to Government Publications, 34
Porter, Sylvia. *Sylvia Porter's Money Book,* 8
Potok, C. *The Chosen,* 136
Preparation for Parenthood (slides and cassettes), 20
Prepositions, handbook of, 164
Print materials, 2
Progressive, The (periodical), 31, 83
Prioia, N.C. and DiGaspari, V.M. *Barron's Handbook of American College Financial Aid,* 59; *Barron's Handbook of Junior and Community College Financial Aid,* 59
Promotional leaflets (job opportunities), 45
Propaedia (*Encyclopaedia Britannica*), 131
Public Affairs Information Service Bulletin, 79
Public library, role of, 21
Publishing advice, sources, 125

Questions and Answers on Middle East Problems (pamphlet), 76
Quotations, books of, 164

R.U.R., 30
Radio and television listings, 87, 124
Rand McNally Cosmopolitan World Atlas, 69
Random House Dictionary of the English Language, 68
Reader's Digest (periodical), 1, 83
Reader's Digest Almanac, 34, 71
Readers' Guide to Periodical Literature, as information source, 36, 150, 163; ethics, 141; health, 31-3; personal finance, 10-11, 14-15; poetry, 121-2; Middle East, 83-5; vocational guidance, 46
Reading Ladders for Human Relations, 137
Recordings, poetry, 107
Recreational books, 136-8, 150
Reference Shelf series, 36
Reid, V. *Reading Ladders for Human Relations* (booklist), 137
Reit, A., comp. *Alone Amid All This Noise,* 92
Reports: preparation of, 30; writing, 154
Research Paper Made Easy (slide-tape program), 154
Research, pattern for procedure, 148-54
Rich, Adrienne, 121
Rights of Students, 16
Roget's Thesaurus of English Words and Phrases, 164
Ronco, W. C. *Jobs: How People Create Their Own,* 49
Rousseau, J.J. *Political Economy,* 21
Russell, M.M., ed. *Occupational Education,* 53

Saturday Review (periodical), 83
Saturday's Child, 48
Schoenbrun, D. and Szekely, L. *The New Israelis,* 73
Scholastic Aptitude Test, 62
Scholes, P. *Concise Oxford Dictionary of Music,* 163

Schwann Record and Tape Guide, 109
Science, information sources, 25-36
Science News (periodical), 31
Scientific American (periodical), 31
Scoring High on College Entrance Examinations (cassettes), 62
See and *see also* references, 131, 149
Seed, S. *Saturday's Child,* 48
Self-Fulfillment: Becoming the Person You Want to Be (slides and cassettes), 42
Senior Scholastic (periodical), 15, 83
Sidewalk Race; and Other Poems of Sports and Motion, 93
Sills, D. L., ed. *International Encyclopedia of the Social Sciences,* 131
Simon, C. *Martin Buber,* 138
Sinacore, J. S. *Health: A Quality of Life,* 29
Slide projectors, 156
Slides, 110
Smith, D. B. and Andrews, E. L., comps. *Subject Index to Poetry for Children and Young People 1957-1975,* 106
Smith, S. *Collected Poems,* 92
Social Ethics, 129
Social Issues Resources Series (SIRS), subject index, 13, 17-18, 35
Social Sciences Index, 86
Social security, information sources, 13-15
Sonnets from the Portuguese, 92
Sounds and Silences, 106
Splaver, S. *Your Career if You're Not Going to College,* 41
Springboard to Education After High School: Five Federal Financial Programs, 61
Statesman's Year-book, 71
Statistical Abstract of the United States, 34
Statistics, information sources, 34, 150
Stevenson, B. *Home Book of Quotations,* 164
Stonaker, F. *Famous Mathematicians,* 163
Stopping Out: A Guide to Leaving College and Getting Back In, 41
Straight Talk About Your Health Care, 29
Subject Guide to Books in Print, 163
Subject headings in library resources, 162; book indexes, 14, 43; card catalog, 5, 8, 10, 15, 20, 28, 48, 73, 134; vertical file, 35, 45, 77
Subject headings in specific areas: behavior, 5; consumer education, 10; family and marriage, 20; health, 28, 35; Middle East, 74, 77; personal finance, 10; philosophy, 134; social security, 14; vocational guidance, 43, 45, 48
Subject Index to Poetry for Children and Young People 1957-1975, 106
Suchar, E. *Official College Entrance Examination Board Guide to Financial Aid for Students and Parents,* 59
Superfilms, 139
Sylvia Porter's Money Book, 8
Synonyms, handbook of, 164
Systems of the Human Body (filmstrips and cassettes), 28

Teacher, encouragement of library use, 170-71
Teenage Jobs, 49
Teenager and the Interview, 49
Television and radio, as information sources, 36, 87, 140, 150
Television: The Critical View, 140
Test questions (review), 168-70
This Way Out, 58
Thoreau, H. D. *Walden,* 138
Three Hundred Years of Great American Poetry (recording), 107
Time (periodical), 83
To Kill A Mockingbird, 136
Today's Health, 31
Toys (film), 139
Transparencies, 159
Trans/vision Book of Health (transparencies), 28
Treasury of Lincoln Quotations, 164
Twentieth Century Poets (recording), 107
Twentieth Century Views series, 114
Two Blocks Apart, 137

U.S. News & World Report (periodical), 15, 31, 83, 85
Ultimate Experiment: Man-made Evolution, 29
Understanding Values (filmstrips and tapes), 135
United States Authors series, 114
United States Department of Labor, Bureau of Labor Statistics, 44

United States Government Printing Office, 44
Untermeyer, L., ed. *Modern British Poetry,* 104; *New Modern American and British Poetry,* 104

Values in Conflict in History (slides and cassettes), 135
Values in Transition, 132
Van Nostrand's Scientific Encyclopedia, 27
Vertical file as information source, 138, 140, 150; college costs, 61; consumer protection, 12; health, 34; Middle East, 76; poetry, 125; vocational guidance, 45
Video cassette recorder, 160
Vital Speeches of the Day (periodical), 83
Vocational guidance file, 45
Vocations, information sources, 40-53

Wade, N. *The Ultimate Experiment: Man-made Evolution,* 29
Wagman, R. J., ed. *Complete Illustrated Book of Better Health,* 29
Walden, 138
Walker in the City, 136
Wall Street Journal (newspaper), 76
War and the Poet, 93
Warriner, J. *English Grammar and Composition,* 164
Webster's Biographical Dictionary, 117
Webster's New Geographical Dictionary, 67
Webster's Third New International Dictionary of the English Language, 68
West, J. *Massacre at Fall Creek,* 136
What About Marriage? (filmstrips and tapes), 20
What About VD?, 29
What Everyone Needs to Know About Law, 16
What Is It Really Like Out There?, 134
When the Legends Die, 136
Where Late the Sweet Birds Sang, 30
Who Are You?, 134
Who Was Who in American Sports, 117
Whole Word Catalogue 2, 125
Who's Who, 72, 150
Who's Who in America, 27, 72, 85
Who's Who in Show Business, 117
Who's Who in the Theatre, 117
Who's Who of American Women, 117
Wiener, P., ed. *Dictionary of the History of Ideas,* 132
Wilhelm, K. *Where Late the Sweet Birds Sang,* 30
Wilson, E. M. *Jerusalem, Key to Peace,* 73
Wilson Author Series, 117
Winn, M. *The Plug-In-Drug,* 140
Wishes, Lies and Dreams, 125
Women in Mathematics, 51
World Almanac, 12, 17, 34
World Authors: 1950-1970, 117
World Book Encyclopedia, 26, 70, 71, 131
World Food Crisis (Reference Shelf), 36
World Politics (periodical), 86
Worldmark Encyclopedia of the Nations, 70
Writer, The, (periodical), 125
Writers and Their Work series, 114
Writing Term Papers and Reports, 154

Yearbooks, 71, 150
Young, L. R. *The Fractured Family,* 20
Young Teens and Money, 10
Your Career if You're Not Going to College, 41
Your Future as a Job Applicant, 49
Your Legal Rights, 16
Your Rights and What They Really Mean (filmstrips and cassettes), 16
Youth and the Law Series (filmstrips and cassettes), 16

Zavatsky, B. and Padgett, R., eds. *The Whole Word Catalogue 2,* 125
Zen and the Art of Motorcycle Maintenance, 138